Dive! Dive!

Dive! Dive!
The Submarine Conflict During
the First World War, 1914-18

War in the Underseas

Harold F. B. Wheeler

Submarines, Mines and Torpedoes
in the War

Charles W. Domville-Fife

Dive! Dive!
The Submarine Conflict During
the First World War, 1914-18
War in the Underseas
by Harold F. B. Wheeler
Submarines, Mines and Torpedoes in the War
by Charles W. Domville-Fife

FIRST EDITION

First published under the titles
War in the Underseas
and
Submarines, Mines and Torpedoes in the War

Leonaur is an imprint
of Oakpast Ltd

Copyright in this form © 2016 Oakpast Ltd

ISBN: 978-1-78282-519-7 (hardcover)
ISBN: 978-1-78282-520-3 (softcover)

http://www.leonaur.com

Publisher's Notes

The views expressed in this book are not necessarily those of the publisher.

Contents

War in the Underseas 7
Submarines, Mines and Torpedoes in the War 165

War in the Underseas

THE LAST OF A PIRATE

Contents

Foreword	13
Clearing the Decks	15
Life as a Latter-day Pirate	34
Germany's Submersible Fleet	42
Pygmies among Giants	50
Tragedy in the Middle Seas	60
Horton, E9, and Others	67
Submarine *v.* Submarine	76
A Chapter of Accidents	81
Sea-hawk and Sword-fish	90
U-Boats that Never Returned	103
Depth Charges in Action	111
Singeing the Sultans Beard	118
On Certain Happenings in the Baltic	127
Blockading the Blockade	141
Bottling up Zeebrugge and Ostend	152
The Great Collapse	159

Dedicated to Geoffrey Charles Taskar Keyes in the sincere hope that if opportunity be his he may emulate the daring of his father, whose achievement at Zeebrugge and Ostend will be related by old boys to their juniors until the Ocean Highway is as dry as a dusty road

Foreword

Sea-power strangled Germany and saved the world. Even when the *Kaiser's* legions were riding roughshod over the greater part of Europe its grip was slowly throttling them. Despite the murderous mission of mine and U-boat, it kept the armies of the Allies supplied with men and munitions, and scoured the world for both. When the British Fleet took up its war stations in the summer of 1914 it became the Heart of Things for civilization. It continued to be so when the major portion of the swaggering High Sea Fleet came out to meet Beatty under the white flag in the chilly days of November 1918. It remains so today, (1919).

The officers and men of the Royal Navy whose march is the Underseas played a perilous and noble part in the Great Conflict. British submarines poked their inquisitive noses into the wet triangle of Heligoland Bight three hours after hostilities were declared; they watched while the Men of Mons crossed the Channel to stay the hand of the invader; they pierced the Dardanelles when mightier units remained impotent; they threaded their way through the icy waters of the Baltic despite the vigilance of a tireless enemy; they fought U-boats, a feat deemed to be impossible; they dodged mines, land batteries, and surface craft, and depleted the High Sea Fleet of many valuable fighting forces. In addition, they had to contend with their own peculiar troubles—shoals, collisions, breakdowns, and a hundred and one ills which a landsman never suspects.

Some set out on their duties and failed to come back. They lie many fathoms deep. Their commanders have made their last report. Sea-power has its price. I am under special obligation to several officers of British submarines for assistance willingly rendered, despite the arduous nature of their duties. Their generous enthusiasm exhibits that "real love for the Grand Old Service it is an honour and pleasure to serve in," as Admiral Beatty wrote to me the other day.

Harold F. B. Wheeler

CHAPTER 1

Clearing the Decks

Society must not remain passive in face of the deliberate provocation of a blind and outrageous tyrant. The common interests of mankind must direct the impulses of political bodies: European society has no other essential purpose.—Schiller.

Surprise is the soul of war. The submarine illustrates this elemental principle, and its astounding development is the most amazing fact of the World Struggle. Given favourable circumstances it can attack when least expected, pounce on its prey at such time as may be most convenient to itself, and return to its lair without so much as being sighted. What has become a vital means to the most important military ends was once described by the British Admiralty as "the weapon of the weaker Power." To a large extent, of course, it is *par excellence* the type of vessel necessary to bidders for Sea Supremacy who would wrest maritime predominance from a stronger Power. On the other hand, it has rendered yeoman service to the British Navy, as many of the following pages will show. Germany, a nation of copyists but also of improvers, diverted the submersible from the path of virtue which previous to the outbreak of hostilities it was expected to pursue. It is safe to say that few people in Great Britain entertained the suspicion that underwater craft would be used by any belligerent for the purpose of piracy.

Up to August 1914 the submarine was intimately associated in the public mind with death and disaster—death for the crew and disaster for the vessel. It is so easy to forget that Science claims martyrs and Progress exacts sacrifice. These are two of the certainties of an uncertain world. The early stages of aviation also were notable for the wreck of hopes, machines, and men. Today aircraft share with submarines and tanks the honour of having altered the aspect of war. The motorcar, once the laughing-stock of everybody other than the enthusiast, and now grown into a Juggernaut mounting powerful guns, is the fosterfather of the three, for the perfection of the internal combustion engine alone made the submarine and the aeroplane practicable.

For good or for ill, the underwater boat has passed from the experimental to the practical. In the hands of the Germans it became a particularly sinister and formidable weapon. The truth is not in us if we attempt to disguise the fact. When there was not so much as a cloud the size of a man's hand on the European sky, and the Betrayer was pursuing the path of peaceful penetration all undisturbed and almost unsuspected, the submarine was regarded by many eminent authorities as a somewhat precocious weakling in the naval nursery. They refused to believe that it would grow up. Even Mr H. G. Wells, who has loosed so many lucky shafts, unhesitatingly damned it in his *Anticipations*. He saw few possibilities in the craft, and virtually limited its use to narrow waterways and harbours.

There were others, however, who thought otherwise, and the controversy between the rival schools of thought was brought to a head by a fierce battle fought in Printing House Square. Sir Percy Scott, who had previously held more than a watching brief for the heavy fathers of the Fleet, bluntly told the nation through the columns of the *Times* that the day of the Dreadnought and the Super-Dreadnought was over. With a scratch of the pen he relegated battleships to the scrap-heap—until other experts brought their guns to bear on the subject. Almost on the conclusion of this war of words the war of actuality began. I do not think I am wrong in saying that the former ended in an inconclusive peace. Practice has proved the efficiency of both surface and underwater craft, but particularly of vessels that do not submerge.

Admiral Sir Percy Scott's prophecy remains unfulfilled. The biggun ship has asserted itself in no uncertain language. It is interesting to note, however, that the ruling of one who took part in the discussion, and whose personal experience in the early stages of the evolution of a practical submarine entitled him to special consideration, has been entirely negatived. Rear-Admiral R. H. S. Bacon, (later Vice-Admiral Sir Reginald H. S. Bacon, K.C.B., K.G.V.O., D.S.O.), the principal designer of the first British type, asserted that "the idea of attack of commerce by submarines is barbarous and, on account of the danger of involving neutrals, impolitic." It is obvious from this that the late commander of the Dover Patrol never contemplated any departure from the acknowledged principles of civilized warfare. The unexpected happened, as it is particularly liable to do in war. One of the main purposes of the enemy's submarines in the World War was piracy, unrestrained, unrestricted, and unashamed. It failed to justify Germany's hope.

Probably Lord Fisher was the first seaman holding high position to actually warn the British Government of the likelihood of Germany's illegitimate use of the submarine. Early in 1914 he handed to Mr Asquith and the First Lord of the Admiralty a memorandum pointing out, among other things, that the enemy would use underwater boats against our commerce. (Reply of Mr Bonar Law to Mr G. Lambert and Commander Bellairs in the House of Commons, 5th March, 1918).

His prescience was forestalled thirteen years before by Commander Sir Trevor Dawson, who had prophesied that the enemy would attack our merchant fleet in much the same way as the Boers were then attacking the army in the Transvaal. He told a meeting of engineer:

> Submarine boats have sufficient speed and radius of action to place themselves in the trade routes before the darkness gives place to day, and they would be capable of doing almost incalculable destruction against unsuspecting and defenceless victims.

Originally Germany was by no means enamoured of the new craft. Her first two submarines did not appear until 1905-6; Great Britain's initial venture was launched at Barrow-in-Furness in 1901. The latter, the first of a batch of five, was ordered on the advice of Lord Goschen. Even then the official attitude was sceptical, not altogether without reason. Mr H. O. Arnold-Forster, speaking in the House of Commons on the 18th March, 1901, after admitting that "there is no disguising the fact that if you can add speed to the other qualities of the submarine boat, it might in certain circumstances become a very formidable vessel," adopted what one might call a misery-loves-company attitude, he averred:

> We are comforted by the judgment of the United States and Germany, which is hostile to these inventions, which I confess I desire shall never prosper.

Dr Flamm, Professor of Ship Construction at the Technical High

School at Charlottenburg, who should and probably does know better, has aided and abetted certain other publicists in foisting on the public of the Fatherland the presumption that the submarine is a German invention. This is not the place for a full history of the underwater craft from its early to its latest stages, but perhaps it is permissible to give a few particulars regarding the toilsome growth of this most formidable type of vessel.

The first underwater craft of which there is anything approaching authentic record was the invention of Cornelius Drebbel, a Dutchman who forsook his own country for England. According to one C. van der Woude, writing in 1645, Drebbel rowed in his submerged boat from Westminster to Greenwich. Legend or truth has it that this "Famous Mechanician and Chymist" managed to keep the air more or less sweet in his craft by means of a secret "Chymicall liquor," and that the structure was covered with skin of some kind to make it watertight. Drebbel, who also professed to have discovered the secret of perpetual motion, is stated to have hit upon the idea of his invention by the simple process of keeping his eyes open. He noticed some fishermen towing behind their smacks a number of baskets heavily laden with their staple commodity. When the ropes were not taut the vessels naturally rose a little in the water. He came to the conclusion that a boat could be weighted in much the same way to remain entirely below the surface, and propelled by means similar to a rowing-boat. It is even said that King James travelled at a depth of from twelve to fifteen feet in one of the two vessels constructed by Drebbel, whose invention is referred to in Ben Jonson's *Staple of News*.

The submarine may be said to have remained in this essentially elementary stage until 1775, when David Bushnell, an American, launched a little one-man submarine after five years of planning and preparation. The shape of the vessel resembled a walnut held upright, the torpedo being carried outside near the top. At the bottom was an aperture fitted with a valve for admitting water, while a couple of pumps were provided for ejecting it. About 200 lb. of lead served as ballast, which could be lowered by ropes for the purpose of giving immediate increase of buoyancy should emergency require it. Bushnell writes:

> When the skilful operator had obtained an equilibrium, he could row upward and downward, or continue at any particular depth, with an oar placed near the top of the vessel, formed

upon the principle of the screw, the axis of the oar entering the vessel; by turning the oar one way he raised the vessel, by turning it the other way he depressed it.

A similar apparatus, worked by hand or foot, whichever was the more convenient, propelled the submarine forward or backward. The rudder could also be utilised as a paddle.

Bushnell provided his little wooden craft with what he called a crown and we should designate a conning tower. In this there were several glass windows. Neither artificial light nor means of freshening the air was carried, though the submarine could remain submerged for thirty minutes before the condition of the atmosphere made it necessary to ascend sufficiently near the surface to enable the two ventilator pipes to be brought into action. The water-gauge and compass were rendered discernible by means of phosphorus.

The torpedo—Bushnell termed it a magazine—was an oak box containing 150 lb. of gunpowder and a clockwork apparatus which was set in operation immediately the affair was unshipped. It was attached to a wooden screw carried in a tube in the brim of the 'crown.' Having arrived beneath an enemy vessel, the screw was fixed in the victim's hull from within the submarine, and the 'U-boat' made off. At the time required the mechanism fired what to all intents and purposes was a gun-lock, and the torpedo blew up.

The wooden screw was the least successful of the various appliances. An attempt was made in 1776 to annihilate H.M.S. *Eagle*, then lying off Governor's Island, New York. The operator apparently tried to drive his screw into iron, and quite naturally failed. Writing to Thomas Jefferson on the subject, Bushnell suggests that had the operator shifted the submarine a few inches he could have carried out his operation, even though the bottom was covered with copper. Two other unsuccessful trials were made in the Hudson River. Owing to ill-health and lack of means, the inventor then abandoned his submarine, though in the following year he attempted to 'discharge' one of his magazines from a whaleboat, the object of attack being H.M.S. *Cerberus*. It failed to reach the British frigate, and blew up a prize schooner anchored astern of her. Washington was fully alive to the possibilities of Bushnell's invention, but was evidently of opinion that it was too crude to warrant his serious attention. Writing to Jefferson, he says:

I thought, and still think, that it was an effort of genius, but that too many things were necessary to be combined to expect much from the issue against an enemy who are always upon guard.

Incidentally this was a remarkable testimonial to the men on look-out duty on the British vessels. Keen sight is still a recognised weapon against submarine attack.

In 1797 Robert Fulton, also an American, brought his fertile brain to bear on the submarine, possibly on hearing or reading of David Bushnell's boat. One would have anticipated that the era of the Revolutionary and Napoleonic wars would be propitious for the introduction of new plans and methods calculated to bring a seemingly never-ending state of hostilities to an end. Novel propositions were certainly brought forward; few were utilized. Fulton, an artist by profession, simply bubbled over with ideas connected with maritime operations. Moreover, he had extraordinary tenacity and enthusiasm. Set-backs seemed to give him added momentum. He tried to do business with Napoleon in France, with Pitt in England, with Schimmelpenninck on behalf of Holland, not always without success, before returning to the United States and running the steamer *Clermont* at five miles an hour on the Hudson.

At the end of 1797 the enterprising American proposed to the French Directory to construct a submarine, to be christened the *Nautilus*, or, as he frequently spelled it, the *Nautulus*. So great was his faith in the project for "A Machine which flatters me with much hope of being Able to Annihilate" the British Navy, that he was willing to be remunerated by results, *viz.*, 4000 *francs* per gun for every ship of forty guns and upward that he destroyed, and half that amount per gun for smaller vessels. All captures were to become the property of "the *Nautulus* Company." A little chary of being caught red-handed by the enemy and dealt with as a pirate, he asked that he might be given a commission in the Service, which would ensure for him and his crew the treatment of belligerents. Pléville le Pelley, Minister of Marine, deeming that such warfare was "atrocious," and yet not altogether unkindly disposed toward it, refused the latter request, which would obviously give the submarine official sanction. The proposed payment by results he reduced by fifty *per cent*. All the arrangements were subsequently cancelled.

Nothing further was done until July 1798, when Bruix was Minister of Marine. Fulton renewed his proposition, and certain inquiries by scientists of repute were made at the instigation of Bruix. The report was distinctly favourable, but again there was disagreement as to terms. Fulton, impatient of delay, built the Nautilus. This little vessel, twenty feet long and five feet beam, was launched at Rouen in July 1800. On the trial trip the inventor and two companions made two dives in the boat, the time of submersion varying from eight minutes to seventeen minutes. Proceeding to Havre, Fulton made various improvements in the *Nautilus*, including the introduction of a screw propeller worked by hand, and the addition of wings placed horizontally in the bows for the purpose of ascending or descending. While at Havre the submarine remained below over an hour at a depth of fifteen feet with her crew and a lighted candle. On another occasion the *Nautilus* was submerged for six hours, air being supplied by means of a little tube projecting above the water.

For sailing on the surface the boat was fitted with a single jury-mast carrying a mainsail jib, which could be unshipped when submarine navigation was required. By admitting water she sank to the required depth, and was then propelled by the method already referred to. A glass dome, a compass, a pump for expelling the water when necessary, and a gauge for testing depth, which Fulton called a bathometer, constituted the 'works.' The torpedo was an apparatus made of copper filled with gunpowder:

> Arranged in such a manner that if it strikes a vessel or the vessel runs against it, the explosion will take place and the bottom of the vessel be blown in or so shattered as to ensure her destruction. (Fulton's report, 9th September, 1801).

The weapon was to be fixed to the bottom of the victim by means of a barbed point on the chain used for towing it.

Fulton approached Napoleon, who authorised Forfait, the latest Minister of Marine, to advance the sum of 10,000 *francs* for the purpose of perfecting the *Nautilus*. He also granted Fulton an interview. When, in the autumn of 1801, he expressed a wish to see the submarine, the vessel had been broken up. Here the matter ended, and the ingenious American turned his thoughts in the direction of steam navigation. The *Nautilus* was his one and only experiment in underwater craft. The first ship to be actually sunk during hostilities by submarine was the Federal 13-gun frigate *Housatonic*, of 1264 tons. She went down off Charleston on the 17th February, 1864, during the American Civil War, as the result of being attacked by a spar-torpedo carried by the Confederate submarine *Hunley*, so named after her designer, Captain Horace L. Hunley. Unfortunately the underwater boat was also a victim, and she carried with her her fourth crew to meet with death as a consequence of misadventure. On the first occasion the boat was swamped and eight men were drowned, on the second a similar disaster overtook her, with the loss of six of her crew, on the third she descended and failed to come up. Small wonder that the *Hunley* came to be known as 'the Peripatetic Coffin.'

The shape of the *Hunley* was cylindrical. For'ard and aft were water ballast tanks operated by valves, and additional stability was given by a sort of false keel consisting of pieces of cast iron bolted inside so as to be easily detachable should it be necessary to reach the surface quickly. On each side of the propeller, worked by the hand-power of eight men, were two iron blades which could be moved so as to change the depth of the vessel. The pilot steered from a position near the fore hatchway.

The torpedo, a copper cylinder containing explosive and percussion and primer mechanism, was fired by triggers. It was carried on a boom, twenty-two feet long, attached to the bow. The speed was seldom more than four miles an hour on a calm day. As there was no means of replenishing the air other than by coming to the surface and lifting one of the hatchways, it was obviously a fair-weather ship.

On the afternoon of the 17th February, 1864, the *Hunley* set out on her final trip. While attacking the submarine was only partly submerged, and one of the hatches was uncovered; why will never be known. She made straight toward the *Housatonic*, with the evident intention of striking the vessel near the magazines with her torpedo. There was an explosion, the ship heeled to port, and went down by the stern. When divers examined the extent of her injuries the plucky little *Hunley* was found with her nose buried in the gaping wound in her victim's hull. Her crew were dead, but apparently the officer was saved.

Other submarines or partly submersible boats were used by the defenders of the Southern cause. They were usually termed 'Davids' because they were built to sink the Goliaths of the Federal Navy. The *New Ironsides*, the *Minnesota*, and the *Memphis* were all damaged as a result of their operations.

The only weapon of the submerged submarine is the torpedo. The World War brought no surprise in this direction. For surface work the calibre of the guns mounted on the disappearing platforms has increased very considerably. In 1914 a 14-pdr. was considered ample armament. With added displacement, gun-power has grown enormously. Some German underwater craft in 1918 carried 5.9-in. guns—that is to say, weapons larger than those used by many destroyers.

During the past decade torpedoes and submarines have made almost parallel progress. Of the various types of the former, the Whitehead is first favourite in the Navies of Great Britain, Japan, Russia, and Austria-Hungary, while France uses both the Whitehead and the Schneider, and Germany was exclusively devoted to the Schwartzkopf (Blackhead). The extreme effective range of each may be taken as from 10,000 to 12,000 yards. The essential difference between a torpedo and the usual run of naval ammunition for guns is that the torpedo retains its propellant, while the shell does not.

The torpedo is really an explosive submarine mine forced through the water at a rate varying from 28 knots to 42 knots by twin-screws worked by compressed air engines. Any deviation from the course is automatically corrected by a gyroscope. Some torpedoes are now fitted with an apparatus which causes the torpedo to go in circles should it miss its mark and meet with the wash of passing ships. There is the added possibility, therefore, that the weapon may strike a vessel at which it was not aimed when a squadron is proceeding in line ahead.

To a certain extent the submarine has enabled the torpedo to come into its own. It is not at all an easy task to hit a rapidly moving ship from a platform also ploughing the water at a great rate. Among other things the speed and distance of the opponent have to be taken into consideration, and the missile aimed ahead of the enemy so that it and the target shall arrive at a given point at the same moment. The late Mr Robert Whitehead's invention, an improvement on that of Commandant Lupuis, of the Austrian Navy, who had sold his patent to the former, was tested by the British Admiralty at Sheerness in 1871. Although extremely crude when compared with its successor of to-day, the sum of £15,000 was paid for the English rights. It was first put to a practical test in the Russo-Turkish War of 1877, when Lieutenant Rozhdestvensky, who afterward suffered defeat at the hands of the Japanese in May 1905, sank a Turkish warship by its means.

Viscount Jellicoe has told us that the arrival of the submarine led to certain alterations in strategy. I quote from an interview which the former First Sea Lord granted to a representative of the Associated Press in the spring of 1917. Sir John, as he then was, said:

The most striking feature of the change in our historic naval policy resulting from the illegal use of submarines, and from the fact that the enemy surface ships have been driven from the sea, is that we have been compelled to abandon a definite offensive policy for one which may be called an offensive defensive, since our only active enemy is the submarine engaged in piracy and murder.

Mr Winston Churchill, First Lord of the Admiralty in August 19 14, put the matter a little more bluntly, he wrote:

But for the submarine and the mine, the British Navy would, at the outset of the war, have been able to force the fighting to an issue on their old battleground—outside the enemy's ports.

This did not mean that every other type of ship had been rendered obsolete or even obsolescent by the coming of the vessel that can float on or under the waves. Admiral von Capelle, Secretary of State for the German Imperial Navy, told the Main Committee of the Reichstag that the submarine was an "important and effective weapon," but added that "big battleships are not wholly indispensable. Their construction depends on the procedure of other nations." (Speech of 27th April, 1917). For instance, the submarine has emphasised the importance of the torpedo-boat destroyer, which some seamen thought it would supersede. The T.B.D. has more than maintained its own. Not only is it useful for acting independently, righting its own breed, but as the safeguard of the battleships and battle-cruisers at sea, and also as the keenest weapon against submarines, the naval maid-of-all-work has proved extraordinarily efficient, (see particularly chapter 10).

In the general operations of naval warfare it cannot be said that the enemy U-boats were particularly successful. In the five battles that were fought the work of German submarines was negligible so far as actual fighting was concerned. In two of them, namely Coronel and the Falklands, they were unrepresented on account of the actions taking place many thousands of miles from European waters. This limitation of range of action is a difficulty that time and experiment were beginning to solve when hostilities came to an abrupt conclusion.

The battles of Heligoland Bight and Dogger Bank are profoundly interesting to the student of War in the Underseas. Sir David Beatty, who commanded the Battle Cruiser Squadron in the first big naval engagement in which submarines were used, while admitting that he did not lose sight of "the risk" from them, says in his dispatch that:

Our high speed . . . made submarine attack difficult, and the smoothness of the sea made their detection comparatively easy.

These two antidotes will be noted by the reader. The same distinguished officer, perched on the forebridge of the *Lion* in his shirtsleeves while pursuing the German Fleet near the Dogger Bank, personally observed the wash of a periscope on his starboard bow. By turning immediately to port he entirely upset the calculations of the enemy commander, who was not afforded a further opportunity to torpedo the flagship. A like manoeuvre defeated a similar projected attack on the *Queen Mary* in the Bight. The helm is therefore a third instrument of defence. Apparently the service rendered by enemy U-boats at these two battles was worthless. If they fired at all they missed. On the other hand, any attempt to sink them likewise failed.

In the dispatches on the Battle of Jutland, which a well-known admiral tells me were severely edited before publication, there are several references to enemy submarines, none to our own. The first attempted attack took place about half an hour after Sir David Beatty had opened fire, and immediately following the entry of the 5th Battle Squadron into the fight. The destroyer *Landrail* sighted a periscope on her port quarter. With the *Lydiard* she formed a smoke screen which "undoubtedly preserved the battle-cruisers from closer submarine attack." The light cruiser *Nottingham* also reported a submarine to starboard. We are also informed that:

> *Fearless* and the 1st Flotilla were very usefully employed as a submarine screen during the earlier part of May 31.
>
> The *Marlborough*, flagship of Vice-Admiral Sir Cecil Burney's First Battle Squadron, after having been torpedoed—whether by submarine or other craft is not mentioned—drove off a U-boat attack while proceeding to harbour for repairs. Sir John Jellicoe adds:

> The British Fleet remained in the proximity of the battlefield and near the line of approach to German ports until 11 a.m. on June 1, in spite of the disadvantages of long distances from fleet bases and the danger incurred in waters adjacent to enemy coasts from submarines and torpedo craft.

In the British list of enemy vessels put out of action, one submarine figures as sunk.

Admiral Beatty justly remarks that the German losses were "eloquent testimony to the very high standard of gunnery and torpedo efficiency of His Majesty's ships." Of the twenty-one vessels lost or severely damaged, it would appear as though nine were accounted for by torpedoes, although this does not necessarily mean that they had not been engaged by gunfire as well. At Dogger Bank, it may be recollected, a torpedo finally settled the *Blücher*, which had already been rendered *hors de combat* by shell fired from more old-fashioned weapons.

The German High Sea Fleet adopted a prolonged attitude of caution after Jutland, but the All-Highest thought it well to issue an Imperial Order calculated to inspire the officers and men of the submarine flotillas. "The impending decisive battle" mentioned in the following message, which is dated Main Headquarters, 1st February, 1917, evidently refers to the 'unlimited' phase of U-boat warfare and not to a general action, as one might imagine at first glance. This highly interesting document runs:

> To my Navy
>
> In the impending decisive battle the task falls on my Navy of turning the English war method of starvation, with which our most hated and most obstinate enemy intends to overthrow the German people, against him and his Allies by combating their sea traffic with all the means in our power.
>
> In this work the submarine will stand in the first rank. I expect that this weapon, technically developed with wise foresight at our admirable yards, in co-operation with all our other naval fighting weapons, and supported by the spirit which during the whole course of the war has enabled us to perform brilliant deeds, will break our enemy's war designs.
>
> Wilhelm

The defensive policy of the Imperial Navy was summed up by a writer in the *Deutsche Tageszeitung* seven months after the publication of the above.

> Above all else, the German High Sea Fleet has rendered possible the conduct of the submarine war. Without it the enemy would have threatened our submarine bases and restricted our submarine warfare, or made it impossible.

It was not a valorous role to play, but there was wisdom in it. The submarine campaign passed through several phases. In its earliest stages it was mainly directed by Grand Admiral von Tirpitz, the predominant personality associated with the growth of the Imperial Navy. In December 1914 this Bluebeard of the Seas asserted that as England wished to starve Germany, "we might play the same game and encircle England, torpedoing every British ship, every ship belonging to the Allies that approached any British or Scottish port, and thereby cut off the greater part of England's food supply." The 'game' was started on the 18th February, 1915, and enthusiastically applauded throughout the German Empire.

All the waters surrounding the United Kingdom, and "all English seas," were declared to be a war area. Every vessel of the British Mercantile Marine was to be destroyed, "and it will not always be possible to avoid danger to the crews and passengers thereon." (Proclamation of 5th February, 1915). Peaceful shipping was warned that there was a possibility of neutrals being "confused with ships serving warlike purposes" if they ventured within the danger zone. Great Britain had declared the North Sea a military area in November 1914, and every care was taken to respect the rights of neutral shipping. The enemy, on the contrary, speedily showed utter disregard of international law. The submarine programme was started before the day advertised for the opening performance.

The sinking of the *Lusitania* on the 7th May, 1915, with the loss of 1225 lives, showed in no uncertain way that the Germans intended nothing less than an orgy of cold-blooded devilry. In the following month the always strident German Navy League stated that the fleet which it had done so much to bring into being "was not in a position to break the endless chain of transports carrying munitions in such a manner as blockade regulations had hitherto required." To search ships was "in most cases impossible." In the same manifesto the sinking of the giant Cunarder was 'explained' by arguing that as submarines had no means to compel vessels to stop, and there was ammunition on board, sinking without warning was justified. "Such must continue to be the case, and the army has a just claim to this service of the Fleet."

As a protest against armed traders, the campaign was intensified on the 1st March, 1916. These ships were "not entitled to be regarded as peaceful merchantmen." The plain English of the move was that Germany wanted some kind of excuse for ordering her submarines to sink vessels at sight. According to her, none other than naval ships had the least excuse to assume so much as the defensive. In President Wilson's so-called *Sussex* note of the 18th April, 1916, attention is called to the:

....relentless and indiscriminate warfare against vessels of commerce by the use of submarines without regard to what the Government of the United States must consider the sacred and indisputable rules of international law and the universally recognised dictates of humanity.

The third phase was that of "unlimited submarine war," announced on the last day of January 1917.

Within the barred zones around Great Britain, France, Italy, and in the Eastern Mediterranean, all sea traffic will henceforth be oppressed by all means.

Neutral ships in those areas would traverse the waters "at their own risk." To a large extent they had done so before. Notwithstanding repeated 'regrets' and pledges given by Germany to the United States, murder on the high seas was now to be an acknowledged weapon of German warfare. It culminated in a declaration of war on the part of the United States on the 6th April, 1917, by which time over 230 Americans had lost their lives by the enemy's illegal measures. The date is worth remembering; it will loom big in the history books of tomorrow. Zimmermann, Germany's Minister for Foreign Affairs, had already expressed the opinion that ruthless submarine warfare promised "to compel England to make peace in a few months." (Note to the German Minister in Mexico, dated Berlin, 19th January, 1917). In this expectation, as in several others, he miscalculated. The Lord Chancellor declared that submarine warfare, as carried on by the enemy, was absolutely illegal by international law, and was mere piracy. (Speech in the House of Lords, 10th August, 1917).

As to mines, which were also greatly favoured by the Huns and sown by their U-boats, it may be mentioned that such weapons laid to maintain a general commercial blockade are equally illegal, although perfectly legitimate outside naval bases. This was a small matter to the *Kaiser* and his satellites, who were out to win at any and all costs. No British mines were placed in position until many weeks after the declaration of hostilities, although the enemy had scattered them indiscriminately in the trade routes either before or immediately following the outbreak of war. When we resorted to the use of mines they were anchored in all cases, and constructed to become harmless if they broke loose.

The reply of England and of France to these measures was to stop supplies from entering Germany by means of a blockade controlled

A U-BOAT GLIDING, SUBMERGED, OVER HER VICTIM.

by cruiser cordon, to quote the British Declaration to Neutral Governments, (dated 1st March, 1915):

> The law and custom of nations in regard to attacks on commerce, have always presumed that the first duty of the captor of a merchant vessel is to bring it before a Prize Court, where it may be tried, where the regularity of the capture may be challenged, and where neutrals may recover their cargoes.

With delicate consideration for the convenience of neutrals, which some folk held to be wisdom and others lunacy, the British Government declared their intention:

> ... to refrain altogether from the exercise of the right to confiscate ships or cargoes which belligerents have always claimed in respect of breaches of blockade. They restrict their claim to the stopping of cargoes destined for or coming from the enemy's territory. (Sir Edward Grey to Mr Page, 15th March, 1915).

Much ado was made about the stoppage of food for the civil population of the Central Empires. It was barbarous, inhuman, and so on. Yet the principle had been upheld by both Bismarck and Caprivi, and practised at the siege of Paris. As Sir Edward Grey delightfully put it, this method of bringing pressure to bear on an enemy country "therefore presumably is not repugnant to German morality." (Sir Edward Grey to Mr Page, 15th March, 1915).

A great deal has been said and written to show that the Prussian Government was not the German People, that instead of Representation there was Misrepresentation. It is still extremely difficult to secure reliable information on any subject connected with intimate Germany, and the contemporary views of so-called neutrals are often more than suspect. A study of German newspapers at the time certainly led one to believe that opposition to the submarine campaign had been more or less negligible. A change of view only came when the people realised that ruthlessness did not pay, and it was the business of the British Navy to demonstrate this—as it did. Meantime the German official accounts of sinkings were grossly exaggerated, and the nation had no means of discovering the loss of submarines other than when relatives serving in them failed to return to their families. There was no one to contradict the grossly exaggerated statement made by Dr Helfferich, Minister for the Interior, that in the first two months of unrestricted U-boat warfare over 1,600,000 tons of shipping had been sunk at the cost of the loss of a mere half-dozen submarines. (In the Reichstag Main Committee, 28th April, 1917).

Dr Michaelis, a more noisy sabre-rattler than his predecessor in the Chancellorship, asserted that "the submarine warfare is accomplishing all, and more than all, that was expected of it." (Speech in the Reichstag, July 1917). Like many other of his countrymen, to him the crews of the Imperial Pirate Service were more of the nature of soldiers than of sailors. Certainly their callous behaviour suggested that they were strangers to the proverbial comradeship of the sea, and one with the glorious band that hacked a way through Belgium, drove their bayonets through babies, and crucified their prisoners. Loud cheers followed the remark that "We can look forward to the further labours of our brave submarine warriors with complete confidence," and also to a reference to greetings sent home to the Fatherland by "our troops on all fronts on land and sea, in the air and under the sea."

As to the thoroughness with which commanders of U-boats performed their task, there is no need to speak. There is plentiful evidence to prove that so elementary a duty as that of examining a ship's papers seldom interested them. They had no respect for law or life. Witness a case that has a direct bearing on this matter, (heard before Mr Justice Hill and Elder Brethren of the Trinity House, 20th March, 1918). It arose in connexion with the salving of the s.s. *Ambon*, a neutral vessel bound for the Dutch East Indies, after having been torpedoed on the 21st February, 1916, when about seven miles off Start Point. A shell was fired from an enemy submarine. Immediately the engines of the steamship were stopped, a lifeboat was lowered, and the chief engineer sent off with the ship's papers and instructions. The latter included a copy of a telegram from the owners advising that the steamer was to call at a certain port on a specified day, in accordance with an agreement between the Dutch and German Governments.

The German commander did not so much as look at the documents, and peremptorily told the crew to leave the *Ambon*. "My orders admit of no variation," he remarked. They were "to sink every ship in the blockade area." The steamer was then torpedoed, but did not founder, and was subsequently towed into Plymouth.

No reliance whatever could be placed on Germany's word, as neutrals early discovered to their cost. Having provided a so-called 'safe' zone, the Dutch steamer *Amsterdam* was torpedoed within it. At Germany's own suggestion, an International Committee, composed of Dutch, Swedish, and German naval officers, was formed to investigate the circumstances. Their finding was that the vessel had been sunk in the 'safe' zone.

There was a time when the French authorities seemed to be in favour of the submarine above all other types of naval ships. The result was that France lost her position in the race for second place in the world's fleets, though it is to her credit that in 1888 she launched the *Gymnote*, the first modern submarine to be commissioned. Nordenfeldt, of gun fame, had already achieved a certain amount of success with steam-driven underwater boats, but they had many disadvantages when compared with those of Mr John P. Holland, who hailed from the same country as Fulton. The first submarines built for the British Government were of the Holland type, of 120 tons displacement when submerged, and having a speed of five knots when travelling below. Germany's pioneer U-boat was built in 1890. In 1918 she boasted giant diving cruisers of 5000 tons, with a radius of action of 8000 miles, and mounting 5.9-in. guns.

As to the vexed question of the number of submarines possessed by Great Britain and Germany respectively at the beginning of the war, one can only say that authorities differ. According to an interview granted by Mr Winston Churchill to M. Hugues le Roux which appeared in *Le Matin* in the first week of February 1915, we then had more underwater boats than the enemy, but Lord Jellicoe afterward asserted that in August 1914 "the German Navy possessed a great many more oversea submarines than we did."

******

Speech delivered in Sheffield, 24th October, 1917. In reviewing the naval situation in the House of Commons on the 27th November, 1914, Mr Churchill had remarked that "our power in submarines is much greater than that of our enemies."

******

Unless there is a subtle distinction between the general term used by the then First Lord and the oversea type referred to by the former Commander-in-Chief of the Grand Fleet, it is impossible to reconcile the two statements, for it is obvious that the leeway mentioned by the latter cannot have been made up in five months.

According to the Berlin official naval annual *Nautilus*, published in June 1914, the total number of completed German submarines up to the previous month was twenty-eight. Commander Carlyon Bellairs, R.N., M.P., estimated them at "fifty built, building, and projected." Austria had six ready, four under construction at Pola, and five on the stocks in Germany. In the five years immediately preceding the beginning of the struggle Germany certainly spent more on underwater craft than Great Britain, the figure for the former being £5,354.206, and for the latter £4,159,670.

Chapter 2

Life as a Latter-day Pirate

> The unrestricted U-boat war means a very strong naval offensive against the *Entente*.—Admiral von Capelle.

Writing in the early summer of 1915, a neutral who visited the once busy ports of Danzig, Stettin, Hamburg, and Bremen remarked that:

> Wherever one goes in these cities, wherever one takes one's meals, one hears the word *Unterseeboot*. Amazing, and often untrue, stories are told of the number of submarines that are being constructed, the size and speed of the latest ones, and the great number of English ships that have been sunk, but whose loss has been 'concealed from the British public.'

The submarine barometer was Set Fair. It soon dropped to Change. Within six months the industrious and outspoken Captain Persius was confessing in the *Berliner Tageblatt* that:

> Regarding the effectiveness of our U-boats in the trade war, one hears frequently nowadays views that bear little resemblance to the views uttered a year ago. Then, alas, hopes were extravagant, owing to a disregard of facts which the informed expert, indeed, observed, but which remained concealed from the layman

A confession of failure, notwithstanding the offer of substantial rewards for every merchant vessel sunk, and pensions for each man in a submarine which destroyed a transport.

Twenty months later Admiral von Scheer asserted that German submarine losses were more than equalized by new construction.

Note the definite acknowledgment of losses and of the necessity for replacing them. In April 1918 Admiral von Capelle, Imperial Secretary of State for the Navy, endeavoured to explain the declining maritime death-rate of the enemy by assuring the Main Committee of the Reichstag that the average loss of British ships from submarine attacks alone, during 1917, was 600,000 tons per month. The truth of the matter was that the average loss from all causes was not more than 333,000 gross tons.

According to an official statement circulated to the German Press on the 4th of the following June, food conditions in England were "extraordinarily bad," because the U-boat campaign was "having the intended result of constantly diminishing England's food supply." In actual fact, the U-boats were then having a particularly rough time. So far as the German Independent Socialists were concerned, they did not "look forward with complete confidence," as Dr Michaelis had professed to do in July 1917, "to the further labours of our brave submarine warriors." Herr Vogtherr, a member of the party, bluntly remarked that:

> It cannot be seen that U-boat warfare has brought peace nearer. Meanwhile we continue to destroy tonnage which we shall need after the war in order to obtain necessary raw materials.

As to the latter clause, the British Mercantile Marine has already had something to say. It lost 14,661 gallant fellows through enemy action.

According to the statement of a member of the crew of the British destroyer which rammed U12, some of the prisoners at least were thankful to be in despised England. They said that the coxswain had been a North Sea pilot for fifteen years previous to the outbreak of war, and though the veriest tyro in matters relating to underwater craft, was compelled to take service, presumably because he was well acquainted with the east coast of the United Kingdom. The story of crews being forced with the gentle persuasion of a revolver to board other U-boats while their own was docked to undergo repairs was not necessarily exaggerated. There is evidence that on occasion German seamen were shot for refusing to go on board a submarine.

The mate of the Brazilian steamer *Rio Branco*, when taking the ship's papers to the commander of an enemy U-boat, asked a member of the crew what life was like as a latter-day pirate. He replied in a single word usually taken to denote eternal misery, and added that although he and his mates would like to mutiny, opportunity was never afforded them, because they were shot on the slightest pretext. There is no reason to doubt that crews were sent to sea with insufficient training, and that their moral steadily declined as Allied efforts to tackle the foe developed.

With a stoical philosophy which may have been specially intended for neutral consumption, (the United States had not then declared war), Lieutenant-Commander Claus Hansen informed the Kiel representative of the *New York World* that:

> We need neither doctors nor undertakers aboard U 16; if anything goes wrong with our craft when below no doctor can help; and we carry our coffin with us.

One can thoroughly appreciate his remark that the work "is fearfully trying on the nerves. Every man does not stand it."

The same article also furnishes other interesting particulars of the life of a modern pirate which bear *prima facie* evidence of truth. "We steer entirely by chart and compass," the commander averred. "As the air heats it gets poor, and, mixed with odours of oil from machinery, the atmosphere becomes fearful. An overpowering sleepiness often attacks new men, who require the utmost will-power to remain awake. Day after day in such cramped quarters, where there is hardly room to stretch the legs, where one must be constantly alert, is a tremendous strain on the nerves. I have sat or stood for eight hours with my eyes glued to the periscope, peering into the brilliant glass until my eyes and head have ached. When the crew is worn out, we seek a good sleep and rest under the water, the boat often rocking gently, with a movement like that of a cradle. Before ascending I always order silence for several minutes, to determine whether one can hear any propellers in the vicinity through the shell-like sides of the submarine, which act like a sounding-board."

Hansen gave the interviewer to understand that lying dormant many fathoms deep was not exactly a treat to his crew.

> When the weather or the proximity of the enemy make it necessary to remain down so long that the air becomes unusually bad, every man except those actually on duty is ordered to lie down, and to remain absolutely quiet, making no unnecessary movements, as movement causes the lungs to use more oxygen, and oxygen must be saved, just as the famished man in the desert tries to make the most of his last drop of water. As there can

be no fire, because fire burns oxygen, and the electric power from the accumulators is too precious to be wasted for cooking, we have to dine cold when cruising.

This chat, it is necessary to add, took place in March 1915. Since then many improvements have been made in submarines, including ventilation and roominess.

At this particular period everything possible was being done to arouse the enthusiasm of the German nation for the Underseas War. Carefully written articles by naval men, syndicated by official or semi-official Press bureaux, made their appearance with almost bewildering frequency. German submarines had found their way to the Dardanelles, a feat attended by much metaphorical trumpet-blowing and flag-waving. To quote Captain von Kühlewetter, a devout worshipper at the shrine of Tirpitz:

> The layman can hardly imagine what it means for a craft of only 1000 tons displacement, about 230 feet long and 19 or 20 feet beam at its widest point, to make with a crew of thirty a trip as far as from Hamburg to New York. The little vessel can only travel at moderate speed in order that the petrol may last. It is always ready to meet the enemy without help of any kind on a journey through hostile waters for the entire distance. And these submarines did meet the enemy often.

There is a charming *naïveté* about the narrative of a U-boat man who spent some time reconnoitring the coast of Scotland. His vessel left her base in company with several others, including U15, which failed to return. "She fell before the enemy" is his pathetic little epitaph to her memory. Each of the ten days spent on the trip was divided into four shifts for alternate sleep and work. For variety there was "a little while under, a little while on top." The only sensational phase of the cruise appears to have been when:

> One after another had to leave his place for a minute and take a peep through the periscope. It was the prettiest picture I ever saw. Up there, like a flock of peaceful lambs, lay an English squadron without a care, as if there were no German sea-wolves in armoured clothing. For two hours we lay there under water on the outposts. We could with certainty have succeeded in bringing under a big cruiser, but we must not. We were on patrol. Our boat had other work to do. It was a lot to expect

from our commander. So near to the enemy, and the torpedo must remain in its tube! He must have felt like a hunter who, before deer-stalking begins, suddenly sights a fine buck thirty paces in front of him.

The reference to British cruisers resembling peaceful lambs is delicious. The writer seems to have forgotten that so far as 'armoured clothing' goes they are considerably better provided than the toughest submarine afloat. And what kind of a wolf was it to let such easy prey escape? One surmises a reason connected with the British patrol rather than with its German counterfeit.

An American sailor-boy was taken on board U39 after that submarine had torpedoed his ship. The lad afterward characterized the unenviable experience as "a dog's life in a steel can," accompanied by a constant succession of rings of the gong that sent every member to his appointed station as though the Last Trump had blown. The usual menu was stew and coffee, the liquid refreshment being varied on occasion by the substitution of raspberry juice.

Three captains—a Briton, an American, and a Norwegian—were made prisoners on U49. For days they were confined in a tiny cabin containing three bunks. They took turns in the solitary chair that was the only furniture other than a folding table. As no light was allowed, conversation and change of position were their only occupations. They found plenty to talk about, but even desultory chatter becomes irksome when it is centred around the topic, What will happen? Still, misery loves company, even if it does not appreciate cramp. The prisoners were kept in this Dark Hole of the Underseas except for occasional airings on deck when the craft was running awash and there was 'nothin' doin'' in the piracy or anti-piracy line. Even then they were closely watched by armed guards. Their rations consisted of an unpalatable concoction called stew, black bread, rancid butter, and alleged marmalade, any one of which might have been guaranteed to engender *mal de mer*.

When off the coast of Spain the commander of U49 hailed a Swedish steamer. The captain must have been deeply relieved when he found that his services were merely required as temporary gaoler. He was peremptorily told to take charge of the prisoners, and land them in the neighbourhood of Camarina. Neither ship nor cargo was interfered with. Never were mariners more pleased to set foot on solid earth.

This particular barbarian was not quite so callous as the presiding genius of U34. Four of the crew of the trawler *Victoria*, of Milford, which he had sunk, were picked up by the submarine. Six of their comrades had passed to where there is no sea, and required no favours from enemy or friend. As though they were not sufficiently well acquainted with the ways of U34, the survivors were summoned on deck the following morning to receive a further object-lesson in humanity as the Hun understands it. They were compelled to watch the death and burial of a Cardiff trawler. One of the German officers explained:

> England began the war, and we shall sink every ship we see flying the British flag.

When the latest victim of U34 had gone to her watery grave, the men were given a handful of biscuits, placed in a boat, and left to the mercy of the sea.

Apparently U-boats were not keen on fine weather. Dr Helfferich, the Vice-Chancellor said:

> A smooth sea and a lull in the wind are very disagreeable for U-boats, especially in view of the enemy's defensive measures, particularly as regards aircraft. Some U-boat commanders are of opinion that U-boat warfare can be carried on with still better results when the weather is not too fine and the nights are longer.

A certain submarine left her lair at Zeebrugge a few days before Vice-Admiral Sir Roger Keyes and his band of heroes gave an enforced holiday to those that remained. She had not proceeded any great distance before she encountered a mine. It did not completely put her 'out of mess,' but sent her staggering backward in inky darkness to the bottom. The electric light had failed with the quickness of a candle meeting a sudden draught. To restore the current was obviously the first thing to do. It was not easy working with the aid of torches, the boat tipped up on end, her stern buried deep in the bed of the sea. Primitive man, his tail not yet worn off, would have fared better. Eventually the supply was restored, and it became possible to make a more thorough survey of the damage. The engineers found that the shock had paralysed the nervous system of the machinery. Not only was the boat leaking badly, but the pumps refused to blow out the ballast tanks.

On an even keel the problem would be easier to tackle. The men were therefore ordered to assemble in the stern and rush forward on the word of command. Their combined movement had the desired effect. Slowly the extra weight in the bow caused the ooze to loose its grip. The submarine sank down with languid grace. There was now nothing to hamper movement. Each member of the crew had a pair of hands ready for service instead of having to employ one for the purpose of hanging on.

The engineers tried to start the motors. They refused to budge. Seawater found its way into the accumulators, adding a further terror to the overwrought men by the introduction of poison gas in an atmosphere already charged with death. Pirates might laugh when they saw British sailors struggling for life in icy water, might derive entertainment from shelling frail craft laden to the gunwale with survivors from ships sunk in pursuance of the German cult of frightfulness, but they failed to appreciate the humour of the situation when they were the victims and the tragedy was enacted 100 feet beneath the surface. The traditional Nero would never have riddled had he felt the scorch of the flames that burnt Rome. There is little enough of the alleged glory of war in being trapped like a rat. Much of its glamour in any circumstance is imaginary, and exists chiefly in the minds of scribblers. This is not pacificism, but fact.

The sea mounted higher and higher in the lonely prison cell. Officers and crew tried to staunch the inflow, to stop the leaks with tow and other likely material. These devices held for a little, then burst away. Some sought to make their escape through the conning-tower, as Goodhart of the British Navy had done; others tried to force a way out *via* the torpedo-tubes. Bolts were wrenched off, fastenings filed through. The doors held firm. The mighty efforts of the men met with no reward. They fell back exhausted and covered with sweat. The pressure from without would have thwarted a score of Samsons. The hatches remained immovable.

They read the handwriting on the curved walls of their prison: "No hope!" The crew must have cursed the Hohenzollerns then. Despair robbed them of reason. One fellow went mad, then another, followed by a third. A man plunged into the water, now up to his knees. His overwrought brain could stand the terrible strain no longer. He drowned in two feet of water. Nobody moved to pull him out. The place became a Bedlam. A comrade tried to shoot himself. The revolver merely clicked. In a passion of rage he flung both weapon and himself into the rising flood. Death was the most desired of all things.

A plate burst, letting in a Niagara. The swirl of waters increased the pressure of air against the hatches. One of them burst open. Those who remained alive were carried off their feet and hurled through the aperture. The blind forces of Nature succeeded where man had failed. A mangled mass of human flotsam was flung to the surface. Two maimed bodies alone had life in them when a British trawler steamed by. A boat was lowered, the half-dead forms fished out of the sea. Then the enemy, potential victims of these men but an hour before, did what they could to alleviate their agony. That is the spirit and the tradition of the British Sea Service, though the sufferer be the Devil himself.

A survivor of a neutral ship blown up by a U-boat, who was kept swimming about for ten minutes before being rescued because the officers wanted to take some snap-shots, avowed that he and his mates were compelled to lend a hand with the ammunition. That was the Huns' method of making them pay their way. Their 'dungeon,' to quote the narrator, was "furnished with tubes, pressure gauges, fly-wheels, torpedoes, and the floor paved with shells." The life he characterized as "monotonous." During their stay of twelve days five vessels were sunk.

As "a recognition of meritorious work during the war" the *Kaiser* created a special decoration for officers, petty officers, and crews of submarines on the completion of their third voyage. That did not make them any the more enamoured of mines and *wasserbomben*.

CHAPTER 3

Germany's Submersible Fleet

The submarine is the hunted today.—Sir Eric Geddes.

In the first phase of the Underseas War torpedoes were the favourite weapons of the U-boat. The work was done more effectively and quicker than was possible with the comparatively small guns then mounted. Later, the number of ships attacked by shellfire rapidly increased. This was due to several reasons. The second method of attack was considerably less expensive, for a torpedo costs anything from £750 to £1000. Comparatively few merchant vessels had any means of defence, for ramming was seldom practicable, and other dodges, such as obscuring the vessel by voluminous smoke from the funnels, and steering stern on, thus presenting a relatively small target, were equally uncertain.

Altogether the submarine had things very much her own way. She could carry an augmented provision of ammunition, and the difficulties of supply were more easily met. It takes longer to make a torpedo than to turn a shell; to train a torpedo expert than a gunner. If no British patrol were at hand, the German commander could safely risk waging war on the surface. He did not have to return to his base so frequently for the purpose of replenishing empty magazines, and he was saving money for the dear Fatherland. With increasing range of action the necessity for conserving torpedoes became more pronounced. The menace grew to such proportions in the Mediterranean that it was found necessary to send vessels by the long Cape route instead of *via* the Suez Canal.

When slow-moving John Bull at last bestirred himself and decided to arm merchantmen, the risks of an exposed U-boat were considerably increased. The torpedo again came into her own. As Mr Winston

Churchill told the House of Commons, (21st February, 1917):

> The effect of putting guns on a merchant ship is to drive the submarine to abandon the use of the gun, to lose its surface speed, and to fall back on the much slower speed under water and the use of the torpedo. The torpedo, compared with the gun, is a weapon of much more limited application.

Germany's maritime faith being based on the U-boat, despite the *Kaiser's dictum* that "our future lies on the water," many keen scientific brains there had a part in its recent evolution. Whereas in 1914 the latest type, such as U30, could travel 300 miles submerged or 3500 miles entirely on the surface—the latter trip an impossibility, of course, with the British Navy in being—at least 8800 miles were traversed by the submarine which in 1918 bombarded Monrovia, the capital of Liberia, on the west coast of Africa. This is assuming that she returned to her home port in Europe.

The following table, in which round figures are used, will help us to appraise Germany's progress in the construction of U-boats previous to the outbreak of hostilities. It is based on what is considered to be reliable evidence, although the difficulty of obtaining accurate figures will be appreciated. I shall refer to the larger types later.

> U1 (1905).—Submerged displacement, 236 tons. Surface engines, 250 H.P.; electric motors, 100 H.P. Speed, 10 knots on surface, 7 knots submerged. Surface range, from 700 to 800 miles. Armament, one torpedo-tube in bow. Complement, nine officers and men.
>
> U2-U8 (1907-10).—Submerged displacement, 250 tons. Surface engines, 400 H.P.; electric motors, 160 H.P. Speed, 12 knots on surface, 8 knots submerged. Surface range, 1000 miles. Armament, two torpedo-tubes in bow. Fitted with submarine signalling apparatus. Complement, eleven officers and men.
>
> U9-U18 (1910-12).—Submerged displacement, 300 tons. Surface engines, 600 H.P. Speed, 13 knots on surface, 8 knots submerged. Surface range, 1500 miles. Armament, two torpedo-tubes in bow, one torpedo-tube in stern. With U13 anti-aircraft weapons were introduced.
>
> U19-U20 (1912-13).—Submerged displacement, 450 tons. Surface engines, 650 H.P.; electric motors, 300 H.P. Speed, 13½ knots on surface, 8 knots submerged. Surface range, 2000 miles.

Armament, two torpedo-tubes in bow, one torpedo-tube in stern, two 14-pdr. Q.F. guns. Complement, seventeen officers and men.

U 21-U 24 (1912-13).—Submerged displacement, 800 tons. Surface engines, 1200 H.P.; electric motors, 500 H.P. Speed, 14 knots on surface, 9 knots submerged. Surface range, 3000 miles. Armament, two torpedo-tubes in bow, two torpedo-tubes in stern, one 14-pdr. Q.F. gun, two 1-pdr. anti-aircraft guns. Complement, twenty-five officers and men.

U25-U30 (1913-14).—Submerged displacement, 900 tons. Surface engines, 2000 H.P.; electric motors, 900 H.P. Speed, 18 knots on surface, 10 knots submerged. Surface range, 4000 miles. Submerged range, 300 miles. Armament, two torpedo-tubes in bow, two torpedo-tubes in stern, two 14-pdr. Q.F. guns, two 1-pdr. anti-aircraft guns. Complement, thirty to thirty-five officers and men. Upper works lightly armoured. Fitted with wireless."

German U-boats are really submersibles. That is to say, the outer shell conforms to the shape of an ordinary ship, with a broad deck, whereas British submarines resemble a fat cigar. Internally they are cylindrical, the space intervening between the compartments and the shell affording accommodation for the ballast tanks. The theory is that vessels built to this design are more seaworthy and easier to handle. U36, which was building when war broke out, was divided into ten compartments, below which were the steel cylinders containing compressed air for freshening the atmosphere, oil fuel, lubricating oil, and water-ballast tanks, and the accumulators for driving the dynamos when travelling beneath the surface. The officers' combined wardroom and sleeping quarters were for'ard, immediately behind the bow torpedo compartment.

Adjoining were the crew's quarters, divided by a steel bulkhead from the control chamber, situated below the conning-tower. In the control chamber the steering wheel, periscope, projection table on which a surface view was thrown after the manner of a camera obscura, water-pressure dial, and other delicate and necessary instruments for the safety and navigation of the ship were distributed. Proceeding toward the stern, the petty officers' quarters, the machine-room with its heavy oil engines for surface work and electric motors for progression when submerged, and the stern torpedo compartment were to

THE INTERIOR OF A GERMAN SUBMARINE
Showing the internal combustion engines for surface work, and the motor-generators for driving the propellers when submerged.

be found. U36 was one of the "new super-Dreadnought submarines," to quote an American correspondent who saw them under construction at Kiel. On these, he added, "the Germans appear to be banking."

The autumn of 1915 witnessed the introduction of mine-laying submersibles. The trotyl-filled cylinders were dropped on recognised trade routes without the slightest regard for the rights of neutrals. The mines were kept in a special chamber, ingeniously contrived so that it could be flooded without the water entering elsewhere, and released through a trap-door. Thus another weapon was added to the submarine's armoury. It answered all too well. Sir Edward Carson said:

> They can follow your mine-sweeper, and as quickly as you sweep up mines they can lay new ones without your knowing or suspecting.

In 1914 the enemy had only one means of sowing these canisters of death, namely, by surface vessels. It will be recollected that the *Königin Luise* was sunk in the North Sea on the morning of the 5th August while on this hazardous duty. Germany's opportunity for hurting us in this manner was of short duration. The British Navy asserted itself, with the result that the enemy was perforce compelled to find a new method. He resorted to the use of specially fitted submarines.

In due course 4.1-in. guns, mounted on disappearing platforms, made their debut, followed by U-boats provided with two 5.9-in. guns. With increase of gun-power came a necessary increase in size, and with both several distinct advantages and disadvantages. The boats were less easy to manoeuvre, required augmented crews, and offered a larger area for attack. Against these minus qualities must be set those of increase of cruising range, and the possibility of spoil, the sole excuse of the old-time pirate. Hitherto his more scientific successor could only sink his victim. Now, given favourable conditions, he might carry off goods useful to the Fatherland. One German U-boat secured twenty-two tons of copper from merchantmen destroyed during a 5000-mile cruise.

Germany waxed particularly enthusiastic over her diving-cruisers. These boats displaced 5000 tons, were from 350 feet to 400 feet long, had a much accelerated submerged and surface speed, were protected by an armour belt of tough steel plate, and mounted a couple of 5.9-in. guns. Some of these submersibles seem to have been driven by steam when in surface trim, others by the usual Diesel engines. On the 11th May, 1918, a British Atlantic escort submarine came across one of these fine fellows travelling awash, likely enough anxious to have a shot at the merchant convoy which the representative of His Majesty's Navy was on her way to pick up. A heavy sea was running at the time, but at intervals between the waves the periscope revealed the position of his rival to the British commander. One torpedo sufficed. The *Tauchkreuzer* went down, carrying with her the sixty or seventy men who constituted her company. There were no survivors. She had the distinction of being the first of the type to be destroyed.

Germany's merchant service, prizes of war, or driven off the seven seas and growing barnacles in neutral or home ports, virtually ceased to exist at the outbreak of hostilities. The mammoth liners which formerly competed with our own no longer sailed the seas with their holds full of cheap goods and their saloons alive with travellers bent on 'peaceful penetration' —and other things. It rankled in the bosoms of her shipping magnates that the much-vaunted High Sea Fleet was impotent to prevent Britain 'carrying on' commercially while conducting campaigns in all parts of the world. It was true that Germany's U-boats were making inroads on the maritime resources of her enemy, that when hostilities were over they might compete on more than even terms because of these losses, but today rankled though tomorrow was full of hope. Likewise the Economic Conference in Paris had declared its firm intention to impose special conditions on German shipping after the war. *After* the war! The Director-General of the North German Lloyd Line said that the English were not so unpractical as to reject a favourable freightage or passage.

I cannot give you the name of the man or woman who first suggested the possibilities of the submarine for business purposes. The idea was certainly not a particularly novel one. All I can say definitely is that the concern which owned the pioneer vessels was called the Ocean Navigation Company, and that the president was Herr Alfred Lohmann. If British merchantmen could use American ports, why not German commercial submarines? The *Deutschland* was built with this object in view. Officially she was described as "a vessel engaged in the freight trade between Bremen and Boston and other Eastern Atlantic ports."

She left Heligoland on the 23rd June, 1916, and arrived at Norfolk News, Virginia, seventeen days later. The German Press quite naturally went into ecstasies over the achievement. Yet it was not quite such a unique event as they imagined. Ten submarines built in Montreal had crossed the Atlantic nine months before. The *Deutschland* duly discharged her cargo, stayed three weeks or so, and returned to Germany. The *Kaiser* showed his pleasure by conferring decorations on Herr Lohmann and the crew. Germany was again a maritime nation—of sorts.

The submersible had travelled no fewer than 8500 nautical miles. She made a second voyage to America in October. This time her port of arrival was New London, Connecticut. When starting on her return journey she managed to get in collision with one of the escorting tugs, which sank with the loss of seven of her crew. The *Deutschland* was the pioneer of seven similar boats said to be in course of construction. A sister vessel, the *Bremen*, was launched and started on a voyage. She is now some two years overdue.

Official Germany revealed no great faith in the possibilities of the commercial submarine, though this does not necessarily mean that the autocrats of the Wilhelmstrasse showed their real belief. It sometimes suited them to lie. According to the *Frankfurter Zeitung*, £15,000,000 *per annum* was earmarked for the fostering of Germany's moribund merchant service in the next decade.

In October 1916 the depredations of U53 off the American coast were hailed by the population of Berlin and other German towns as a sure prelude to peace. She was the first armed U-boat to cross the Atlantic, but the German nation saw her multiplied by scores, if not by hundreds. Many optimistic folk held the belief, based on the wonderful tales that were told of huge Allied shipping losses, that the war would be over before the dawn of a new year. Britons are not the only people who have hugged delusions. After having put in at Newport News for a few hours and been visited by various notabilities, U53 took up a position off the Nantucket Lightship, so well known to all Atlantic voyagers. She then calmly proceeded to sink half a dozen ships—British, Dutch, and Norwegian—under the nose of U.S. destroyers. According to accounts that were published in American newspapers at the time, the submersible had four torpedo-tubes, one 4-in. gun forward and one 3-in. gun aft, three periscopes, wireless apparatus, and engines of 1200 h.p. that enabled her to travel on the surface at eighteen knots. Her submerged speed was understood to be some four knots less.

U-boats were built at the Vulkan and Blohm and Voss shipyards of Hamburg; at Hoboken, in the former yards of the Société John Cockerill, (an Englishman, who started the famous engineering works in Belgium at Seraing at the early age of twenty-seven); at Puers, near

Termonde; and at the great naval bases of Kiel and Wilhelmshaven. Here the parts were assembled, for it is fairly evident that the thousand and one units of a modern submersible were constructed on many lathes in many parts of the Fatherland. For example, it is believed that UC5, the small mine-layer of 200 tons displacement captured by the British Navy and exhibited off the Thames Embankment, was brought in sections to Zeebrugge and put together there.

When German liners were compelled to keep in American ports owing to the pressure of British sea-power, there seemed not the slightest likelihood that the United States would become an active participant in the war. In 1917 these selfsame steamers were traversing 3000 miles of ocean with armed tourists bound for Germany, giving the lie direct to the Imperial Chancellor's hopeful message that Uncle Sam could not:

> Send and maintain an army in Europe without injuring the transport and supply of the existing Entente armies and jeopardizing the feeding of the Entente people.

The mercantile marine of the United States is small, but with the aid of former German vessels and British ships her troops defied the submarine menace and were landed by the hundred thousand in France as America's splendid contribution toward the liberation of the world. The spectacular appearance of the *Deutschland* and U53 fade into insignificance before this amazing triumph.

Speaking at a luncheon given in London, (by the English-Speaking Union, 11th October, 1918), in honour of American Press representatives visiting England, Vice-Admiral Sims remarked that some of his countrymen regarded it as a miracle of their navy that it had got a million and a half troops across the Atlantic in a few months and had protected them on the way, he avowed:

> We didn't do that, Great Britain did. She brought over two-thirds of them and escorted a half. We escort only one-third of the merchant vessels that come here.

America has been most generous in her appreciation of the part played by Britain in the war.

CHAPTER 4

Pygmies among Giants

> This is the first time since the Creation that all the world has been obliged to unite to crush the Devil.—Rudyard Kipling.

Two weeks after the declaration of war Count von Reventlow was cock-a-hoop regarding the "attitude of reserve" of what he was kind enough to term the "alleged sea-commanding Fleet of the greatest naval Power in the world." He asserted:

> This fleet has now been lying idle for more than a fortnight, so far from the German coast that no cruiser and no German lightship has been able to discover it, and it is repeatedly declared officially, 'German waters are free of the enemy.'

Whether the count was aware of the fact or not, British submarines were watching in the vicinity of the ironclad fortress of Heligoland three hours after hostilities had begun. Had the High Sea Fleet ventured out it would have been greeted with anything but an "attitude of reserve," as part of it found to its cost on the 28th August, 1914. The initiative on that splendid occasion was taken by the British, who compelled the enemy to give battle by means of a delightful little ruse in which submarines not only played the leading part, but had "supplied the information on which these operations were based."

At midnight on the 26th August Commodore Roger Keyes hoisted his broad pennant on the *Lurcher*, a small T.B.D. of only 765 tons, and accompanied by the *Firedrake*, of similar displacement, escorted eight submarines to sea. On the night of the 27th the vessels parted company, the submarines to take up positions preparatory to the following day's work. Destroyer flotillas, the Battle Cruiser Squadron, the First Light Cruiser Squadron, and the Seventh Cruiser Squadron also left their various bases and made toward the Bight.

At dawn the *Lurcher* and the *Firedrake* carefully searched for U-boats the area that would be traversed by the battle cruisers in the succeeding operations, and then began to spread the net into which it was hoped the Germans would fall. E6, E7, and E8, travelling awash, proceeded in the direction of Heligoland, the destroyers following at some distance. They were "exposing themselves with the object of inducing the enemy to chase them to the westward." In this decoy work the submarines were eminently successful. In the ensuing action they played no active part. To quote the commodore's dispatch:

> On approaching Heligoland the visibility, which had been very good to seaward, reduced to 5000 to 6000 yards, and this added considerably to the anxieties and responsibilities of the commanding officers of submarines, who handled their vessels with coolness and judgment in an area which was necessarily occupied by friends as well as foes. Low visibility and calm sea are the most unfavourable conditions under which submarines can operate, and no opportunity occurred of closing with the enemy's cruisers to within torpedo range.

The German U-boats were no more fortunate. Three of them attacked the Battle Cruiser Squadron before it was engaged, to be frustrated by rapid manoeuvring and the attention of four destroyers. The use of the helm also saved the *Queen Mary* and the *Lowestoft* during the battle.

The most enthralling incident in the fight centres around E4, whose commander witnessed the sinking of the German torpedo-boat U187 through his periscope. British destroyers immediately lowered their boats to pick up survivors. They were rewarded by salvoes from a cruiser. Lieutenant-Commander Ernest W. Leir prepared to torpedo the vessel, but before he could do so she had altered course and got out of range. Having covered the retirement of the destroyers, he went to the rescue of the boats, which had necessarily been abandoned. The story of what followed is well told by a lieutenant in a letter to the *Morning Post*.

> The *Defender*, having sunk an enemy, lowered a whaler to pick up her swimming survivors; before the whaler got back an enemy's cruiser came up and chased the *Defender*, and thus she abandoned her whaler. Imagine their feelings; alone in an open boat without food; twenty-five miles from the nearest land, and

that land the enemy's fortress, with nothing but fog and foes around them. Suddenly a whirl alongside, and up, if you please, pops His Britannic Majesty's submarine E4, opens his conningtower, takes them all on board, shuts up again, dives, and brings them home 250 miles! Is not that magnificent? No novelist would dare face the critics with an episode like that in his book, except, perhaps, Jules Verne; and all true!

Another survivor asserts that while he was in the whaler about two hundred shells burst within twenty yards without doing the slightest damage to the company. A lieutenant and nine men of the *Defender* were stowed below in E4, while a German officer, six unwounded men, and twenty-six others who had sustained injuries of various kinds were provided with water, biscuit, and a compass, and told to make for land. A German officer and two A.B.s were taken prisoners of war. The commodore justly remarks:

> Lieutenant-Commander Leir's action, in remaining on the surface in the vicinity of the enemy, and in a visibility that would have placed his vessel within easy gun range of an enemy appearing out of the mist, was altogether admirable.

The enemy suffered the loss of three cruisers and a destroyer, and one cruiser and at least seven torpedo-boats were badly mauled.

Reference has already been made to the running fight in the North Sea on the 24th of the following January, when Sir David Beatty very effectively prevented a raid on the Northeast Coast, and to the Battle of Jutland. The former affair, characterized by the Germans as having been broken off by the British, and in which they sank a hypothetical battle-cruiser, ended in the loss of the *Blücher* and serious damage to two other enemy battle-cruisers. The enemy squadron escaped because Sir David Beatty had chased them to the verge of "an area where danger from German submarines and mines prevented further pursuit." The Germans were so keen on meeting the hated British that they sheered off immediately they sighted our ships and laid a straight course for home. Although the *Lion* and the destroyer *Meteor* were disabled, they reached harbour safely and the necessary repairs were speedily effected.

These are some of the highlights of a picture which has in it many dark and sombre shadows. Enemy submarines exacted a heavy toll of the British Navy. It would be a tedious business to detail the loss of every man-of-war lost by enemy action. Casualty lists make uncongenial reading, but it is well to bear in mind that Germany's campaign was not entirely devoted to commerce-destroying. I shall therefore deal with some of the more outstanding triumphs of her attempt to control the Empire of the Ocean from below before dealing with the victories of her British rivals in the Realm of the Underseas.

H.M.S. *Pathfinder* was the first naval vessel to be lost by submarine action in the Great War. When the news was given to the public, it was announced that this fast light cruiser of 2700 tons had struck a mine "about twenty miles off the East Coast," a geographical expression conveying the minimum of information. The intimation sent to relatives of those who lost their lives stated that the ship had been sunk by a submarine, which was the case. The discrepancy in the two statements was due to a belief that the *Pathfinder* had been blown up in the manner originally described. Subsequent investigation proved this to be incorrect. It was not contradicted at once because the Admiralty held that possibly the intelligence might hamper operations for catching the offender.

It must have occurred to many people, however, that a notice issued shortly after the original *communiqué*, that all aids to navigation on the East Coast of England and Scotland were liable to be removed, was more or less connected with the loss of the cruiser and the presence of enemy submarines. When letters from survivors began to appear in the newspapers it was clear that a torpedo had caused the loss of the ship, which foundered twelve miles north of St Abb's Head, Berwickshire. The approach of the weapon was observed by some of those on board, and the order was given for the engines to be stopped and reversed. It was too late. The explosion took place close to the bridge, causing the magazine to blow up. A survivor says:

> I saw a flash, and the ship seemed to lift right out of the water. Down went the mast and forward funnel and fore part of the ship, and all the men there must have been blown to atoms.

When the order to man the boats was given it was found that only one boat was left whole; it capsized on reaching the water. Nothing could be done to save the *Pathfinder*, now partly on fire and *in extremis*. The death-knell of hope rang out sharp and clear: "Every man for himself." Officers and crew jumped overboard and made for anything floatable that had been flung adrift by the explosion or thrown out by the men themselves when the last dread order had been given. Wonderful work was done by a lieutenant and a chief petty officer. Both of them powerful swimmers, they paddled about collecting wreckage, and pushing it toward those in need of help. One of the most miraculous escapes was that of Staff-Surgeon T. A. Smyth, who got jammed beneath a gun, was carried down with the ship, and escaped with a few bruises.

The dramatic swiftness attending the loss of the *Aboukir*, the *Hogue*, and the *Cressy* accentuated the ruthless nature of the sea campaign in the public mind. The three armoured cruisers were struck down within an hour by the same submarine. They were patrolling in company, and two of them were lost while going to the assistance of the *Aboukir*, which was believed to have struck a mine.

Sixty officers and over 1400 men, many of them reservists, perished as a sequel to Otto Weddigen's prowess and their own humanity, or more than the total British losses at the battles of the Glorious First of June, St Vincent, the Nile, and Trafalgar. From a naval point of view the loss of the ships was unimportant. One is apt to forget that men-of war have often a floating population equal to many a place in the United Kingdom which prides itself on being called a town. If several hundred inhabitants of such a spot were wiped out in a few minutes it would be regarded as a terrible happening. The tragedy of the affair would come home to us because a similar thing might occur where we live. Yet often enough a naval disaster arouses nothing more than scant sympathy and a mere comment. During the Great War those at sea in our big ships faced such disasters every hour of every day and every night.

Fortunately the *Aboukir*, the *Rogue*, and the *Cressy* did not constitute the "British North Sea Fleet," as ultra-patriotic German newspapers inferred. According to his own statement, the commander of U9 was eighteen nautical miles to the north-west of the Hook of Holland when he first sighted the cruisers, time 6.10 a.m. The vessels were proceeding slowly in line ahead, and the first torpedo struck the *Aboukir*, which was the middle ship. The reverberations of the explosion could be felt in the submarine, for "the shot had gone straight and true." The *Aboukir'* s consorts closed on her, intent on offering assistance, but, as Weddigen points out, this was playing his game. They were torpedoed in rapid succession.

> I had scarcely to move out of my position, which was a great aid, since it helped to keep me from detection.
>
> One shot from the *Cressy*, he adds, "came unpleasantly near to us."

The commander pays a generous tribute to his foes:

They were brave, true to their country's sea traditions.

In one thing only was he unsuccessful. The cruisers were unattended by a covering force of destroyers, but while U9 was returning to her lair he came across some of these vessels. By exposing his periscope at intervals Weddigen hoped to entice them into a zone where capture or destruction by German warships was probable. Although the destroyers failed to put an end to his career, he likewise failed to get the flies into the spider's parlour.

The Admiralty held that the commanders of the *Rogue* and the *Cressy* committed a pardonable error of judgment, and noted that:

> The conditions which prevail when one vessel of a squadron is injured in a mine-field or is exposed to submarine attack are analogous to those which occur in an action, and that the rule of leaving disabled ships to their own resources is applicable, so far at any rate as large vessels are concerned.

The *Hawke*, a cruiser of 7350 tons, with an armament of two 9.2-in., ten 6-in., twelve 6-pdr., and five 3-pdr. guns, plus two 18-in. submerged torpedo-tubes, was characterized by some of those in the Service as an unlucky ship. She had collided with the White Star liner *Olympic* when that vessel was on her maiden voyage, an incident deemed quite sufficient to justify sinister prophecies of an untimely end. On that occasion she lost her ram, which was replaced by a straight stem. On the 15th October, 1914, when the war was only a little over two months old, she was torpedoed by U29, with the loss of some three hundred officers and men. Her enemies were subsequently decorated with the Iron Cross at the hands of the crown princess.

H.M.S. *Theseus*, a vessel of the same class which was patrolling with the *Hawke* in northern waters at the time, was attacked first, but managed to escape. The submarine then aimed at the *Hawke*, hitting her amidships on the starboard side aft of the fore funnel, and probably blowing up the magazine, as in the case of the *Pathfinder*. She settled very rapidly, "at God knows what angle," according to an eye-witness. She had nearly a hundred watertight doors, but even they can buckle and jam, and are not explosive-proof. When the order was given to abandon ship a few of the crew managed to get into one of the boats, while about forty others scrambled on to a raft.

Commander Bernhard Pratt-Barlow was of the company. "There

are too many on this raft," he remarked, "I will swim to another." He dived in, but was never seen again. It was merely prolonging the agony for most of those who remained. Before night many of the poor fellows had succumbed to exposure and the bitter cold. After being on the raft for twenty-three hours the survivors were picked up by a destroyer, and after recovery proceeded to Portsmouth for a new kit. The last seven words epitomize the splendid spirit of the British Navy.

The *Hermes*, an old cruiser used as a seaplane-carrying ship, was sunk in the Straits of Dover in October 1914, while returning from Dunkirk. She was the victim of two torpedoes fired by a U-boat. The sea was choppy, which may account for the submarine's escape, for she was not seen. As the *Hermes* was near the warships engaged in bombarding the Dunes in support of the Belgians, it is more than likely that the enemy vessel had been hopeful of catching larger fry, an expectation which did not materialise. One sailor who endeavoured to make himself more or less comfortable on an upturned table was asked if he was training for the next Derby, while two fellows in similar straits informed their friends in the water that they were Oxford and Cambridge. The *Hermes* must have been what is called a 'matey' ship. The majority of her company were saved.

Another loss to the navy in 1914 was the *Niger*, a torpedo gunboat built in 1892 and sister ship to the *Speedy*, mined on the 3rd September.

The little vessel of 810 tons was torpedoed while on patrol duty by the first U-boat which succeeded in dealing destruction in the Downs. Despite a high wind and a heavy sea, all the officers and seventy-seven men were saved, thanks in no small measure to the efforts of three Deal boats and the fact that many of the bluejackets were wearing life-saving collars. The submarine was seen approaching from the direction of South Sand Head Lightship, but as the *Niger* was anchored she was an easy prey. At the moment of impact the wireless operator was actually sending the S.O.S. signal. When the explosion occurred Lieutenant-Commander A. T. Muir was on the navigation bridge, which, despite severe injuries, he vacated only after every other person had left the sinking vessel.

The gunboat was struck abaft the foremast. Although the bow was soon under water, she kept afloat for quite twenty minutes, probably because orders had been given for the watertight doors to be closed. One poor fellow was lugged through one of the portholes; another scrambled aboard after he had been rescued, hauled down the flag, and returned to the boat.

The torpedoing of the *Formidable* was an inauspicious omen for 1915. This, the fourth ship to bear the name of one of *Hawke's* prizes in the Battle of Quiberon Bay, was a preDreadnought of 15,000 tons, armed with four 12-in. and twelve 6-in. guns, twenty-six smaller weapons, and four submerged torpedo-tubes. She was encountering a south-west gale in the Channel at 2.20 a.m. on New Year's Day when a torpedo struck her abaft the starboard magazine and abreast of No. 1 stokehold.

The *Formidable* was the first victim of a submarine attack in the darkness of night. While boats were being got away, and chairs, tables, and other floating articles thrown overboard for use as life-savers, a torpedo exploded on her port side. Captain Loxley, puffing at a cigarette, gave orders from the bridge as coolly and collectedly as though the *Formidable* was making her way to Portsmouth Harbour on an even keel in the piping times of peace. "Into the water with you! She's going!" he sang out. "Goodbye, lads. Every man for himself, and may God help you all!" He went down with his vessel and as goodly a company of seadogs as ever trod the deck of a British battleship. Over five hundred officers and men were coffined in the *Formidable* or drowned in attempting to get away. (I have dealt with the loss of the three cruisers and of the *Formidable* at much greater length in *Stirring Deeds of Britain's Sea-dogs,).*

The loss of this useful, if obsolescent, vessel was severely criticized by Admiral Lord Charles Beresford, (later Admiral Lord Beresford). He commented on the fact that the squadron of which the battleship was a unit had started from port with destroyers and afterward sent them back, also that the ship had slackened speed in an area known to be infested with submarines.

Although it was announced that the battleship *Russell* struck a mine in the Mediterranean, the Germans claimed that she was sunk by one of their U-boats. This was the second pre-Dreadnought and the third flagship to pay the price of Admiralty during the war. The *Russell*, named after one of six famous admirals, was commissioned in 1903, and completed her career on the 27th April, 1916. She carried four 12-in., twelve 6-in., ten 12-pdr., and two 3-pdr. guns, and four torpedo-tubes. Although Rear-Admiral S. R. Fremantle, M.V.O., the captain, twenty-four other officers, and 676 men were saved, over 100 of her complement were reported as missing.

Of the five capital ships lost by Britain in the Dardanelles campaign, the *Ocean* and the *Irresistible* were lost by mines or torpedoed from the shore, the *Goliath* was torpedoed in a destroyer attack, and the *Triumph* and the *Majestic* were submarined. On the 22nd May, 1915, the periscope of a U-boat was sighted from the battleship *Prince George*. A couple of rounds made the submersible take cover. That was the first occasion on which enemy underwater craft had put in an appearance in the vicinity of the Gallipoli peninsula. Three days later the *Swiftsure* was on the verge of being attacked, but her gunners proved too wide-awake and drove off the enemy. A little later the submarine discharged a torpedo at the *Vengeance*, and missed.

On the 26th the enemy was seen again, escaped, and plugged two or three torpedoes into the *Triumph*, lying stationary off the now famous, or infamous, Gaba Tepe. Her nets were down, but the weapons went through them with almost as much ease as a circus clown jumps through a hoop covered with tissue-paper. Henceforth devotees of this form of protection had little to say. The battleship disappeared in fifteen minutes, fortunately without a heavy roll of casualties. Three officers and fifty-three of her considerable company were lost. Like the *Swiftsure*, her sister ship, the *Triumph* was built for the Chilian Government and purchased by Britain. An enemy submarine exacted another toll on the following day, when the *Majestic*, one of the oldest battleships on active service, was sunk while supporting the troops against an attack by the Turks. Within four minutes of the explosion, says a member of the French Expeditionary Force who witnessed the catastrophe, the *Majestic* turned completely over and went down.

> It was a terrible moment, but it was also sublime when 600 men, facing death mute and strong, were thrown into the sea, covered and caught in the torpedo nets, which ensnared them like an immense cast-net among the gigantic eddies and the profound sobs of their dear annihilated battleship. I shall never forget that infernal instant when submarines, aeroplanes, cannons, and quick-firing guns dealt death around me. And yet this vision only lasted the space of a flash of lightning, for we too looked death in the face, and in our own ship's boats we took part in the finest rescue that the palette of an artist ever represented.

So the French have forgiven us for Nelson and Trafalgar!

The last battleship to be sunk by a U-boat in the World War was H.M.S. *Britannia*, lost near Gibraltar on the 9th November, 1918. Two explosions occurred, killing some forty of the crew. An hour and a half later, while she was still afloat, the periscope of a submersible was spotted. The guns of the stricken leviathan were trained and fired, with what success is uncertain. Then two destroyers dropped depth charges where the enemy was seen to submerge. If her ugly sides ever rose again they certainly did not do so in the vicinity of the *Britannia*. Shortly afterward the battleship turned turtle in deep water.

CHAPTER 5

Tragedy in the Middle Seas

> Germany must for all time to come maintain her claim to seapower.—Lt.-Gen. Baron von Freytag-Loringhoven, Deputy Chief of the German General Staff.

The Adriatic afforded much interesting naval news. The strategy of the Austrians was exactly that of the High Sea Fleet—tip-and-run raids and avoidance of battle whenever possible. During the blockade of the Austro-Hungarian naval ports of Pola and Cattaro previous to Italy's becoming an active participant in the war, the battleships and cruisers of the French Fleet were frequent objects of attacks on the part of enemy underwater craft. The armoured cruiser *Léon Gambetta* escaped being submarined on the 2nd September, 1914, only to fall a victim on the 27th April, 1915. The Austrian U5, a small boat with a surface displacement of 235 tons, commanded by Lieutenant von Trapp, picked her up some twenty miles south-west of Cape Leuca.

It was a brilliant moonlight night, the armoured cruiser was steaming slowly, and hitherto no U-boat in the Adriatic had betrayed activity after the passing of day. The great black shape, with its four massive funnels, stood out a mammoth silhouette as the first torpedo sped on its devastating errand. It struck the port side, wrecked the dynamos, and plunged the ship in darkness, precluding the possibility of a momentary flash of a searchlight to discover the assailant. The wireless was also put out of action by the same cause. A second torpedo wrought havoc in one of the boiler-rooms. A Vienna account says:

> From the heeling of the cruiser Lieutenant Trapp concluded that a further torpedo was unnecessary.
>
> An effort was made to beach the ship. This failing, it became the

difficult task of Captain Andre to provide for the safety of his crew, a task not only hampered by lack of illumination, but by the boats having been swung inboard to ensure the more effective use of anti-torpedo guns. "The boats are for you; we officers will remain," Admiral Sénès told the crew without the slightest affectation of heroism, although neither he nor any single individual on the quarterdeck was to be saved. He called the men his children, told them to keep steady and take to the boats. "Forward, sailors of France!" he cried.

"My destiny is here," said Commander Depérière, the worthy colleague of so gallant an officer. "I die with my ship. *Vive la France!*"

Portable torches were used to show the way to the wounded and the sick. To make escape easier the captain issued orders to fill the starboard compartments so as to counterbalance the intake of water on the other side. He did not want the great ship to turn turtle before *mes enfants* had been afforded an opportunity to escape. One officer, anxious to restrain any undue haste that would retard escape, took out a cigar from his case, lit it, and puffed away as calmly as though he were in Toulon Harbour instead of standing in a foot of water on a ship that was rapidly sinking under him. "*Vive la France!*" shouted the officers on the bridge; "*Vive la France!*" echoed the many who had failed to get away.

With that ringing cheer of Victory and not of Defeat, the *Léon Gambetta* and 684 officers and men of the gallant company disappeared out of the night into the greater darkness. From first to last the tragedy took just ten minutes.

Those who were saved owed their lives to the fine courage of the commanders of Italian torpedo-boats and destroyers, who ran the risk of being mistaken for French men-of-war. (Italy was then a neutral). Jean and Jacques are never at a loss when it comes to paying a compliment. Had they been British sailors who were pulled out of the water, a gruff but well-meant "Much obliged" would probably have sufficed. Frenchmen are more artistic. They cried "*Vive l'Italie!*" As for U5, when she returned to Cattaro she was naturally received with honours.

The *Danton*, a French battleship with a displacement of 18,028 tons, completed at Brest in the spring of 1909, was on the point of celebrating the seventh anniversary of her launching when she was struck down in the Mediterranean on the 19th March, 1917. She had taken many months to build, but took only thirty minutes to sink. Destruction comes easier to man than construction. Two torpedoes accomplished her end. Fortunately the catastrophe occurred in the afternoon, and the tragedy of the personnel of the *Léon Gambetta* was not repeated, although even then 296 of her company lost their lives. The destroyer *Massue* and patrol vessels rescued the remaining 806 officers and men.

The story of how Lieutenant-Captain Robert Moraht sent the *Danton* to her doom was subsequently told by himself. The following is based on his lively narrative.

At midday the U-boat was off the southwest point of Sardinia, and those of the crew not actually required for the working of the ship were enjoying a breath of fresh air on deck with a delightful sense of having nothing whatever to do. Moraht was below, when the whistle of the speaking-tube blew a short, sharp blast. He answered the summons readily enough. "A steamer on the port bow," came the message, spoken in a tone of some urgency. Almost before the commander had taken his ear from the instrument the men were clattering down the ladders and taking up action stations. Reaching the conning-tower with some difficulty by reason of the undue haste, Moraht distinctly saw the outlines of the vessel whose appearance had so suddenly changed their programme for the afternoon. The commander picked it up with his glasses. "French battleship!" announced a fellow officer who was standing at the telescope. At the moment the commander's thoughts were centred on whether the U-boat had been seen, whether hunter and hare were both aware of the other's presence.

Apparently not. The *Danton* kept on her zigzag course, as yet far out of range. Had she sighted the submarine she could have got clear away; there was little chance now, for Moraht had submerged. Presently a destroyer made her appearance, likewise zigzagging, and in advance of the battleship. The U-boat was nearer the object of her vengeance, and likewise nearer danger. Destroyers are to submarines what terriers are to rats. Moraht felt a shade uncomfortable. Besides, a battleship in the Mediterranean, or any other sea for the matter of that, does not go about blind. Keen eyes look out for her safety and their own.

What the men on the destroyer might miss, those on the *Danton* might find. The commander of the submarine was sparing in the use of the periscope. There is a tell-tale wake when that apparatus is above the surface that human device cannot dispel. The waters, parted by the tube, embrace as though long separated, leaving a trail of emotion behind. Moraht popped it up now and again as necessity compelled, took his bearings, lowered it, and checked his course.

The weather conditions on this 'Mediterranean Front' changed in favour of the Germans, as they usually did in France, according to popular belief, whenever the Allies took the offensive. Listen to the commander:

> A considerable lightening of the mist was rolling up from the north-west, and the wind was freshening; thick white tufts of foam stood on the deep blue sea. That was the light we wanted. Anyhow, nobody saw us. The destroyer raced past without suspicion about in 600 yards off, then the giant ship herself came before our bow. Everything was just right today. 'Both tubes, attention! No. 1—let go! No. 2—let go.'

The periscope vanished, its wash was replaced by that of the torpedoes and a liberal accompaniment of bubbles. The weapons, at an interval of five seconds between them, tore the ship asunder. Later, from a safer distance, Moraht took a peep at his victim in her death-agony. The rudder was hard to port, proof that the twin harbingers of destruction had been seen and a fruitless attempt made to dodge them. The torpedoes could scarcely have performed their duty more loyally. The *Danton's* massive keel was where her turrets ought to have been; her bulgy side, with casemates resembling a fortress, revealed "two holes like barn doors."

Moraht says that his boat 'buck-jumped' after the shots. This means that the compensating tanks, which fill with water to make up for loss of displacement when a torpedo leaves the tube, did not act quickly enough. As a consequence the periscope and the upper part of the superstructure appeared above the surface for a second or two. The *Massue* dropped depth charges, and the 'buck-jump' may not have been entirely unconnected with them.

Today, (1919), the submarine that robbed the Allies of a fine ship mounting four 12-in., a dozen 9.4-in., and sixteen 2.9-in. guns does not figure as a fighting unit in what remains of the German Navy. She has joined the *Danton,*

Visiting the bottom of the monstrous world.

Austrian submarines depleted the ranks of Italy's naval forces by several ships, but the hereditary enemy of the Land of Dante lost considerably more at the hands of Italy, which also policed some 300 miles of coast with flotillas of hydroplanes in addition to the regular naval units. During a reconnaissance in force in the Upper Adriatic, the *Amalfi*, an armoured cruiser of 9958 tons displacement, carrying four 10-in. and eight 7.5-in. guns, was torpedoed at dawn on the 7th July, 1915. According to information received, it was the intention of the Austrians to bombard the Italian coast. While searching the Dalmatian littoral for the enemy, with the idea of bringing him to battle before he could carry out his object, the cruiser was lost. The ship listed heavily to port almost immediately, and sank in less than thirty minutes. Nearly all her officers and crew, numbering 684, were saved. Before giving orders to leave the ship the commander lined up his men on the quarterdeck and shouted, "Long live the King! Long live Italy!" The response was not less hearty than if they had been given a week's leave.

One instance of extraordinary bravery stands out conspicuously, though the discipline was exemplary in every respect. While in the water the chief engineer was drawn toward the revolving propellers, and one of his arms was completely severed. A surgeon witnessed the incident when swimming at no great distance away. With powerful strokes he reached the injured officer, took off his own belt, applied it as a tourniquet, and then supported the sufferer until help arrived. The surgeon was on the verge of collapse, but he had performed a feat probably unique in the annals of first aid.

The second armoured ship to be lost by Italy was torpedoed three weeks later in the same sea. She bore the honoured name of *Giuseppe Garibaldi*, whose presentation swords of gold were kept on board as treasures beyond price. The cruiser formed part of a squadron that had been bombarding the railway and fortifications at Cattaro, where a number of Austrian battleships had taken refuge, unwilling to face four Italian vessels which had outlived their youth. The enemy adopted much more stealthy tactics. As the *Giuseppe Garibaldi*, the *Vettor Pisani*, the *Varese*, and the *Ferruccio* were steaming away they sent out a flotilla of submarines. The first attack was skilfully fended. Subjected to a withering fire, in which the *Giuseppe Garibaldi* joined, two of the U-boats sought safety in flight. U4 was so badly damaged that she sank. A fourth either lay 'doggo' for a time or returned to the attack a little later. Her first torpedo, fired at the close range of about 500 yards, missed, but the second did such damage, despite the cruiser's belt of 6-in. armour, that saving her was out of the question. The majority of her crew of 540 were rescued.

When Germany and Austria arranged to drench Europe in blood

in pursuit of Teutonic ambitions, the Austro-Hungarian Navy possessed three completed Dreadnoughts, of which the *Viribus Unitis* was one. This powerful battleship of 22,000 tons, carrying twelve 13-in. guns, twelve 5.9-in. quick-firers, six torpedo-tubes, and a complement of nearly 1000 officers and men, was attacked in Pola Harbour by an intrepid French submarine, which succeeded in damaging her to such an extent that she was rendered useless for a considerable time. Had she been at sea it is probable the *Viribus Unitis* would have sunk, but plenty of assistance was handy, and she reached dry dock with a very ugly wound in her hull and certain portions of her engines so badly wrecked that the workshops at Trieste had to get busy to provide new parts.

This was in December 1914. She was still in Pola Harbour in May 1918, when a little Italian motor-boat penetrated the mine-field, cables, and steel nets guarding the entrance and completed the discomfiture of the great vessel. Captain Pellegrini and three volunteers discharged two torpedoes at the *Viribus Unitis*, and after seeing them take effect, sank their own tiny craft to prevent it from falling into the hands of the enemy. This was the thirteenth operation by the Italian Navy against enemy bases, and was completely successful. Apparently the Dreadnought was resurrected, for she was again sunk in November 1918 by means of a time-charge laid by two Italian officers.

Italy also lost several fine destroyers by attack from Austrian or German U-boats. The *Impetuoso* was submarined in the Straits of Otranto on the 10th July, 1916, with small loss of personnel, but the fate which befell the *Nembo* was more tragic and more romantic. The *Nembo* was escorting a transport to Valona. The submarine was sighted on board the destroyer, whose commander at once changed course so as to cover his charge, which had some 3000 soldiers on board. He succeeded in doing this, and the torpedo intended for the transport struck the *Nembo* with full force. She at once began to settle, but the indomitable officer swung his ship round with the intention of ramming his assailant.

Loss of speed and gain of water on the part of the destroyer gave the U-boat time to submerge, but the commander still had another card to play. He ordered depth charges to be dropped overboard. There was a mammoth upheaval of water, followed by the reappearance of the enemy showing evident signs of distress. Shortly afterward destroyer and submarine went to a common grave, the *Nembo* carrying with her most of her gallant crew, while eleven men from U16 managed to scramble into one of the destroyer's boats that floated by without a solitary occupant.

Vienna newspapers, like those of Berlin, endeavoured to bolster up the naval cause of the Central Powers by deliberately manufacturing desirable news. In January 1915 the Austrians were told that their E12 had sunk the French battleship *Courbet*, a Dreadnought armed with a dozen 12-in. guns. That was sufficiently wide of the mark in all conscience, for it was absolutely untrue, but the loss of the *Jean Bart* by colliding with her when going to her assistance was tagged on to make the victory still more complete. E12 certainly did succeed in hitting the *Jean Bart* with a torpedo, but the material damage was of slight importance and was speedily repaired. At the time the *Courbet* was many miles away from the scene of the imaginary action—"in excellent trim," as the French Ministry of Marine stated. On another occasion the French battleship *Véritè* was alleged to have been seriously damaged by a German submarine.

This tale of disaster, terrible in the loss of great ships and greater men, is at the worst only a record of what is legitimate in modern naval warfare. Those who thought, like Nobel, that the more violent the agencies to be employed in conflict the more likelihood of preserving peace had their fond delusions shattered in the saturnalia of the centuries. Likewise those who sow the wind often reap the whirlwind.

CHAPTER 6

Horton, E9, and Others

If the submarine had succeeded our Army in France would have withered away.—D. Lloyd George.

Previous pages have had much to say about U-boats. The northern mists, from the obscurity of which the Grand Fleet occasionally emerged into the broad sunlight of publicity, were as nothing compared with the fog of war which veiled the hourly activities of British and Allied submarines. Scouting is notoriously hazardous and necessarily private. Our underseas craft had sufficient of it. In the performance of this task they also tackled much other business, tracked and sent to the bottom vessels of their own species though not of their own tribe, wormed their way through waters sealed to surface ships, ferreted a course through strings of floating mines, dodged unanchored infernal machines, convoyed in safety hundreds of thousands of troops, and stalked men-of-war. They proved themselves friends to all but the Ishmael of the seas; and when opportunity served they snatched him from a watery grave when he ought to have perished.

The first German warship to be sunk by a British submarine was the *Hela*. She fell to E9 on the 13th September, 1914. Heaven knows it was not for lack of searching for legitimate prey that nothing had been secured by our underwater craft ere the second month of the war. Like Villeneuve's ships before Trafalgar, if any German vessels occasionally took an airing they also took good care to keep near home. The *Hela*, a light cruiser of 2040 tons displacement, with a complement of 178, of little consequence for fighting purposes because her heaviest guns were 15½-pdrs., was only six miles south of Heligoland when she was torpedoed by Lieutenant-Commander Max K. Horton.

E9, it may be well to note, had already won her spurs in the prelude to the Battle of Heligoland Bight. Two torpedoes were fired, with an interval of fifteen seconds between. One hit. Greatly daring, about a quarter of an hour later Horton took just the suspicion of a glance in her direction through the periscope, and saw that she was heeling over to starboard. When he again ventured to use his 'eye' there was no *Hela*, and a trawler had gone to the rescue of her crew. One of the crew wrote:

> What we are so proud about is that it is the first torpedo fired from a British submarine that made a hit, and it has been a great competition among all our boats to get first one in, and of course we consider ourselves 'the cock of the submarine flotilla' now.

A number of German torpedo-boats hunted for E9 during several hours after the destruction of the cruiser. Yet the following day saw her calmly at work examining the outer anchorage of the island fortress, "a service attended by considerable risk." An exceptionally heavy westerly gale was blowing on the 14th and continued for a week. On a lee shore, with short, steep seas, the lot of the submarines in the Bight was both hazardous and unpleasant. the commodore says:

> There was no rest to be obtained, and when cruising at a depth of sixty feet the submarines were rolling considerably, and pumping—*i.e.* vertically moving about twenty feet.

Officers and men were granted prize bounty amounting to £1050 for sinking the *Hela*, an exploit which the crew regarded as avenging the *Pathfinder*.

Further insight into the hazardous life of those who operated in the Bight is afforded by the following extract from another official report:

> When a submarine is submerged, her captain alone is able to see what is taking place. The success of the enterprise and the safety of the vessel depend on his skill and nerve and the prompt, precise execution of his orders by the officers and men under his command. Our submarines have been pioneers in waters that have been mined. They have been subjected to skilful and well-thought-out antisubmarine tactics by a highly trained and determined enemy, attacked by gunfire and torpedo, driven to lie at the bottom at a great depth to preserve battery power, hunted for hours at a time by hostile torpedo-craft, and at times

forced to dive under our own warships to avoid interfering with their movements. Sudden alterations of course and depth, the swirl of propellers overhead and the concussion of bursting shells, give an indication to the crew of the risks to which they are being exposed, and it speaks well for the morale of these young officers and men, and their gallant faith in their captains, that they have invariably carried out their duties quietly, keenly, and confidently under conditions that might well have tried the hardened veteran.

On the 6th of the succeeding month E9 was 'at it again.' She was patrolling off the estuary of the Ems, near the much-advertised island of Borkum, which boasted some of the most powerful guns ever mounted for coast defence. Presently the enemy's torpedo-boat S126 came along, entirely unsuspecting. (We should call S126 a destroyer, but the term is unknown in the German Navy. All vessels of the type are dubbed torpedo-boats, irrespective of size).

Horton was really after bigger game, but when out shooting pheasants one does not disdain a pigeon if nothing else is available. He was keen on a battleship, and only a little while before had spotted a fair-sized cruiser, an excellent 'second best.' When enthusiasm was at its height, and triumph reasonably sure, circumstances compelled him to dive. We are not told what those circumstances were. Perhaps we should not be far wrong if we ventured the opinion that they were intimately connected with the noisome presence of fleeter craft whose pet particular prey is the British submarine. When the officer had another opportunity to observe what was going on in the upper world, the larger ship had gone out of sight and a smaller vessel come into view.

Within a hundred yards of E9 was S126, followed at some distance by a second T.B. Horton waited until the leader had travelled another 500 yards, ensuring a 'comfortable' range, and then fired. The commander evidently believed in even numbers, for he discharged two 'rooties' at his quarry, as he had done when attacking the *Hela*. It was just as well that he did, for one missed. The other struck the enemy amidships and worked deadly havoc. Coastguards on the Dutch island of Schiermonnikoog, opposite Borkum, and some seven miles from the scene, heard the roar of the explosion, and saw a great column of water shoot up near the forepart of the ship. In three minutes all that remained of S126 was flotsam. She went down bow foremost, like a leaping salmon. As the stern rose her men took to the water. Most of them appear to have been rescued by a cruiser which came up a little later, but did not consider it advisable to make a long stay. "Look at her!" Horton cried. "The beggar's going down!" as though it was the most surprising thing in the world for a ship to sink after having a 21-in. torpedo plugged in her side.

The second torpedo-boat, unwilling to run the risk of sharing her consort's fate, made off, leaving the shipwrecked crew of thirty-six to fend for themselves. The lost vessel, launched in 1905, had a displacement of 420 tons, and carried three 6-pdr. guns and three torpedo-tubes.

When E9 swung into Harwich safe and sound the crews of destroyers and other craft based there knew that Horton and his gallant little band had scored another hit. No wireless conveyed the intelligence. She was displaying the White Ensign, plus two unofficial flags that are the pride and glory of the Submarine Squadron. These little bits of bunting, one yellow and the other white, bore the death's-head and cross-bones so intimately associated with the pirate of yester-year, and more appropriate to the Huns. The former represented the 'tuft' of the *Hela*, the latter that of the latest victim. The officers and crew received further prize money to the tune of £350 for 'digging out' S126. Horton was awarded the D.S.O., and noted for early promotion. On the last day of 1914 he became Commander.

The news was spread abroad by Germany that the action had taken place in Dutch territorial waters, within a mile of the shore. The Dutch Naval Staff promptly contradicted this report, pointing out that sands extend for two and a half miles from Schiermonnikoog, off which it was alleged E9 had committed this grave misdeed.

Horton's succeeding *coup* took place in the Baltic, and rightly belongs to a later chapter. I introduce it here because it will better help us to appreciate his worth.

Shortly after the Germans had occupied Libau, Russia's most southerly port in the Baltic, a certain mysterious submarine made her presence felt in the Mediterranean of the North. An official bulletin from Petrograd stated that the boat was British, and that she had sunk the pre-Dreadnought *Pommern* off Danzig on the 2nd July, 1915. The censor in London removed the reference to the nationality of the submarine, but a little later it leaked out that E9 had resumed operations and was responsible for the disaster. In reply to a question put by Commander Bellairs, Dr Macnamara answered that no official report

The Second Exploit of E9
When Lieutenant-Commander Max K. Horton torpedoed S126 in the mouth of the Ems

had been transmitted to the Admiralty, "but from a semi-official communication received from the Russian Government it appears that the name of the officer referred to is Commander Max K. Horton, D.S.O.," which statement was received with enthusiastic cheers by the House of Commons.

The *Pommern* was completed in 1907, and displaced 13,200 tons. She carried four 11-in. and fourteen 6.7-in. guns, and a crew of over seven hundred officers and men. The *Pommern* was the first German battleship to be sunk in the war. The coveted Order of St George (Fourth Class) was bestowed on the Commander by Tsar Nicholas. The German Government vigorously denied that a battleship had been lost, but

All the King's horses and all the King's men
Couldn't put Humpty Dumpty together again,

and all the contradictions in the world failed to resurrect the *Pommern*.

The energetic E boats did not remain in obscurity very long. In the following month the enemy endeavoured to secure naval control of the Gulf of Riga. Their first attempt, made on the 8th August with nine battleships, twelve cruisers, and a brave showing of torpedo-boats, was a complete failure. It was followed up eight days later by a more ambitious force. Favoured by heavy sea fog, the enemy cleared a channel through the mines and net defences at the entrance within forty-eight hours, and were then ready to penetrate farther. If we accept the assertion of the Russians, the Germans paid dearly for their adventure. Against their own losses of two gunboats and several torpedo craft they assessed those of the Germans at two cruisers, and eight torpedo-boats either sunk or badly damaged. In addition, the *Moltke*, a battle-cruiser, was torpedoed by E1. She was not mortally wounded, and was towed back to harbour, where she remained until Beatty claimed her. The Huns gained nothing and lost much in this attempt to dominate the Gulf.

On the 19th August, 1916, Lieut.-Commander Robert R. Turner of E23 attacked an enemy battleship. The vessel, a member of the *Nassau* family, the first type of Dreadnought to be built in a German yard, was powerfully armed with twelve 11-in., twelve 5.9-in., and sixteen 21-pdr. guns, in addition to half a dozen submerged torpedo-tubes. The displacement was 18,600 tons, and the speed 19-20 knots, but experts held that the class was a failure when compared with our own earlier Dreadnoughts.

The first torpedo fired by E23 badly damaged the battleship. Of that there is not the slightest doubt. Five destroyers immediately went to her assistance. While these were engaged in escorting her, a second torpedo hit the target, and the officer in command of the submarine reported that he "believed she was sunk." Then began a war of contradiction. The Germans stated that one of their submarines had attacked a British destroyer and a cruiser, both of which went down shortly afterward. They admitted that the submarine was rammed, but added the rider that she had returned to harbour 'badly damaged.' The question of the loss of a second U-boat was carefully hedged.

The statement can only be verified when all reports from our submarines are to hand.

An ingenious ruse. The report anent British losses was without foundation.

As in the above case, it is not always possible to ascertain the result of a shot. Many other instances of likely losses could be cited. A British submarine saw four battleships of the *Kaiser* class off the Danish coast. After making all ready to attack, the boat broke surface of her own accord owing to the exceedingly heavy swell. This terrible risk was run quite accidentally, but she got under again. Four torpedoes were discharged at a range of 4000 yards at the third ship in the line. Two explosions proved that the weapons had performed their tasks, and the commander was of opinion that the third and fourth ships had both been hit. He was about to verify his belief when a destroyer was heard racing in his direction, followed by others. For two hours they patrolled in search of the boat that had shot this '*bolt from the blue*.' They failed to find her. Two depth charges nearly did, but not quite, and a sweep dragged ominously over her hull. Puzzle: Did the battleships founder? The *Marineamt* in Berlin knows but does not say. In fifty-one months of conflict British submarines successfully attacked forty-three enemy warships.

A British submarine, referred to in a Dutch official communication as C55, was patrolling in the North Sea on the 27th July, 1917, when she picked up a German steamer. This was the *Batavier II*, of 1328 tons net, proceeding in the direction of Hamburg. The North Sea, or 'German Ocean' as those who dwell on its eastern fringe fondly call it, had not been darkened by a mercantile ship of that nationality for many long months, and even the *Batavier II* was British-built and had been captured from the Dutch. The submarine overhauled her, and after having sustained damage by gunfire, she was captured, her crew escaping in their boats. A prize crew took possession of the vessel and endeavoured to bring her to port. The idea had to be abandoned because she made so much water. The opening of her sea-cocks speedily sent her beneath the waves. Twenty-eight survivors of the steamer's crew were subsequently landed at Texel.

According to the Dutch Navy Department, the steamer was towing the motor-ship *Zeemeeuw* at the time, and at the opening of the engagement both vessels were outside territorial waters. When they were abandoned they had again entered the three-mile limit. The prize crew succeeded in getting the *Batavier II* outside, but owing to her disability and a strong current she again drifted within the Dutch sphere of influence. A Dutch torpedo-boat then hoisted the signal "Respect neutrality," and the submarine retired. The *Zeemeeuw* was taken in tow and conducted to Nieuwediep.

Less than a month later the *Renate Leonhardt*, another German steamer, attempted to run the blockade. Instead she ran ashore near the Helder, and after being refloated was met on the high seas by a British submarine, which made short work of her. The crew were picked up and taken to Holland.

Let me close this chapter with a contrast. Fiendish brutality characterised the behaviour of most German U-boat commanders. It mattered not whether the ship attacked was sailing under the colours of the Allies or of neutrals. To them war was a biological necessity, a phase in the development of life, to be waged relentlessly and vitriolic ally. The more cruel the method, the shorter the conflict. That was the Prussian theory, and the Great Conflict proved it false. To the German the neutral country was only neutral when it was working for the Fatherland. Often enough, even in these circumstances, he preferred to regard it as an open enemy. The lanes of the ocean are strewn with the wrecks of neutral craft and dead men assassinated by "our sea-warriors" in their hideous attempt at world-conquest. I quote a report received from the commander of a British submarine. The statements are corroborated by the neutrals of the world:

> On the morning of March 14 1917 His Majesty's submarine E——, when proceeding on the surface in the North Sea, sighted two suspicious craft ahead. On approaching them, however, she found them to be ship's boats sailing south, and containing

some thirty members of the crew of the Dutch steamship *L. M. Casteig*, which had been torpedoed and sunk by a German submarine some distance to the northward over twenty-four hours previously.

After ascertaining that there was both food and water in the boats, E— took them in tow at once, and proceeded toward the Dutch coast at the greatest possible speed consistent with safety, in view of the state of the weather. Some four hours later the Norwegian steamship *Norden* was sighted, and as she showed some natural reluctance about approaching the submarine, not knowing that it was a British one, the boats containing the Dutch crew cast off the tow and pulled toward her. E— kept the boats in sight until they were seen to have been picked up by the *Norden*, and then proceeded on the course which had been interrupted for this act of mercy.

Mercy as a biological necessity of war! It is a suggestive thought, of British origin. It compares favourably with the treatment of forty of the crew of the s.s. *Belgian Prince*, who were lined up on U44 and drowned as the submersible plunged. About a fortnight later Paul Wagenführ, the instigator of this diabolical outrage, was drowned with his confederates. U44 was their coffin.

CHAPTER 7

Submarine *v.* Submarine

Grapple your minds to sternage of this navy.—Shakespeare

At the beginning of the war it was freely stated that the one ship a submarine could not fight was the submarine. This theory, like so many others, went by the board in the process of time. Finally the notion was completely reversed. Allied underwater craft ferreted out many an enemy submersible. Indeed, if we accept the authority of Rear-Admiral S. S. Robison, of the United States Navy, they did "more than any other class of vessel" to defeat the U-boats.

The French and Italians name the units of their underseas navy. They are not vague, impersonal things denoted by a letter and a number, after the fashion of an inhabitant of Portland Prison. The first recorded action between submarines took place in June 1915. It remains one of the mysteries of the war. The Italian submarine *Medusa*, after carrying out several daring reconnaissances, was torpedoed by an Austrian submersible of almost similar type and size. The *Medusa* was quite a small boat, built at Spezzia in 1911, with a displacement of 241 tons on the surface and 295 tons below water. Her crew numbered seventeen. She was scouting in the Adriatic when the incident occurred, and we must presume her to have been comparatively close to the enemy without being aware of the fact, otherwise her action is unaccountable.

For some reason or other she came to the surface, whereupon the commander of the Austrian U-boat sighted her through his periscope and torpedoed her. An officer and four men were picked up. According to a later report, divers were sent down to examine the condition of the *Medusa* with a view to salvage operations. They made the startling discovery that the wreck of an Austrian submersible was lying close to that of the Italian, suggesting that the two vessels had participated in a duel in which both had got a fatal shot home and neither was the victor.

In August of the same year an Italian destroyer was escorting a submarine, when the commander of the former became aware that his ship was the object of attention on the part of an Austrian U-boat. He could see the periscope just sticking out of the water. Judging by her movements the enemy was manoeuvring for a favourable position from which to strike. The destroyer sought to cover her charge, and did so. At the same time the submarine took advantage of the protection thus afforded, and played the same game as her rival. Everything being ready for the projected attack, the destroyer changed course so as to give her consort an unlimited field for operations.

The Austrian opened fire from one of her bow tubes, and scored a miss. The Italian, not satisfied with the target presented, made no reply. Both tried to outmanoeuvre the other, and admirably succeeded for an hour and a half. It was the most skilful game of 'touch' ever played. At last the Italian secured a slight advantage and fired. Almost at the same moment her adversary did the same, but whereas the Italian escaped without a scratch, the Austrian received the full force of the blow amidships. Not a man of the crew of U12 survived, though the destroyer reached the spot shortly after the submersible had disappeared.

On one of those evenings which the tourist in Venice calls perfect because the sea and sky seem to have less imperfection in them than most things deemed of the earth earthy, the commander of an Italian submarine was taking a look round. A wilderness of blue water, calm as the proverbial millpond, had met his gaze all day, and was becoming tedious. Perfection depends so much on the point of view. To him the sea which pleases and fascinates the traveller was a medium for work, and had become the abomination of desolation by reason of enforced inaction. He had almost completed the circle of his observations when a blot representing something maritime appeared squatting on the waters. He held on his course, his eyes strained on the far-away object.

As the submarine and 'it' grew nearer, 'it' assumed definite shape. A submersible of Austrian origin without doubt, lying on the surface as listless as a dead whale. At first men were busy on the deck, then they disappeared one by one down the hatches until there was not a living soul visible. Apparently the Italian boat had not been seen. By great good fortune it might escape observation if the enemy did not bring his periscopes into early service.

The Italian broke surface, stealthily approached, found the range. There must be no mistake, no 'giving the show away,' and likewise no hesitation. She was discovered nevertheless, though not through lack of caution on the commander's part. One of the enemy's 'eyes' moved in her direction, revealing its owner's dire peril, and at the same time making the Italian's task more risky. At the moment the Austrian was broadside on—a lovely target. Slowly the Austrian began to turn so as to bring her torpedo-tubes to bear on her rival. A few more seconds would have sufficed, but the Italian officer got his blow in first. It literally disembowelled his enemy, and she sank like a stone.

Ramming submarines was formerly regarded as the special prerogative of surface vessels. Submersibles were certainly more inclined to fight duels by other means, but several instances could be cited of British commanders who did not hesitate to turn and rend an enemy without so much as a shot or a torpedo being fired. A British submarine was patrolling her beat in the North Sea. Suddenly her commander caught sight of a couple of periscopes that had no right to be there. He tackled the U-boat, ramming the nose of his vessel so far into her side that he could not back it out again. It was a horrible predicament for both of them. Thanks to the German's effort the British submarine got clear. By pumping out the ballast tanks the U-boat managed to rise to the surface, bringing her assailant with her. The wounded vessel slowly drew away, making water rapidly. Already the bow was submerged, and she betrayed an unhealthy list to starboard. Less than two minutes later the stricken pirate gave a lurch and disappeared.

On another occasion a British submarine and a German U-boat sought to come to grips for nearly half an hour. As soon as one had taken up a position the other dodged. At last the British commander ventured a torpedo. It missed by a few feet. Again the game of hide-and-seek began with renewed zest. It went on for exactly eight minutes, when another torpedo went speeding through the water in the direction of the U-boat. There was a terrific noise as the weapon struck the enemy's stern, which rose completely out of the water with, judging by the smoke, one or more of the aft compartments on fire. Another U-boat had finished her career. She rose almost as straight as a church steeple, then slid under.

One of our submarines chased a U-boat for nearly two hours before she finally sent her quarry to the bottom. When the commander first became aware of the enemy's presence the latter was making ready for a cruise on the surface. She was then too far away to warrant a shot, and consequently there was every likelihood that the German would escape unless swift measures were taken for dealing with her. The British officer dogged the U-boat with grim determination, then struck a patch of shallow water. If he could safely navigate this he knew that the other's 'number was up'; if he avoided it by taking a circuitous route he was equally confident that the enemy would escape. He took the risk, bumping the bottom heavily several times, and stealthily approached to a distance of 550 yards. Two torpedoes were fired simultaneously. From his place of safety, several fathoms below, the commander heard them explode. When he took a peep no submersible was visible, though the water was bubbling where she had floated a few minutes before.

Some of the commanders of British submarines are exceedingly cryptic in their reports. They give the barest information and the fewest possible details. Here is one in its brief entirety:

> 10.30 a.m.—Sighted enemy submarine, so dived and altered course.
>
> 10.47 a.m.—Enemy picked up in periscope.
>
> 10.50 a.m.—Again altered course.
>
> 10.52 a.m.—Stern tube torpedo fired.
>
> 10.53 a.m.—Sharp explosion heard.
>
> 11.10 a.m.—Came to surface and sighted oil right ahead, with three men swimming in it. Two were picked up, but the third sank before we could reach him. Dived. Survivors stated that submarine U— was hit in a full tank just before conning-tower and sank very rapidly by the head, rolling over at the same time.

Here is a chapter of thrilling heroism told in less than fifty words:

> 10 a.m.—Sighted hostile submarine. Attacked same.
>
> 10.3 a.m.—Torpedoed submarine. Hit with one torpedo amidships. Submarine seen to blow up and disappear. Surface to look for survivors. Put down immediately by destroyers, who fired at me.

Had the periscope been in good health—it was suffering from a stiff neck that took three men to move—the commander might have bagged one or two of the destroyers in addition to the submarine. As it was he dared not risk the operation, particularly as he knew that the surface craft would be scouring the sea in every direction and dropping pills all round him. He put a distance of four miles between himself and the scene of his prowess, then awaited events. Depth charges were used in great profusion. He lay at the bottom and heeded them not, though the noise of discharge was heard right enough. For hours he listened to vessels passing above, and once a wire sweep scraped along the port side with an ominous grating. It was not particularly inviting waiting for something to happen, but the commander had the satisfaction of knowing that he had scored a victory over his rival. Through the ill-behaved periscope he had seen a torpedo take effect forward of the conning-tower, send up a tall column of water and yellow smoke, and had watched the U-boat disappear.

While returning home after an arduous cruise, a British submarine, travelling on the surface, came across a U-boat prowling about for merchantmen. She also was unsubmerged, and apparently so engrossed in searching the horizon for fat cargoes that the patrol was not noticed. The Britisher went under, took careful aim, fired a couple of torpedoes, and waited. The weapons took effect. After the German had disappeared, the submarine came up and searched for possible survivors. One was bobbing up and down in the water. He was the captain of the U-boat.

The *Nereide*, an Italian submarine of 297 tons, was unloading supplies for the garrison at Pelagosa when an Austrian U-boat suddenly appeared. Although the commander of the *Nereide* made instant preparation to meet the enemy he had insufficient time at his disposal. Two torpedoes struck the boat and she went down with her crew.

Another of these unusual encounters occurred on the 19th June, 1917, when the French submarine *Ariane* was sunk by a U-boat in the Mediterranean. The vessel carried a crew of about thirty, of whom nine were saved.

I began this chapter by quoting a remark of Rear-Admiral Robison. I will end it with another anent Britain's stalking submarines, whose duty he regarded as the most hazardous occupation of the war. He stated that at Harwich, in June 1918:

> There was a record of twenty-five submarines which had gone out of port and had not come back.

CHAPTER 8

A Chapter of Accidents

In the future as in the past, the German people will have to seek firm cohesion in its glorious Army and in its belaurelled young Fleet.—Lt.-Gen. Baron von Freytag-Loringhoven.

All kinds of queer accidents happen to submarines. It was one thing to have a 'joy-ride' standing on the conning-tower of a spick-and-span craft in the neighbourhood of Haslar, and quite another to be compelled to lie 'doggo' hundreds of miles from the base owing to the near presence of German torpedo-boats out for slaughter. The following story has been told before, but may be thought worthy of repetition because it reveals the calm philosophy which is the submarine man's sheet-anchor. Without it he would speedily be reduced to nothing more than a nervous wreck.

A British submarine, intent on business intimately connected with the enemy, broke surface at an awkward moment. A shell whizzed close enough to assure the commander that somebody was on the watch for the Paul Prys of the British Navy. She went under, and after lying quiet for four hours again ascended for the purpose of finding out things. She discovered them all right, although they were not exactly of the kind she sought. One of the shots made a hole that necessitated a certain amount of plugging in double-quick time. The submarine submerged until after dark, then made off to report. "What did you do while you were at the bottom?" an inquisitive friend asked the commander as he was stretching his legs on the quay and forming a miniature smoke screen with whiffs of Navy Cut.

"I did fine," was the answer; "we played auction bridge all the time, and I made 4s. 11½d."

The officers and crew of a French submarine had a much more

exciting experience while engaged on similar duty in the early days of the war. They were proceeding cautiously toward the entrance of an enemy harbour. The periscope showed a delightful bag, but unfortunately the battleships that constituted it were protected by nets sufficiently substantial to make poaching impossible. There was no sign of movement other than in the smoke issuing languidly from the funnels. While the commander was taking observations, the ships began to show signs of life, and, with a number of torpedo-boats, denoted by their actions that they had every intention of weighing anchor. Here was an opportunity in a thousand, an unexpected one too, and the French officer seized it with avidity. As the enemy approached, he decided to go ahead a short distance so as to make assurance doubly sure. He wanted his aim to be absolutely certain. The submarine had not proceeded more than a few yards when there was a nasty jar. The rudder had become fixed as in a vice. It was caught so tightly in a steel cable that the boat could not budge an inch.

The crews of the T.B.s knew exactly what had happened, though how they came by the knowledge remains their secret. The vessels raced to the spot, hoping that the submarine was sufficiently near the surface to be rammed. Providentially she was not, though her crew heard the thrashing of the screws as they passed perilously close to her carcase. Immediately they had gone a furious hail of shells ploughed the sea, and one or two torpedoes were discharged by the enemy on the off chance that they might hit the intruder. It was a hot spot, despite the cold water. One who was on board says it was a miracle they were not struck:

> We thought we were done for, and we patiently awaited the explosion which would deliver us from the cruel suspense.

Meanwhile something had to be done, and quickly. Death by being blown to pieces is infinitely preferable to suffocation. The one is speedy and certain; the other slow and agonising. The water tanks were filled until they could hold no more. It was hoped that the added weight would force the craft down and snap the cable. Nothing happened. Then some one suggested that if the steering-wheel were compelled to move, possibly the wire would snap. If it failed to do so, and merely smashed the rudder, it could scarcely add to their anxieties. A doomed ship might as well be without steering gear as otherwise.

Half a dozen men exerted their full strength on the spokes. The wheel remained rigid for one, two, three seconds, then spun round with a sudden jerk that was not good for the equilibrium of the sailors but entirely satisfactory from every other point of view. The submarine went down several fathoms before she was brought under control.

The commander thought it was time to make tracks for a healthier clime without further spying. Risks are to be run only when necessary. Some hours later he ventured to use his periscope, only to find that an enemy vessel was no great distance off, evidently on the watch for such as he. The craft reached her base somewhat overdue. "*All's well that ends well*," but there is often a painful interim.

Explosions in underwater boats are not frequent, though they have occurred. Several men were either killed or injured in a disaster of this nature in a U.S. submarine cruising off Cavite, in the Philippines. The 'blow' was due to gasoline fumes, but the cause of ignition is unknown. U.S. submarine E2 also sank as the result of a similar mishap in the Brooklyn Navy Yard in January 1916.

Spain, a neutral country, was treated by the Germans as though she were an admitted combatant on the side of the Allies. Yet after torpedoing Spanish ships and leaving their crews to look after themselves as best they could, U-boat commanders were very thankful to take shelter in her ports on more than one occasion, despite the risk of internment. Here is a typical case. A French seaplane caught sight of U56 while on the prowl in the Mediterranean, dropped what bombs she possessed on the shadowy target, and proceeded on her way. She could do no more. U56 found herself in difficulties.

Damage had been done to the diving gear. The second officer was for 'risking it' and making an attempt to reach home. The commander thought otherwise, and as he had the casting vote in this as in other matters, the submarine limped into Santander. Kissvetter, the officer in question, after seeing that his ship was safely berthed, lined up his crew and marched them to the naval headquarters of the port. On giving his parole, he indulged in a lively chat with the officer in charge, during the course of which he was good enough to volunteer the information that the British bluejackets who had taken part in the raids on Zeebrugge and Ostend had displayed great valour.

Another French aeroplane distinguished itself in a similar manner off the Moroccan coast. It succeeded in so badly damaging U39 that the submarine could not reach Cartagena unassisted. There was an ugly dent in her bow, the upper structure was damaged, and part of the machinery put out of commission. Although his craft had sustained these injuries, the commander found no difficulty in submerging, which proves that the more modern U-boat was not so easily defeated as some people imagined. Presumably the submarine waited until another of her tribe was due to come along, possibly at dusk, and then made her presence known. At any rate, a sister boat towed her within easy distance of Cartagena Harbour, cast off, and disappeared. In response to signals of distress, a tug took the battered submersible in charge and berthed her alongside a Spanish cruiser. Commander Metzger, wearing the Iron Cross, was taken with his crew of forty men to Madrid and interned.

Fog is usually accepted as one of the plagues of the sea, but on occasion it proved an excellent friend to the enemy when British patrol craft were hot on the scent. This was not the case, however, with a small German submarine which went ashore near Hellevoetsluis in perfectly clear weather. The officer seems to have lost his bearings completely. After spending several fruitless hours hoping that the incoming tide would refloat his ship, the crew of fifteen men were compelled to abandon her.

Their action was certainly less desperate than the means adopted by the officers and men of a German mine-laying submarine which grounded on the French coast to the west of Calais. She 'touched bottom' at high tide, the worst possible time to choose for such a performance, and remained as immovable as a rock. At daybreak the coastguards saw the boat lying like a stranded whale, and promptly secured her. The officers and men offered no resistance. They had made their plans when they realised that the 'game was up.' By flooding the submarine with inflammable oil and applying a match they effectively prevented the boat from passing into the service of the French Navy.

Occasionally the hunter got more than he bargained for and was *'hoist with his own petard.'* The pirate commander of a U-boat was congratulating himself on having disposed of a British steamer with the minimum of trouble, when the victim blew up. He had attacked a vessel loaded with ammunition without knowing what was in her hold, and at comparatively short range. The explosion was so violent that it upset the stability of the submersible, and did so much damage in other ways that for a time it was believed she would founder. She was a sorry spectacle when the cliffs and frowning guns of Heligoland were sighted through the periscope.

In the early days of submarines their constitution could only be described as delicate. At each stage of progress the craft has taken on strength, until it has now anything but a fragile frame. That was one

"*Kamerad! Kamerad!*"

of the reasons why the British Admiralty was chary of issuing definite statements as to U-boat losses. Oil rising to the surface might be a sign that a submarine had been wounded, but was no definite guarantee that the patient would bleed to death. U-boats had a little trick of letting out oil when attacked in the hope that it would deceive the enemy. Take the case of a certain British submarine which had the very undesirable misfortune to barge into a German mine.

These submerged canisters were filled with a heavy charge of trotyl. You will better appreciate what this means when I add that T.N.T. has a bursting force when confined of 128,000 lb. per square inch. Yet this British-built ship is still afloat, and her crew alive to tell the tale. Vessel and men owed their escape from death to a mighty good bulkhead. She struck the mine bow on. Bulkheads 1 and 2 were burst open; her two fore torpedo-tubes, both loaded, were so twisted and jammed that they were rendered useless; the glass of the dials of the various recording instruments was scattered in all directions; every member of the crew was knocked flat, and the vessel sent to the bottom, nose foremost. A landsman would have said it was the end of all things; the men most concerned merely admitted that it was 'a nasty jar.'

When they had regained their feet the crew went back to their allotted stations to await orders. There was no need for them to puzzle why their craft was in this predicament. Neither a sunken wreck nor a submerged rock goes off with a bang. Meanwhile, there were some nasty leaks to divert the mind. They would be attended to later, when orders had been given. Discipline, like explosive, is a mighty force.

The commander picked himself up, carefully brushed his uniform with his hands, and went to his post. *"Let all things be done decently and in order"* is the acknowledged, if unwritten, motto of British submarines. The officer's action was the outward and visible sign that he had not forgotten it. He gave instructions for the pumps to be set in motion—if they were capable of movement. Everything depended on the answer. There were moments of tense anxiety before it came. No one, even the bravest of the brave, likes to be drowned like a rat in a trap. The motors were going. They had not stopped. But the pumps?

They started! With the beating of their pulse hope flowed in where before it had been on the ebb. The submarine came to the surface as game as ever, though terribly bruised. If *"God tempers the wind to the shorn lamb,"* a kindly Providence most assuredly watched over this craft. In enemy waters, three hundred odd miles from home, with a broken nose and internal injuries, she had not too much strength for the journey. She accomplished it satisfactorily enough, and was back again in her old haunts within a few weeks.

There is a particularly poignant note of tragedy in a strange mishap that befell another British submarine. The why and the wherefore of the accident have now been revealed. She was on her trials, and the ventilating shafts had been left open, flooding the rear compartments and drowning thirty-one men. She took an unexpected plunge of thirty-eight feet, stuck fast in the mud, and positively refused to budge. She lay like a dead thing. Every conceivable means of resurrection was tried; each failed. One has read of wonderful life-saving devices that are supposed to be donned by submarine men when their boat is in difficulties. They look like smoke-helmets. All that is required is to don one of these affairs, enter the conning-tower, open the lid, and pop up like a cork. It sounds simple, even entertaining, and might be introduced as a side show at an exhibition as a change from the Flip-Flap . Whatever other submarines may have of this kind, this particular boat either did not possess or could not use.

Officers and crew watched the hands of the clock complete the circle several times. There was little else to do. One does not talk much when waiting for eternity. Each felt that he was a doomed man, that ere long his wife would be a widow and his children fatherless. There was 'a war on,' but was this war? No enemy had done this, unless Destiny be an enemy. The forty-two men who still lived were within a comparatively short distance of the Scottish shore.

A terrible way out suggested itself to Commander Francis Herbert Heaveningham Goodhart. It is a formidable name to remember in its lengthy entirety, but one to make a note of. No future Book of Sea Heroes will omit it and be reasonably complete. The surname, although it is without an 'e,' fitted the man and the deed. He already had the D.S.O. to his credit; his next award, the Albert Medal in gold, was posthumous. Now you know the tragedy of the story. The story of the tragedy remains to be told.

Goodhart's "terrible way out" was this. The conning-tower of a submarine may be cut off from the boat by a trap-door. He proposed that a tin cylinder with a message giving full particulars of the position of the craft, the approximate length of time the men could hold out, and other details should be given to him, and that he should be blown up with it through the conning-tower. To effect this it was necessary to partly fill the chamber with water, turn on the high-pressure air, and release the clips that secured the lid. Placing the little cylinder in his belt, Goodhart set out on his last desperate adventure. Together with the commanding officer, who was to open and close the hatch, he stepped into the conning-tower. "If I don't get up, the tin cylinder will," he remarked quite casually to his colleague.

Water was admitted, then air. The lid fell back, and Goodhart made his escape. At this point Destiny, the unknown and the unknowable, intervened. It reversed the order of affairs that man had so carefully planned. Goodhart was flung back against the structure and killed outright. At the same moment the officer who was to retire into the submarine was shot upward and reached the surface. According to the official account in the *London Gazette*:

> Commander Goodhart displayed extreme and heroic daring, and thoroughly realised the forlorn nature of his act.

This does not go quite far enough. Had it not been for the dead man's attempt the instructions which were of such vital consequence to the imprisoned men would never have reached the rescuers. In due course fresh air, food, and water were sent to those below by methods private to the printed page. That night the survivors slept on shore as a slight compensation for their long and awful vigil.

In October 1916 the Danish submarine *Dykkeren* met with a somewhat similar mishap, although the cause of her sudden disappearance was a collision with a Norwegian steamer in the Sound. Divers entrusted with the salvage operations hammered messages of good cheer in the Morse code on the side of the sunken boat, to which the prisoners promptly responded. The commander alone lost his life. He was found dead in the conning-tower.

The pirate chiefs of Germany did not have it all their own way even when the absence of Allied patrol vessels, mines, and anti-submarine nets rendered existence a little less worrying than was usually the case with these pariahs of the deep. Lieutenant-Commander Schneider, who had won renown in the Fatherland as an instrument of the 'Blockade,' was swept overboard from his conning-tower while his craft was travelling awash. When his body was recovered life was extinct. It was consigned to the deep, whither the commander had sent many another during his career as a pirate. Some men from a U-boat in the Baltic were investigating the papers of a schooner, when a German cruiser put in an appearance.

Being uncertain whether the submarine was a foreigner or not, as no colours were displayed, the man-of-war ventured too close, and crashed into the bow of the stationary vessel. Both U-boat and cruiser were compelled to retire for repairs. Off Norway a German submarine mistook another of her own nationality for a British representative of the underseas and promptly torpedoed her.

CHAPTER 9

Sea-hawk and Sword-fish

The present submarine difficulty is the result of our undisputed supremacy upon the sea surface. The whole ingenuity, building power, and resource of Germany are devoted to submarine methods, because they cannot otherwise seriously damage us.—Lord Montagu of Beaulieu.

They call them 'blimps' in the navy. The term conveys to the landsman about as much information as 'Blighty' to a Chinaman. Blimps are speedy little airships driven by a single propeller, with a gondola capable of holding two or three men and a supply of munitions of war. These miniature Zeppelins are handy little craft not given to high flying and acrobatic feats, therefore less interesting to the general public than aeroplanes, though not less useful to the commonwealth. They were the guardian angels of the Merchant Service in the war. As such they played an important part in combating the submarine evil. These tractor balloons, with envelopes conforming to the shape of a fish, can hover over a suspected spot for hours at a time, which a seaplane cannot do. On the other hand, they are useless for raiding purposes on account of their vulnerability. Blimps are submarine spotters, and frequently submarine sinkers.

From the height at which it is accustomed to travel, the blimp, given fair weather conditions, is able to see the shadowy form of a 'dip chick' when not so much as her periscope is showing, and it can cover a fairly wide area of observation. If you stand on the bank of a broad and deep brook you will not be able to see so far into the water as if you were standing on a bridge that spans it and leaning over the parapet. That is why a gull looks for its food above the sea, and having glimpsed a toothsome, or rather beaksome, morsel, dives after it. This is also the secret of the spotter's sight. Many a German and Austrian U-boat disappeared in a welter of oil and bubbles by reason of the fact.

It was during Lord Jellicoe's term of office as First Sea Lord that increasing attention was paid to aircraft as an ally of the Senior Service. At the same time it is only fair to mention that when the British Expeditionary Force crossed to France in 1914, aircraft patrolled the marches of the sea between the French, Belgian, and English coasts.

The navy and the army have their own schemes of warfare, but in one particular plan of operations there is marked similarity. Just as the land is divided into sectors for fighting purposes, so the sea is divided into sections for the purpose of patrol. Destroyers and hydroplanes, auxiliaries and trawlers, airships and seaplanes have their beats mapped out for them like a City policeman. This does not mean that every square yard of salt water is covered—an obvious impossibility—but it does mean that as many square yards are watched as is humanly and practicably possible. In one month 90,000 miles were travelled by seaplanes on patrol, and 80,000 miles by airships.

When the war was very young, a seaplane containing an officer and a petty officer was scouting. Without any preliminary warning the engine broke down, and they were compelled to descend and drift on the surface with a heavy sea running. Of rescue there seemed to be little hope. Fog completely enveloped them. A survey of the damage proved that patching up was altogether out of the question. Nothing short of a lathe would suffice. The airmen fell back on tobacco, "the lonely man's friend." Even this comfort speedily failed them. Cigarettes and sea-sickness do not go well together. The poor fellows held on and watched their machine gradually break up. They were horribly ill, and on the verge of despair, when the throb of machinery suddenly fell on their ears, and a destroyer peered in through the opaque surroundings of their little world. They were no longer face to face with death. Other men have not always been so fortunate. One does not necessarily have to be washed overboard to be "lost at sea."

A couple of seaplanes on outpost duty were watching the waters below with great interest when one of them sighted a submarine travelling on the surface. They were up a good height, but the observers duly noted a couple of men on the conning-tower. Apparently the Germans were too intent on the business in hand to observe the sky-pilots, who kept on a steady course. They suffered a rude awakening a few minutes later. A weighty bomb fell plumb on the starboard side of the sea pest, midway between the conning-tower and the stern. That bomb 'did its bit' for King and Country. Slowly but surely the U-boat heeled over, ceased to make progress, and lay like a log on the water. Then the bow rose at an awkward angle, and the vessel began to settle rapidly. Another bomb, released by the second seaplane, burst close to the conning-tower, followed by a third bomb, "to make assurance doubly sure." This particular submarine was not handed over to Sir Reginald Tyrwhitt.

America did much excellent work in helping the British Navy to rid the seas of underwater pests. An ensign in the U.S. Naval Reserve attached to the Aviation Service was patrolling in a British seaplane with a British observer. Within thirty minutes of having started, "we sighted the periscope of a submarine directly in front of us," he reports:

> Immediately I opened the engine full out and attacked, dropping a bomb which landed a few feet ahead of the periscope and directly in line with it. A moment later a great quantity of air bubbles came to the surface. The water all about began to boil. I turned and attacked again. This time I dropped a bomb of twice the size. It landed nearly in the centre of the first disturbance. A mass of oil now appeared on the surface in addition to the debris left by the bomb itself. The second disturbance continued for some time. Then I circled round for two hours before returning to warn merchant ships in the vicinity and inform a destroyer escorting a British submarine of what I had done and seen.

From his point of vantage the look-out of a British airship noticed a steamer limping along in a manner which distinctly suggested that she was in difficulties. That had been a fairly familiar sight since the opening of Germany's illegal warfare. The cause of her crippled condition was evidently of enemy origin, though her assailant was invisible. Sea-wolves did not make a regular habit of gloating over their victims. That little hobby was only indulged in when the 'coast' was clear. The coxswain headed the airship in the direction of the stricken steamer, but before reaching her tugs had made their welcome appearance and lent the assistance of a stout steel hawser that worked wonders.

As a precaution against surprise the airship accompanied the miniature squadron. They proceeded quietly enough for a time, making fair speed, when a U-boat broke surface about five miles off. Signalling by wireless the position of the pest to all and sundry, the airship accelerated her engine and lowered to a height from which she could make the best use of her weapons. The submarine was not taken entirely unawares; she submerged before the sea-hawk was immediately above. Two bombs, released simultaneously, caused a terrible commotion and effected a kill. A destroyer which had picked up the wireless subsequently dragged the spot, and signalled the cheering news, "You've undoubtedly bagged her."

Better luck attended this effort than befell the pilot of a seaplane who came across a large submersible travelling awash. Here early demise seemed a certainty . Unfortunately there is many a slip 'twixt the bomb and the U-boat. One packet of high explosive fell ahead and another astern of the grey monster. The third was a marvellous shot. It did the aviator's heart good to see it strike. It landed directly in the centre of the deck. He had scored a bull's-eye. I am afraid I cannot quote what he said when the missile failed to detonate. His anger was not appeased by the knowledge that his supply of ammunition was exhausted. The enemy submerged, descended to the lowest depths, and made off.

Observation balloons, towed by destroyers, although they obviously lack the initiative of airship and seaplane, have their uses like their more energetic brethren of the sky. On one occasion an observer telephoned that there was a U-boat in the neighbourhood. Depth charges were thrown overboard, but achieved nothing more than causing the boat to shift her position. She passed from mortal ken so far as her hunters were concerned. Later on, however, the submarine came to the surface and began shelling a poor little helpless sailing vessel that could neither escape nor offer effective resistance.

The destroyer opened fire, and as a submersible is no match for this type of vessel, she promptly went below. Her rapidity of movement failed to evade Nemesis, though her smartness in this respect was highly commendable. Guided by the balloon, the parent ship took up the trail, and nine 'pills' were sent overboard with the compliments of the captain. Then followed such a display of oil as is rarely seen. No fake oil squirt ever succeeded in covering a mile of sea with the colours of the rainbow. The U-boat had gone to her doom.

The task undertaken by blimps and seaplanes in their daily warfare against the pirates was far from selfish. The Mistress of the Seas and her Allies kept guard over the welfare of neutral nations as well as of their own. While journeying homeward the Danish steamer *Odense* was met by a German submersible. It signalled her to stop. The order was complied with without hesitation, but instead of making an examination of the ship's papers the U-boat opened fire, killing two of the crew. The enemy commander then ordered the survivors into the boat. This was really inviting them to commit suicide, for the weather was such as to render the likelihood of the men's being saved extremely remote. While this little tragedy of the sea was being acted, a British submarine put in an appearance, apparently from nowhere. She had been summoned by aircraft. The U-boat did not stay to fire further shells into the steamer. Not long afterward a British patrol ship on its ceaseless vigil came across the Danes in their cockleshell, took them on board, gave them warm food and dry clothes, and amply demonstrated the fact that the British Navy was neither spiteful nor cruel because it did not own the globe.

A British coastal airship was scouting for a convoy bound westward. The voyage had been uneventful, when a look-out spied the track of a torpedo aimed with deadly certainty at one of the steamers. With marvellous agility the course of the airship was altered and traversed the trail still outlined on the water. It is said that she travelled at a rate approaching ninety miles an hour. There was the gaunt form of the submarine right enough, though submerged. Well-placed bombs did the rest.

Another airship, quietly sailing in the upper air, also came across a British convoy. The reply to the pilot's request for news was entirely unsatisfactory from his point of view. No U-boats had been seen or reported. Things were slow. They continued so for several hours after the two branches of the Service had parted, but brightened up a bit when a wireless message was received that a merchantman was being attacked by a pirate. Details as to position proved correct. The submersible was floating awash. Blimps being pre-eminently handy affairs which readily respond to helm and engine control, the airship was hovering over the U-boat before the latter was completely submerged. It boded ill for the intended victim, whose ballast tanks were slower in filling than the airship's mechanical appliances in accelerating.

The first bomb was a good shot, but not a hit. It fell three feet short of the mark, and exploded astern of the propellers. That it did the enemy no good was evident. Streams of oil, too voluminous to be make-believe, spurted to the surface. The second bomb was a direct hit aft of the conning-tower, causing the stern to rise upward. It would have been waste of good ammunition to spend more on the wreck that lay below. She slowly turned turtle, and was no more seen. Another U-boat had paid the price of her perfidy. The blimp had scored a full triumph that admitted of no question.

A seaplane was patrolling her section, keeping a sharp eye on possibilities in the nether regions that failed to eventuate. Presumed periscopes are sometimes in reality nothing more than mops or spars. After the novelty of flying has worn off it is apt to become a trifle boring without action. As the pilot was proceeding on his way, doubtless thinking that his luck was most decidedly out, he picked up a wireless message. Judging by its purport it was evidently sent by a U-boat no great distance off. He had not proceeded very far before he spotted his prey, comfortably squatting on the surface about a mile ahead.

The seaplane was 'all out' in a trice. Seahawk and sword-fish exchanged greetings, the one with a bomb, the other with a shell. The latter burst quite harmlessly within fifty feet of the aircraft, then splashed over the sea like a shower of pebbles. The bomb went more than one better. It fell on the U-boat and tore a great rent in her deck. While this battle royal was proceeding, three German U-boats, three torpedo-boats, and a couple of seaplanes were speeding in the direction of the firing. The weather was somewhat misty, but they sighted the solitary seaplane and tried to wing her. The pilot treated them with contempt, and calmly proceeded with the business immediately in hand. The firing in his direction became so heavy that it formed a barrage through which the German aircraft were totally unable to penetrate. The officer gave his enemy another dose of bomb, photographed her as she was going down, took a picture of her friends, and having exhausted his ammunition, returned to report.

A gunner on a British submarine cruising off Denmark proved himself a better shot than his German rivals in the afore-mentioned incident. Two enemy seaplanes saw the boat and dropped their highly explosive eggs. The bombs burst, made a great noise, but did no damage. A shell from the submarine sped straight and true and one of the seaplanes was brought down, whereupon her companion, realizing that the locality was unhealthy, beat a hasty and undignified retreat.

German airmen naturally endeavoured to turn the tables on us. They hunted for British submarines in addition to doing scouting work for their own. Within a month of the outbreak of war an enemy airman and his mechanic got what was at once the greatest shock in their lives and the means of the aforesaid lives being preserved. Their machine had broken down, and they were using it as a raft, when one of His Britannic Majesty's submarines rose to the surface. Instead of making war on them as a 'biological necessity,' the commander rescued the two men and took them into Harwich, after their damaged craft had been satisfactorily disposed of.

During the afternoon of the 6th July, 1918, a British submarine was on guard off the East Coast when five hostile seaplanes swooped down on her and made a vigorous attack with bombs and machine-guns. According to the German official account, the action took place off the mouth of the Thames, and two submarines were severely damaged, one of which, when last observed, was in a sinking condition. The report rather reminds one of occasions when Teutonic imagination has robbed the Grand Fleet of battle-cruisers. As it happened, the British craft sustained only minor injuries, and was towed into harbour by another submarine—presumably the one which the enemy had seen. She had suffered no inconvenience whatever from the seaplanes' attentions. Unhappily an officer and five men were killed in this attack.

Some time since the Berlin Press made much ado about a British submarine being sunk by a German airship. It was when Zeppelins were considered to be rather more substantial assets in the Wilhelmstrasse than they subsequently became. A little later the 'sunken' submarine returned to her base without so much as a scratch on her bulgy sides, and reported that she had been in action with a hostile airship, which she had damaged and driven off. So much for the Truth as propagated in Berlin.

One of the most brilliant exploits of what I may term the aerial phase of war in the underseas took place in March 1918. The scene of the engagement, in which three British seaplanes and five German machines were involved, was just beyond the North Hinder. While the enemy were attacking from the rear, and our men were busily engaged in putting up a stiff fight, a U-boat made its appearance ahead with several officers and men on the conning-tower. The three Britishers dived down, and having nothing else available, fired their machine-guns at the spectators, who disappeared inside and slammed the hatch. They then took up positions to renew the aerial combat. The fight continued for half an hour, to be broken off by the enemy when five British trawlers were sighted.

As for the submarine, she was nowhere to be seen. One of our seaplanes was then out of action owing to a petrol pipe having burst. It returned home without overmuch difficulty.

Meanwhile the remaining two seaplanes carried on with their patrol work, though some of the men were relieved. Almost three hours later they came across as pretty a sight as British airmen could wish to see. The five Germans were floating on the water. The British gave them a round or two from their guns, but before they had got well within range the enemy were up and had taken places in their usual V formation at a height of about 200 feet. This was speedily broken up as our airmen gained on them, the V rapidly assuming the appearance of an elongated I, or single line ahead. Having succeeded in scattering them, the British seaplanes attacked them individually. An enemy twin-seater was hurled down, followed by a second machine, whose observer and gunner were both shot, and a third seaplane was rendered unfit for immediate service. The other machines escaped because not a solitary cartridge was left available for pursuit; in all 2500 rounds had been fired. A solitary casualty was sustained on our side. A wireless operator was wounded in the neck, whereupon his companions administered first aid and returned to their respective duties.

Five British seaplanes were patrolling off the East Coast on the afternoon of the 4th June, 1918. After a particularly 'tame' flight, a similar accident to that which had occurred in the engagement related above compelled one of the machines to descend to the water. A petrol pipe had broken, and as repairs of this nature cannot be effected to a heavier-than-air machine while it is on the wing, there was no alternative but to come down. While the others were on guard, a squadron of five enemy aircraft was seen approaching. The seaplanes at once gave battle, but the Germans were in no mood for fighting, and made off as fast as their propellers would take them. When it was obvious that they could not be brought to action, the British machines returned to their crippled comrade. Two more hostile seaplanes appeared a little later, and were similarly disposed of.

Before the wounded sea-hawk was fit for further righting, no fewer than ten hostile seaplanes came in view. Probably they were the previous flock concentrated and augmented. There was no thought of "retiring according to plan." The Britons went to meet the enemy, as is their wont. By taking the offensive they would also best screen their comrades below, who were working with an energy seldom equalled. They, like the others, wanted to be up and at them. The aerial battle was sharp and furious. Two of the German craft were shot down; one of our machines fought till she could fight no longer. The latter eventually landed in Vlieland, Holland. Finding that the task of putting their craft in order was impossible with the appliances at their command, the crew of the other maimed machine set it on fire when they reached Dutch territorial waters, and made their escape by swimming to land.

During the course of the action a British seaplane was attacked by two of the enemy, and the assistant pilot was shot dead. Five other German 'planes then closed with the British machine. The pilot made a nose-dive, shook off his assailants, and put up such a hot fight with the gun in the stern that they broke off the contest. A little later the petrol pipe of this machine also broke, and the seaplane was forced to descend for the needful repairs. Petrol pipes are the *bêtes noires* of the airman's life. The engineer air-mechanic did his work with such dexterity that within ten minutes everything was in running order again and the machine was climbing up to rejoin its companions. When it reached them they set out in search of the enemy. They met with no luck, and returned to their base.

In such ways as these aircraft fought fish with steel fins and winged creatures after their own kind. There remained yet another method of warfare known to them, namely, bombing submarine bases, of which Ostend, Zeebrugge, and Bruges were probably the most important. Time after time one read in the newspapers that these places had been attacked by aircraft, until one wondered how it was that so much as a stone or a stick of timber was left. The reason is that a bomb explosion is entirely local in its effects. It does not spread like fire in a gale, though it may cause buildings to be gutted. It was only now and again that direct hits were scored on submarines, torpedo-boats, and other vessels in the docks. But there was another important factor to be taken into consideration. The soldiers, sailors, tinkers and tailors who inhabited these places could not possibly produce their best work under the strain of constant attacks from the air. They must have suffered from the 'jumps' pretty frequently; and Napoleon said truly that the moral is to the physical as three to one.

Submarines, aircraft, and surface fighting forces were involved in the famous Christmas Day attack on the heavily fortified base of Cuxhaven in 1914. This was a sequel to the German naval raid on Scarborough, Whitby, and the Hartlepools ten days before. Seven seaplanes, three seaplane-carriers, escorted by the light cruisers *Undaunted*, and *Arethusa*, several destroyers and submarines, duly arrived in the neighbourhood of Heligoland. When they had left England the previous afternoon the coast was bathed in sunshine, but the mouth of the

Elbe was fog-bound. However, the aircraft got away, their principal objective being the warships lying in Schillig Roads. The surface craft then toured about while awaiting their return, and were seen from Heligoland. Two Zeppelins, several seaplanes, and a number of U-boats came out to attack, but it is significant that although the British ships were off the German coast for three hours not a solitary surface vessel attempted to face them. They doubtless foresaw a second battle of Heligoland Bight and were anxious to avoid it.

Bombs from the aircraft dropped fast and furious; they merely ploughed the sea. Maxims, antiaircraft weapons, rifles, and 6-in. guns took up the challenge and put the Zeppelins to flight; torpedoes were fired at the *Arethusa*, and skilfully avoided by swift manoeuvring. A Taube spotted one of our submarines, made half a dozen attempts to sink her, and failed. In this matter they were no more successful than the British seaplanes, which tried to hit an enemy torpedo-boat and a submersible. What actual damage was achieved by the airmen is unknown, but the Germans certainly scored at Langeoog. Under the impression that T.B.D.s were hiding in the fog off the island they dropped a number of bombs, thereby killing several civilians.

Of the six British airmen who returned, three were picked up by our surface ships, the others by submarines. In the case of the latter the machines were sunk. For a time it was feared that Flight-Commander Hewlett had been brought down or was drowned, but he eventually turned up none the worse for his exciting adventure, having been picked up by a Dutch trawler. Chief Mechanic Gilbert Budds, writing to his father, gives a little glimpse of his exciting experiences:

> Just fancy Christmas Day—first on a ship through mine-fields, on a seaplane over the enemy's fleet and force, and then back in a submarine. During the homeward trip we had the gramophone going with all the latest music, and had chicken, Christmas pudding, custard and jellies for dinner. How's that, Dad, for a submarine in the heart of the enemy's fleet in war-time?

After all, perhaps life in an underwater craft during the war had its compensations.

The French seaplane patrol service also did wonderful things, as was to be expected, for our Allies took aircraft seriously when we only regarded them as expensive toys for wealthy folk with suicidal tendencies. In a single month, and in various samples of weather, their seaplanes made as many as 3139 nights. During the thirty days under review, ten submarines were attacked, six mine-fields were located, and nine night bombardments carried out. French airships also made 141 trips.

So much for statistics, which is the practical in undress uniform. Now for the more picturesque aspect of the Service. A couple of French sea-hawks were watching the Channel, and came across a German submersible on the surface. Apparently the commander of the U-boat had not the slightest notion that there was an enemy "up above the world so high" until he was attacked. When the rude awakening came he began to submerge. The boat was not quite so quick in her movements as the seaplanes. The airmen dived with extraordinary rapidity, and both scored a bull's-eye on the target.

The semi-official note says:

> The leading machine then returned to its base for a further supply of bombs, leaving the other machine to keep a look-out. The latter, a few seconds after the attack, saw the forepart of the submarine emerge at an angle of 45 degrees. Then the submarine slowly rose to the surface, without, however, being able to regain a horizontal position, and again disappeared in a violent whirlpool. Three times at short intervals the submarine attempted to rise to the surface, taking at each attempt a stronger list to starboard. Then the observer saw the whole of the submarine's port side exposed, while the submarine rested on its beam ends. Finally the vessel disappeared without having succeeded in getting its conning-tower above water.

One Sunday a British pilot and a Frenchman attached to the R.N.A.S. were on the spy for U-boats off the Belgian coast. They had scarcely been in the air half an hour, and had reached a height of about 9000 feet, when they saw two submarines lying side by side on the surface. The spot was some five miles west of Nieuport, where the water is shallow. To the aviators it looked very much as though the craft were just above a sandbank. So much the better for the attackers. The boats would have furnished lovely targets had there been no look-out below, but it was first of all necessary to decrease the distance separating the airmen from the objects about to be attacked, and during the descent the Germans saw their enemy. One of the submarines managed to get away, leaving the other to fend for herself. At 600 feet Lieutenant de Sincay dropped a bomb right on the conning-tower. A second missile did such terrible execution that the boat sank like a

A Seaplane of the R.N.A.S keeping a watchful eye on an enemy submarine

stone.

The great Austrian naval bases of Cattaro and Pola were visited several times by Italian airmen. On one occasion a raid was made on the former harbour at night and direct hits were scored on submarines and torpedo-boats, while an aerial attack on Pola was responsible for the destruction of three U-boats undergoing repairs.

It is only doing bare justice to remember that neutral aviators also played a part in making a life under the rolling deep in a U-boat anything but pleasant. Time and again German pirates endeavoured to use the deep fiords of North-western Scandinavia for purposes best known to themselves, but in all probability as convenient rendezvous for stabbing Norwegian vessels in the back. Several tried to hide themselves in Bergen Bay. They were discovered by native airmen and promptly informed that if they did not quit the neutral zone without delay they would be interned. They left.

Chapter 10

U-Boats that Never Returned

Let us march farther, undaunted and confident, along the road of force. Then our future will be secure against British avarice and revenge. The German is too good to become England's vassal.—Admiral von Scheer.

Many U-boats were buried in the same grave as their last victim. This was not adequate retribution, but it left the Navy and the Mercantile Marine with one submarine the less to fight.

Close to the wreck of the great White Star liner *Justicia*, a magnificent steamer of 32,000 tons, lie the remains of one of her attackers. There may be others, but I give the official figure. The submarine in question was sunk by the destroyer *Marne* on the 20th June, 1918, the day the Germans were being driven back across the historic river whose name she bore. The *Justicia* was dogged by submersibles for twenty-two hours, during which time no fewer than seven torpedoes were fired at her. It was the most determined onslaught ever made by U-boats. Moreover, the attack is remarkable by reason of the fact that not only were destroyers and other craft convoying the vessel, but she herself was armed.

The first torpedo struck and exploded in the engine-room, killing fifteen men and injuring the third engineer so terribly that he died later. The second weapon was diverted from its course by the *Justicia's* gunners; the third missed. Depth charges and other means were used to deal with the menace, and apparently with success. During the ensuing night nothing further was seen or heard of the enemy. Early the following morning, however, two torpedoes were fired simultaneously, one taking effect in No. 3 hold, the other in No. 5 hold. When it was realized that there was not the remotest chance of bringing the

Justicia to port, the crew of between six and seven hundred were quietly transferred to another vessel. The liner kept afloat for eight hours after that, a remarkable testimony to the efficient work of those who had built her in the Belfast yards of Messrs Harland and Wolff.

Several commanders of U-boats asserted that a number of attempts had previously been made to sink the *Justicia*, but had failed because she was provided with torpedo-nets. This does not seem altogether an adequate explanation, unless we are to presume that the devices alleged to be in use were not in position when the maritime snipers succeeded in sending her to Davy Jones's locker.

The during-the-war policy of the British Admiralty as regards lost, stolen, and strayed U-boats was one of reserve, and rightly so. When you are on the watch for a gang of burglars you make as little fuss about it as possible. If full publicity had been given to the methods of capture the Central Powers would have speedily become conversant with them. We preferred to let the enemy find out things for himself—if he could. To use an expression common on the Western Front, it 'put the wind up' German crews to find that an ever-increasing number of their friends on U-boats failed to report after a voyage. Except in rare instances no information as to their fate came to relieve their friends' anxiety. They just disappeared from mortal ken. It did not make for ease of mind; it harrowed the nerves of the strongest. The effect on the morale of the enemy was distinctly marked. The plot rebounded. The sea-dogs of the British Merchant Service were to be frightened into submission; their ships were to rust for want of use, moss was to grow on the quayside. It was the U-boat which surrendered to the White Ensign.

The first enemy submersible to be lost was U15, sunk in the North Sea by H.M.S. *Birmingham* on the 9th August, 1914. This was admitted by Mr Winston Churchill in a telegram to the lord mayor of the cruiser's name-place, whose loyal citizens had made a presentation of plate to her officers' mess. U15 was a small vessel of about 300 tons, carrying a crew of twelve officers and men, and appears to have had two or three consorts with her. An A.B. on the *Birmingham*, which was attached to the First Light Cruiser Squadron, sighted the periscope of a submarine, and fire was opened at once. The noise of the guns and the piercing notes of the bugle calling all to action stations brought those who were not on watch to their allotted positions in double quick time. Officers in pyjamas, men with one leg in their trousers and one out, scampered along the upper deck as though joining in a race, anxious only to get to grips with the enemy.

It is said that the first shell struck the periscope and rendered the submarine sightless. If so, it was a marvellous shot at a range of a couple of miles or thereabouts. Probably the sailor who set the story going was indulging in a little game of 'leg-pulling,' a hobby not unknown in the navy. There was a mighty swerve as the captain of the cruiser altered course so as to be out of the line of fire. In another instant the *Birmingham* was racing toward her assailant as though the engines would tear themselves from their pits in the excitement of the chase. Every gun was trained on the U-boat. Another shot rang out, wrecking the conning-tower. The sharp steel bow of the man-of-war did the rest. There were no survivors.

In October 1914 it was announced that the T.B.D. *Badger* had rammed and probably sunk an enemy submarine. This was contradicted by the Germans, who asserted that the vessel in question had returned to her base in a damaged condition. There was less uncertainty about a U-boat casualty that happened in the following month. U18 penetrated a certain harbour in the north of Scotland much frequented by naval vessels. It happened that just as the submarine was going in, a trawler attached to the patrol was coming out. Apparently the tough little craft passed over the U-boat, for the skipper immediately signalled, "Have struck submarine."

Now a submarine chase was much appreciated by those who commanded destroyers. There was sport about it rather more exciting than merely "barging about the North Sea." The T.B.D. *Garry* was first in the field. She slipped along in wonderful style and attempted to ram the enemy as she was endeavouring to get away. According to a seaman, the periscope crumpled up, but the jar that was felt was scarcely enough to warrant his commander in believing that the U-boat had run her course. Accordingly he cruised about for a while, anticipating that eventually she would come to the surface if any life remained in her. This is exactly what happened, and once again the *Garry* worked up to full speed. She was on the verge of crashing into the enemy when the crew appeared on deck. One of them waved a white handkerchief in token of surrender. It was a narrow squeak, but the destroyer rescued three officers and twenty-three of her crew. One of the latter was drowned. He volunteered to stay behind and open the Kingston valve so that the craft might not be captured.

To give a chronological list of the U-boats known to have perished in the war, with particulars of their death, would occupy all the pages in this volume. I can therefore only cite a few instances. The story of the sinking of an unknown marauder by the *Thordis*, a little coasting steamer of 500 tons, is too well known to require retelling. (See my *Daring Deeds of Merchant Seamen,* and *Stirring Deeds of Britain's Seadogs*). Captain Bell was the first master in the Merchant Service to win official recognition as a submarine-sinker.

U8 had been operating in the Straits of Dover and the English Channel for several weeks before she was finally rounded up by a dozen destroyers under the command of Captain C. D. Johnson. This was in the afternoon of the 4th March, 1915. Here again there was an alarming discrepancy in the company the submersible ought to have carried and the number she actually had on board. Her normal complement was twelve officers and men; when she was sunk twenty-nine survivors were picked up.

The sinking of U8 and U12 was made the basis of a threat of reprisals upon British officer prisoners in Germany because the authorities at Whitehall did not "feel justified in extending honourable treatment" to the men of U8. They held that there was "strong probability" of their having "been guilty of attacking and sinking unarmed merchantmen" and "wantonly killing non-combatants." Sir Edward Grey pointed out that up to the time of the incident more than a thousand officers and men of the German Navy had been rescued from the sea, "sometimes in spite of danger to the rescuers, and sometimes to the prejudice of British naval operations." Not a single British sailor had been picked up by the enemy. The widely circulated report that the officers of U8 were guests of Royal Artillery officers at lunch at Dover Castle was a falsehood.

The life of U12 as a pirate was extremely short. She was caught by the destroyer *Ariel* on the 10th March, 1915, before she had been able to do anything approaching appreciable damage, her sole victim being a little steam collier of 60 tons, which she sank by means of a bomb.

A certain amount of mystery is also associated with this particular submarine. Her displacement, if she were the original U12, was 300 tons submerged and 250 tons above water. Fourteen men would have been ample to work her, yet she had a complement of twenty-eight. It is possible, though the idea seems somewhat far-fetched on account of the limited accommodation on board, that the men in excess were being trained. What appears to be far more probable is that an old number had been given to a new boat, just as the name *Arethusa* has been borne by a long line of fighting ships in the Royal Navy. Ten of the pirates were picked up and landed in Scotland; eighteen were drowned.

Although Captain Otto Weddigen achieved momentary fame in Germany as the hero of an exploit that sent the *Aboukir*, the *Cressy*, and the *Hogue* to the bottom of the North Sea, he did not live long to enjoy his popularity. When the U9, the submarine which he commanded on that occasion, was withdrawn from service, he was given the U29, believed to have a displacement of some 800 tons, and to be armed with two quick-firing guns and four or more torpedo tubes. One of the U9's last adventures was to get entangled in the net of a Dutch steam trawler, necessitating the cutting away of the lines.

U29 first appeared as a commerce-destroyer about a fortnight before she was sent to the bottom. Her hunting-ground was the vicinity of the Scillies. Known as 'the Polite Pirate,' Weddigen sank five or six merchant ships, and on occasion regaled the crews with cigars and wine and towed their boats toward land. Not once did he behave with the stupid and blundering brutality of many of his associates in arms. When the crew of the *Adenwen* were taking to the boats, one of the men fell overboard. Weddigen happened to be on the conning-tower at the time. Noticing the sailor's plight and his rescue, the captain of the U-boat sent him a suit of dry clothes.

The German commander's order *Pour le Mérite* and the Iron Cross of the First Class went down with his ship. This misfortune reached the *Kaiser's* ears. That august personage sent duplicates to Weddigen's widow, at the same time condoling with her in:

> The bitter loss of a man whom the entire Fatherland mourns, who achieved unforgettable fame for himself and the Fatherland, and who will live for all time as a shining example of daring, calm, and resolution.

Weddigen's humanity came in very useful when the fate of U 29 had to be explained in the German Press. The *Deutsche Tageszeitung* suggested that:

> British ships surprised U29 while she was busy saving the crew of the steamer. In the midst of this humane work the knightly English must have caught U29 while she was helpless, and it would be easy for them to destroy her. The noble hypocritical sentimentality of the English Press about the captain points to facts of this kind.

Admiral Klaus, writing in the *Vossische Zeitung*, put forward the theory that the submarine was sunk by a British ship flying a neutral merchant flag, and added that as the British Admiralty had seen fit to withhold details there were apparently good reasons for not being proud of the success. The only information vouchsafed by the officials of the Wilhelmstrasse was couched in the baldest of bald language:

> U29 has not yet returned from her last cruise. According to the report of the British Admiralty issued on March 26, 1915, the ship sank with her entire crew. The submarine must therefore be regarded as lost.

The burial of the U-boat in a shroud of mystery must have been horribly galling to the bigwigs of Berlin. The intimation that she was "sunk by one of His Majesty's ships" conveyed nothing to them except the obvious. On the 9th June, 1915, Mr Balfour announced in the House of Commons that a German submarine had been sunk and the entire crew taken prisoners. The German Admiralty subsequently announced that U14 was evidently the vessel in question, as it had "not returned from its last expedition."

Whether the following letter is a typical revelation of the mind of the German underwater sailor or not is more than I can say, but it is particularly interesting as showing that the writer was thankful to a kindly Providence for sparing him when the game of piracy and murder had come to an end and he was safe in British hands. It could scarcely be supposed that every German who sailed in a submarine did it of his own free will or took a delight in the work. I can only suggest that all too often the Prussian Cult makes blackguards of men who are not by nature what they afterward become. The communication runs as follows:

> My dear, good Parents,
>
> Go to church the first Sunday after you receive these lines from me, and thank the good God for having so mercifully watched over and preserved me. I have fallen into the hands of the English, unwounded and whole in body and mind, and have been well treated, quite particularly so by the English naval officers.
>
> It was an extremely sad day for me. First of all in the morning I saw dead on the deck two poor Norwegians who had unhappily fallen victims to our gunfire. The day will be engraved on my memory in letters of blood.
>
> But as for you, dear parents, do not be distressed, and do not

weep for me. The good God Who has protected me hitherto will continue to be my aid, and if it should be His will that I should quit this world I shall know how to die.

The submersible in which the writer of the above letter served was UC39, commanded by Otto Ehrentraut, a personal friend of Prince Henry of Prussia. UC39 was a minelayer, but does not appear to have been so employed when she was destroyed. She was simply indulging in cold-blooded piracy with the aid of torpedoes and shell. Her first victim was the Norwegian s.s. *Hans Kinck*. Although the vessel stopped when summoned to do so, many rounds were fired at the helpless ship. Victim No. 2 was the British s.s. *Hanna Larsen*, which was sunk by bombs and the master and chief engineer made prisoners. Victim No. 3 was another Norwegian steamer, the *Ida*, when the old practice of firing after the vessel had stopped was again indulged. No fewer than twenty shells were hurled at her before Otto Ehrentraut gave the order to cease fire. It was only then that the men in one of the *Ida's* boats ventured to come alongside and inform him that two of their comrades, both wounded, had been left on the sinking vessel. When a German officer clambered on board, the mate and the steward were lying dead on the deck. There they were allowed to remain while the *Ida* was finished off with bombs.

A steamer and a trawler were next attacked. Both escaped in the mist. Another steamer was encountered a little later, but this time UC39 caught a Tartar. A destroyer was close by and opened fire. Before the submarine could dive sufficiently low to make her whereabouts uncertain a depth charge exploded in her near vicinity. Water poured in, making it dangerous to remain submerged. So she came to the surface, to receive a tornado of fire from the man-of-war. Ehrentraut appeared on the conning-tower, and was struck by a shell. His place was taken by another officer. As UC39 continued on her course, the commander of the destroyer yelled through a megaphone for her to stop. Before she answered the summons several of the crew had been killed or wounded, but seventeen survivors were rescued. All these events were crowded into two days.

The French, Italian, and Japanese Navies all displayed splendid prowess in dispatching submarines. The Austrian U3, a small submarine of 300 tons displacement when submerged, was rounded up in the Lower Adriatic by the French T.B.D. *Bisson* after a search in which Italian men-of-war had joined. No sooner was the periscope sighted than the destroyer scored a hit at over 3000 yards. The second shot was not so successful, for it fell short, but the third struck her and exploded in the engine-room. Although U3 went down in half a minute, twelve of her crew were rescued.

The U-boat which wrecked the *Chateaurenault* in the Ionian Sea on the 14th December, 1917, took a lot of killing. After the enemy had sent her first torpedo, the spot where she submerged was riddled with shells. On her reappearance shortly afterward, the gunners of the cruiser opened fire, causing her once more to make a hasty withdrawal. A second torpedo followed, and the U-boat was again shelled, while two seaplanes dropped bombs. Unable to keep under water, she came up for the last time, and was literally blown to pieces.

I have scarcely touched the fringe of a vast topic. In August 1918 Mr Lloyd George stated that 150 enemy submarines had been destroyed by the British Navy alone since the beginning of the war. Before the end forty more had been added to the obituary list, while three were destroyed by the Germans at Zeebrugge, half a dozen foundered in British minefields, and one was lost in the North Sea while crossing to Harwich. Precise particulars of the When and Where of submarine-hunting cannot even now be given, but the How of the matter will be related in fuller detail in later chapters.

CHAPTER 11

Depth Charges in Action

I believe the day is not distant when we shall overcome the submarines as we have overcome the Zeppelins and all the infernal machines started by the Germans in this war.—Lord Milner.

One of the most effective antidotes for the submarine menace when the approximate whereabouts of the enemy is known is the depth charge, already mentioned more than once in these pages. Outwardly it resembles nothing more murderous than a cylindrical drum such as is used for storing paraffin oil. There the likeness ends. Inwardly it is filled with high explosive, and fitted with a fuse that can be set to detonate at any desired depth. Given a reasonable amount of luck, the surprise packet when thrown overboard blows up in the track of the enemy. Very often it strikes a death-blow, sometimes it does such extensive damage that it is only with extreme difficulty that the injured craft can crawl back to port, and occasionally the enemy escapes with nothing worse than a nasty jar. The effect naturally depends on the distance separating the charge from the target.

Some time since a young friend of mine who is an engineer officer on a certain armed auxiliary was asked if he would volunteer to take charge of the engine-room of a minesweeper. "Their man" was in sick bay, and as mine-laying U-boats had become increasingly active in the vicinity, it was highly desirable that operations should be resumed with the least possible delay. As his own ship was not due to sail for several days, he assured the skipper that he would be delighted to render any possible service. Incidentally he looked forward to what he termed "a bit of sport."

It was abominably rough outside the sheltered seclusion of the harbour, and he was beginning to think that 'a willing horse' is a synonym for a fool, when a terrific crash made the ship quake, flung him in anything but a gentle manner against the nearest handrail, and nearly burst his ear-drums. Our friend glued his eyes to the indicator, expecting it to swing round to 'Astern' or 'Stop.' The hand remained motionless. He comforted himself with the reflection that if the bow was blown to bits or the vessel sent sky-high it was none of his business. It was not his duty to interfere with the navigation of the ship, which was certainly ploughing her way through the short and choppy seas as though nothing untoward had happened.

Presently the skipper's burly form appeared at the casemate.

"What on earth was *that?*" asked the engineer.

"Only a depth charge exploding a couple of miles away," was the answer. "There's lots of oil hereabouts."

Unfortunately the Allies were not the sole possessors of the prescription for these quick-acting pills. Depth charges 'made in Germany' were sometimes dropped in the tracks of British submarines. A certain commander, who also knows what it is to face the ugly muzzles of 6-in. guns spitting flame when a submarine is cruising awash, confesses to a preference for the latter weapon. This is the reason why:

He came near the surface at an awkward moment. No sooner had he fixed his eyes to the periscope than he discovered that enemy torpedo-boats—not one but many—were in the immediate neighbourhood. Their movements showed them to be perfectly well aware of his presence. His orders were terse. Any hesitation in translating them into action would have meant disaster. The boat began to descend, nose foremost. She continued travelling in that direction even when it was a matter of urgent importance to maintain an even keel. Something had jammed, and jammed badly. Then there was a terrific report, followed by a concussion that did more than merely shake the submarine.

Some of the crew were knocked down. No need to ask if there had been a seaquake. Everybody knew right enough what had happened, and fully realized that the shock was probably only the prelude to further episodes of a similar kind. Rivets, bolts, and plates held good—so did the beastly jam. The submarine just dived to the bottom. There the officer let her remain without any attempt to repair the trouble. Like Brer Rabbit, he believed there were occasions when it is supreme wisdom to 'lie low' and do nothing. This was one of them. There was no immediate haste. He appeared to be waiting for something.

The 'something' came three minutes later, accompanied by a deafening bang that made rich, warm blood run cold. Another depth charge had been hurled overboard. It made the submarine rock, but a careful investigation of every nook and cranny made it evident that she had not so much as sprung a leak. British shipbuilders are the finest in the world when they like, and they had liked when putting together this underwater craft. With those on board the *Norah Creina* the commander could say, "God bless every man that swung a mallet on that tiny and strong hull! It was not for wages only that they laboured, but to save men's lives."

Evidently the enemy was not quite satisfied that he had killed his prey. There was nothing on which to base a report of death. Surmise is not certainty; it withholds proof. The Germans got out their sweeps and began fishing. The imprisoned men could hear the cable scraping along their boat, and thanked God when it ceased. The wire rope got entangled in nothing. That was a big mercy.

A third depth charge was heard and felt to explode, nearer this time, but still without doing serious injury. The torpedo-boats dropped no more ground-bait after that. The submarine was "missing, believed killed." The Germans were not fond of remaining in one spot for any considerable time. When the victim was dead or mortally wounded, there was no need to attend the funeral. There were always the grey police of the patrol to be reckoned with.

Down below the crew of the "missing, believed killed" were straightening things out and wondering if they were to receive further attention from above. Two, four, six, eight hours passed, daylight with them. Little likelihood of the hunters being about now. Then the submarine, according to the official report, "proceeded to her base."

Before the war I tried to puzzle out why it was that human beings, of their own free will, became firemen on a battleship. One minute in a stokehold is sixty seconds too long for most people. To me the problem remains unsolved. Are they all possessed of the steel nerves of Hotham when he was told to fight his vessel till she sank and was comforted by Duncan's remark that he had taken the depth of the water and that when the *Venerable* went down his flag would still be flying? Stoking is bad enough, but what of those who volunteer for service in a submarine? They do not seem to be out of the ordinary ruck of humanity. Solve the riddle of the 'something' they possess and you will be able to put down in black and white, after the manner of a sum, the secret of Britain's Sea-power.

Seemingly unconscious of the unpleasant fact that a T.B.D. was a mere mile away, a submersible broke surface, presumably to recharge her storage batteries. No sooner had she come to the top than the commander discovered the British vessel racing toward him at full tilt. If the destroyer missed a fine chance of ramming by reason of the Hun's alertness, she certainly seized a rare opportunity for dropping a couple of depth charges. They gave the enemy a terrible shaking. No other reason would have brought the U-boat so perilously near the surface as to uncover the periscope, which appeared at an angle sufficiently rakish to show that the submarine was anything but comfortable. The T.B.D. gave her another dose. One or two other vessels appeared, anxious to render assistance with a further supply of concentrated destruction. In addition to a lavish waste of oil, there came to the surface four significant things: a calcium float, a broken steel buoy, a wooden ladder, and a lifebelt. I do not think there is the least likelihood that that particular U-boat returned to Zeebrugge or any other lair.

Sometimes even more conclusive evidence of decease was furnished by the victim. Motor launches which formerly lived a genteel existence, lifting silver cups at smart regattas, became terribly efficient engines of war as submarine-chasers. One of them sighted the 'eye' of a U-boat not more than 200 yards away. A couple of depth charges were dropped on the spot just after she had disappeared. Some hefty sheets of metal came hurtling up from Neptune's kingdom, flung wide of the attacking vessel by great good fortune. The usual tell-tale streaks of oil, ascending in ever-increasing volume, afforded further testimony to the efficacy of the explosions.

Some U-boats took a lot of killing; they seemed as hydra-skinned as the offspring of Typhon and Echidna was many-headed. They came to resemble the poor patient who has a complication of diseases and yet lives for years. Therefore we usually made assurance doubly sure. A destroyer on patrol gave a submersible a thundering good ramming. There was no doubt about it, because the skipper on the bridge saw a gaping hole in the hull just before the conning-tower, and seeing is believing. Now it was no part of British war methods to impose a lingering death on our enemies, however deep-dyed in sin they might be. We got the killing business over as speedily as possible.

On this occasion two depth charges were flung out to polish off the job with the maximum of celerity. Then the destroyer circled round the spot on the off chance that the U-boat might still be near the surface. There was plenty of oil rising thereabouts, but the commander of the T.B.D. was not quite convinced of a 'kill,' and it was his business to deal with facts rather than probabilities. So he anchored a buoy near the spot, determined to return at daylight. When he came back several hours later rainbow patches were still rising. He used another depth charge before proceeding on the uneven tenor of his way. In due course the position was swept and the wreck located.

Lord Jellicoe has told us that at night a submarine travelling awash is not visible at a distance of more than 200 yards. Moonlight, of course, increases visibility, and on the particular night I have in mind the look-out on a British auxiliary sighted a U-boat in surface trim about half a mile distant. The patrol vessel gave chase, but the submarine managed to submerge before her enemy came up. Half a dozen depth charges were dropped overboard. Their explosion—'some explosion,' as Uncle Sam would say—was followed by what the commander termed a 'disturbance' about 300 yards distant, which may or may not have been the U-boat breaking surface, likely enough inadvertently. At any rate, a shot whistled in that direction. Vast pools of oil settled on the water. Harsh, guttural voices made themselves audible above the tumult. One survivor was picked up. Sir Eric Geddes has said that when the full story of the British Navy in the Great War is told:

> It will surpass in heroism and daring and ingenuity and wonder the tales of Captain Marryat.

The speed of a convoy is necessarily that of the slowest ship, but sometimes bad steaming plays ducks and drakes with the keeping of a correct formation, on which so much depends. Ships have an awkward way of falling behind, necessitating their being shepherded like a flock of sheep, and adding considerably to the risks. The commander of a convoy needs a sweet temper.

A merchantman was forming an involuntary rearguard on her own account. She had fallen behind, and in her isolated position was an ideal target for any U-boat that might happen to be lying low by reason of the presence of lynx-eyed destroyers with the main body. One of the latter was detached to hasten up the sluggard. Scarcely had she reached her before one of the steamers in the van was neatly torpedoed. Heading for the track of the steel fish, the T.B.D. apparently cut across the submarine. She quivered from stem to stern with the force of the bump. The skipper of a sister ship distinctly saw a periscope sticking above the waves, and, coming up, dropped a depth

THE DESTROYER'S SHORT WAY WITH THE U-BOAT
Sighted at a distance of several miles, a British destroyer found a
U-boat in difficulties and ended them in the manner depicted.
Drawn by a naval officer.

charge, which was followed by an explosion and the appearance of the U-boat astern. Both destroyers put their helms right over, and opened fire. The fight was ended by one of them charging the submersible and literally chopping her in half. Both sections kept afloat for a few seconds, then disappeared in two mammoth whirlpools. It was one of the cleanest cuts of the war, though a United States cruiser managed to perform a similar feat a few weeks later.

While escorting a convoy a look-out on the U.S. destroyer *Fanning* noticed a periscope sticking out of the water. Heading for the spot, a single depth charge was unloaded. The U-boat came to the surface, and after a short chase meekly surrendered. According to the evidence of prisoners, the machinery of the submarine was wrecked beyond repair. The Germans referred to depth charges as 'water-bombs.' Frankly, they were not enamoured of them. With that abnormal lack of humour which no Briton can understand, Commander Rose of the *Kaiser's* Undersea Navy explained that "their material effect is only small"—witness the above samples—"but the infernal din of their explosion" had a great moral effect, "especially on an inexperienced crew."

CHAPTER 12

Singeing the Sultans Beard

There must be a beginning of any great matter, but the continuing unto the end until it be thoroughly finished yields the true glory.—Sir Francis Drake.

To win the first Victoria Cross awarded to a naval officer in the Great War, to be the first submarine commander to gain it in any war—these are no mean distinctions. Primarily, of course, Lieutenant Norman Douglas Holbrook, R.N., owed his blue ribbon to "most conspicuous bravery," as the *Gazette* has it, but to this must be added a particularly daring and unique exploit that showed exceptional tactical and executive skill.

The deed was not one of those lightning-stroke affairs that lack premeditation and are accomplished on the spur of the moment in the heat of battle. The elements of conflict were there, guns, ammunition, soldiers, and all the stage scenery necessary to give a picturesque and enthralling setting. The chief actor alone failed to appear in the picture. I would not for the world attempt to minimize the superb heroism of any holder of a much-coveted decoration. Yet there is a marked difference between this particular deed and all others that had gone before. It was accomplished in a place remote from other British battle forces. The young officer neither carried a wounded man on his back amid a storm of bullets, his comrades looking on, nor with a machine-gun held up a horde of Huns.

Harking back, it is interesting to recall that the first person to win the V.C. was a bluejacket—an above-salt-water sailor. Holbrook belonged to the same splendid Service, but to a section unborn when Charles Davis Lucas flung overboard a live shell from H.M.S. *Hecla* off Bomarsund in 1854. The commander of B11 gained his fourpenny worth of bronze in a submarine below the sea. What Holbrook's meritorious action lacks in intensity of swift drama is more than compensated by the cool and calculated daring of the whole proceeding.

Standing quietly in a sealed chamber breathing 'canned air' for nine mortal hours, dodging mines, torpedo-boats, and gunfire from forts, requires a steady nerve and a concentration of mind and purpose beyond what is called for in open fighting. He accomplished what he had to do, brought back his ship, fourteen men and an officer, quite safely, and betrayed an eager anxiety as to what his next task might be.

It was not as though Holbrook had been placed in command of a brand-new vessel of modern type, replete with the latest improvements, spacious, comfortable, and minus the stuffiness so inseparably associated with earlier craft. B11 was one of the smallest, slowest, and oldest submarines in the British Navy. She had been launched in 1906, when Holbrook was still a 'snotty,' which is the service name for midshipman. There was no question as to the risks all on board knew they were about to run. It was an adventure in the truest sense of the word, without a single 'dead cert.' in it. Every man jack of them left letters behind, "in case of accidents," as one of the brave fellows modestly put it, and he added, perhaps half wistfully, that the commander was "a very cool hand."

The latter fact needs no qualification; it is self-evident. For one thing the lieutenant had promised his mother "to be careful" when he bade her goodbye at Portsmouth. He fulfilled his pledge, as is the habit of worthy sons of worthy parents. Later on, when he gave her an account of his deeds, Holbrook gently reminded her of his vow in a subtle way. He signed his letter, "Your affectionate and *careful* son." Which shows that a sense of humour is likewise one of his traits.

Lieutenant Holbrook had been appointed to H.M.S. *Egmont* at Malta for the command of B11 in December 1913. What he and his submarine did in the interim of a year does not concern us. The blue waters of the Mediterranean hid them from the public gaze for exactly twelve months. Then they suddenly turned up in the Ægean Sea, hundreds of miles from their base. The Angel of Peace had retired sadly before the bustling entrance of Mars. A combined British and French squadron was gathered together in the neighbourhood of the entrance to the Dardanelles.

There was an idea that big ships and big guns could smash their way through the Straits and appear before Constantinople. Eminent naval men said that the project was perfectly feasible; others that it was an impossible task. The 'Ayes' had it; the 'Noes' came into their own a little later. The heavy fathers of the Fleet had tuned up for the overture at daybreak on the 3rd November, 1914. On the 13th of the following month Holbrook and his merry men started to pierce the Straits via the underseas.

Wiseacres in the battleships, jealous of the reputation of the giants, and secretly itching to follow in the tracks of Admiral Sir J. Duckworth, who had got through in 1807, before battleships were quite so bulky and the Turks so well prepared, called in superstition to justify their views. The 13th was, and always had been, unlucky. It was the height of foolishness to tempt Providence with that date staring at one from the calendar. Really, the lack of wisdom in their superiors was beyond words!

The commander of the expedition was too eager to get on with the job to be deterred by superstition, and too much occupied with practical affairs to be concerned with old women's tales once the Dardanelles had been entered. The Hellespont of ancient history is a bit of a teaser to a navigation officer. It has all manner of depths and shallows, widths and currents. Mists frequently hang between the rocky heights and the low hills of the landlocked waterway like steam and smoke in a railway tunnel. To these difficulties were added peril from mine, floating and fixed, peril from the guns of forts and land batteries, and peril from whatever naval forces might be in the vicinity.

Holbrook's main object was to torpedo the Turkish battleship *Messudiyeh*. She was guarding the mine-field in the roadstead of Nagara, below the Narrows. Here the distance between the banks is only some 1400 yards, and the current often runs at the rapid rate of four and a half knots. The *Messudiyeh* was a rather curious specimen of naval architecture, the combined product of British and Italian labour. Launched at Blackwall forty years before, she had been rebuilt to a great extent at Genoa in 1902. From the point of view of armament she was by no means to be despised. Although her two 9.2-in. breech-loaders were being overhauled in England and had given place to wooden replicas, she mounted twelve 6-in. quick-firers, and over two dozen smaller weapons—a plentiful selection of guns for service should B11's periscope be sighted. As a matter of fact it *was* sighted, but not before Holbrook had taken his observations and discharged a torpedo, as we shall have occasion to notice a little later.

The 10,000-ton battleship was perhaps the least of the difficulties that confronted the intrepid lieutenant. When beset by so many dangers comparison between one and another is of little consequence. The ship was anchored, and therefore presented as fine a target as a submarine commander could wish. But before she could be reached there was a gauntlet of five rows of live mines to be run. It was no good trying to 'rush' the Straits. For one thing, the motors of B11 could not propel her more than 5½ knots an hour when submerged, and only 11 knots on the surface, and for another, speed would have been a disadvantage rather than a help. Barging into the nearest horned canister is not good for the health of a submarine, and Holbrook realised that he must feel his way in the painful manner of a blind man, with the difference that at intervals he could use his periscope.

The fact that the *Messudiyeh* had been the flagship of a British admiral previous to the outbreak of war lent a sentimental interest to the commander's project. All submarine officers are not compounded of crude blood and iron, as popular belief has it. Holbrook is a particularly human specimen of the species, and has more than a strain of idealism in his make-up. Rear-Admiral Limpus had been engaged in reorganising the Ottoman naval service previous to the winning-over of the Turks by the Germans. To be sure the serviceable material at his disposal, so far as battleships were concerned, was poor enough. These numbered three in all, but three on the effective list are better than none, and two Dreadnoughts were under construction in England. The last-mentioned are now members of the great family that goes under the generic name of the Royal Navy.

Holbrook threaded his way through the mines, as Nelson dodged the shoals at Copenhagen, got within target-distance of his intended victim, took his bearings, and discharged an 18-in. torpedo, the first to be fired by a B boat since the commencement of the war.

Do not run away with the idea that it was a one-sided affair—a game of naval cricket with the British commander as bowler and the batsman out of his wicket. The wash of the periscope had been spotted by a keen-eyed look-out on the *Messudiyeh*. Before Holbrook knew the result of his aim, shells were falling unpleasantly near, and not a few! The enemy peppered the spot with a mighty weight of metal, but B11 was down and under when the Turks got the correct range. Even then things were precious uncomfortable, for the submarine grounded on a shoal, with only about thirty feet of water above her thin skin. It took some little time, plus much bumping and scraping, to get clear, but Holbrook never turned a hair. Flurry is not in his dictionary. He gave an order or two, then waited. On the whole

B11 behaved herself very well. She got into deeper water, from which Holbrook took a look round to ascertain the extent of the damage done. After expressing his satisfaction, he again descended.

During the whole voyage B11 remained submerged for nine of the longest hours that the crew had ever experienced. The early British submarines are cramped and stuffy, with the minimum of accommodation and the maximum of discomfort. At least the crew could congratulate themselves on having accomplished something, for there had been a mighty reverberation a few seconds after the torpedo had started on its travels. It was horribly difficult to keep a straight course on account of the current, but coxswains and men proved themselves worthy of so gallant a skipper.

What of the *Messudiyeh*? It was given out by the Turkish authorities that she had sunk at her anchorage off the Asiatic shore "as the result of a leak," and that part of the ship was still above water. The *communiqué* has a refreshing touch of humour about it not altogether characteristic of the general run of similar announcements. If we may accept the word of 'a reliable source,' the veteran turned turtle in shallow water within five minutes of having received Holbrook's compliments. Of the battleship's crew, which may have numbered 600 or more, the same authority states that only twenty-three escaped. These were got out by the dexterous manipulation of axe and saw.

If Englishmen take their pleasures sadly, they make war with a light heart. Shortly after his return, Lieutenant Holbrook was presented with a specially constructed Iron Cross—a huge metal affair almost as big as his head. Commander Bromley, (later Captain), performed the mock ceremony on board H.M.S. *Indefatigable*, to the immense amusement of the assembled company.

Holbrook was rightly acclaimed the Hero of the Service. Admiral Count Bettolo, voicing the opinion of the countrymen of Columbus, said that the achievement was:

> A magnificent feat which highly honours the British Navy and shows the firm determination to succeed on the part of the English sailors.
> The British Navy wishes the world to know it is capable of heroism and daring not inferior to that of any other navy. The organiser of the raid has demonstrated that he possesses the qualities to triumph at any cost.

In Russia the exploit was hailed as one of enormous military value, which the enthusiasm of the moment doubtless suggested but subsequent events did not justify. It certainly robbed Turkey of the *Messudiyeh*. Most important of all, Lieutenant Norman Douglas Holbrook had blazed a trail.

Lieutenant Sydney T. Winn, second in command of B11, was appointed to the Distinguished Service Order. No one was more delighted to hear of this honour than Lieutenant Holbrook. All the members of the crew were granted the Distinguished Service Medal.

The ill-fated Dardanelles Campaign, so rich in deeds of daring and so poor in practical results, introduced to the world at large two other submarine commanders, each of whom won the V.C. in connexion with it.

Lieutenant-Commander Edward Courtney Boyle, R.N., took E14 beneath the enemy mine-fields and suddenly appeared in the Sea of Marmora on the 27th April, 1915. He was stalking transports, the enemy's favourite method of conveying troops to Gallipoli because the land communications consisted of a solitary road. The submarine, a larger and more powerful boat than B11, with a displacement of 810 tons, did not return to her base until twenty-two days later. When she arrived it was much to the astonishment of many officers and men of the Allied Fleet, who had firmly believed that she and her brave crew had gone to Davy Jones's locker.

During the interim E14 had dodged mines, navigated treacherous currents, kept out of harm from hostile patrols, sunk a couple of gunboats, wrecked two transports—one crowded with 6000 troops—and poked her inquisitive nose into the Bosphorus.

The first week spent in the Sea of Marmora was terribly exciting. E14 was hunted by all the light craft at the disposal of the Turks. Gunboats, destroyers, and torpedo-boats took part in the chase, without achieving the slightest success. Their failure, combined with shortage of coal, caused most of them to be withdrawn from the service. Thenceforth they assumed the more humble role of convoys. This phase lasted a short time only. After Boyle had sunk the large troopship already mentioned, the Turkish soldiers refused to go by sea, preferring to march for three days and three nights rather than run the risk of meeting the terrible submarine.

E14 went into the Marmora on two subsequent occasions. Altogether she spent no fewer than seventy days there. On her last visit she had to break through the net placed across the Dardanelles by Nagara Point. As this formidable obstacle was made of chain and 3½-

in. wire, it "required some breaking," to quote the words of the commanding officer. Then Boyle's first lieutenant developed typhoid, and was ill for the remainder of the voyage, a matter of over a fortnight. About fifty vessels, including *dhows* laden with grain and other useful commodities, were sent to the bottom by E14, but—mark this—no non-combatant ship was ever sunk before the crew had been taken close inshore in their boats and had been fed if they were hungry. Submarines can be good Samaritans, despite German assertions to the contrary. It should also be added that for two days E14, in conjunction with E11, shelled the reinforcing troops marching to repel the Suvla Bay landing.

Boyle superbly earned and won the V.C., his colleagues, Lieutenant E. G. Stanley, R.N., and Acting-Lieutenant R. W. Lawrence, R.N.R., were awarded the Distinguished Service Cross, and each member of the crew was given the Distinguished Service Medal. One can fully appreciate the statement of Admiral de Robeck, that "it is impossible to do full justice to this great achievement." On the occasion of E14's first penetration of the Straits the king sent the gallant commander and his crew a telegram of congratulation.

Another E boat carried this process of anything but peaceful penetration still farther. Lieut.-Commander Martin Eric Nasmith, R.N., not only took E11 through the Dardanelles and crossed the Sea of Marmora, but actually succeeded in entering the Golden Horn, situated no fewer than 170 miles from the entrance to the Straits. At the quay adjoining the arsenal he fired a torpedo, which "was heard to explode." Whether it hit a transport or a lighter laden with firebricks lying near by has not been ascertained with certainty. The Turks and their Teutonic friends are none too keen on telling the truth if it is to their disadvantage. One informant had it that the barge was blown to smithereens, and that part of the debris was flung with such terrific force against the German Levant steamer *Stambul* that she was holed and had to be beached.

Another report stated that the strong current deflected the torpedo, causing it to blow up part of the jetty. All independent observers were at least unanimous as to the effect of the raid on the nerves of the inhabitants of Constantinople. The people were panic-stricken, and when the Turkish guns opened fire on their invisible foe they merely contributed to the ferment. So far as Nasmith was concerned, it was almost a case of *'much ado about nothing.'* E11 escaped with no worse casualty than a jagged wound in her periscope! Many of the Turks thought that the Russian Black Sea Fleet had broken through and was bombarding the capital as a preliminary to the landing of troops. Nasmith was merely singeing the *sultan's* beard, as Drake had singed that of Philip of Spain three centuries before.

Whether the torpedo in question struck troopship, lighter, or jetty at Constantinople does not much matter; the commander's remaining torpedoes found their billets right enough. Nasmith undoubtedly destroyed two heavily laden transports, a large gunboat, an ammunition ship, and three store ships, while another vessel containing supplies was driven ashore. As though this bag were not large enough, he returned to torpedo a fourth transport when his crew were congratulating themselves that the most dangerous part of the homeward voyage had been safely negotiated. The ammunition ship blew up with a terrific explosion. By her loss the enemy was deprived of thousands of charges, a quantity of gun mountings, and a 6-in. gun. Having sunk everything that could be sunk, Nasmith returned to report.

The most unpleasant incident of a whole chapter of exciting passages occurred in the Sea of Marmora. The submarine ran foul of the cable that anchored a mine. As other canisters of death were in the vicinity, it was much too perilous to attempt to go astern in the hope that the steel rope would become disentangled. The mine was the submarine's unwelcome guest for eleven miles. Every officer and man knew it, and each realized only too well exactly what would occur if one of the horns of the beastly thing bumped against the boat or struck some floating object. What with submerged torpedo tubes skilfully rigged up by the Turks on shore, land batteries, forts, floating and anchored mines, there was sufficient food for reflection to say nothing of the sinister appendage, and it is perhaps not surprising that the company was serious. If conversation was not animated this was not entirely due to the somewhat sultry atmosphere of E11. However, Nasmith got rid of the mine at last, and when he emerged among the battleships and cruisers at the other end of the Dardanelles no king or *kaiser* ever received a warmer welcome.

This young hero of thirty-two years, who had already attracted notice by his ready resource when A4 inadvertently sank while exercising at Spithead in 1905, had certainly earned his V.C., and the same may be recorded of his brother-officers, Lieutenant Guy D'Oyle-Hughes, R.N., and Acting-Lieutenant Robert Brown, who were given similar distinctions to those awarded to the subordinate officers of E14. Had Nelson been alive we may be quite sure he would have admitted the heroes of this chapter to his gallant 'band of brothers.' Their exploits are memorable, as Bacon says of another great naval episode:

Even beyond credit, and to the Height of some Heroicall Fable.

CHAPTER 13

On Certain Happenings in the Baltic

British submarines may take to themselves the credit of having damaged our trade and shipping in the Baltic.—Captain Persius.

Before our Russian allies abandoned the sword and the ploughshare for revolution and famine the Baltic was alive with naval doings. Occasionally it even became the scene of intense activity. When the former subjects of the Little Father obtained their liberty, and thereby shackled themselves with a greater tyranny, the inland sea of Northern Europe passed to the enemy. The unweaned democracy of Russia sought peace with paper and not with a sword, hugging the delusion that a new heaven and a new earth could be created with the aid of the devil and the whirlwind. The Baltic became a vast German lake. With the acumen of a committee of Frankfort Jews, and in pursuance of the much-vaunted Mittel-Europa policy that was both commercial and political, the Fatherland at once projected a canal between the Baltic and the Black Sea. This, of course, would have rendered the Empire entirely independent of the sea-water and long-distance route from Odessa, the granary of the South.

Great Britain was Russia's only ally in the Baltic before she surrendered. Two or three battle-cruisers from the neighbourhood of the Orkneys would doubtless have been a desirable addition to her naval strength, but there were good and sufficient reasons why they were withheld. What would have happened had there been no revolution can only be surmised. Certainly there was a time when the appearance of large British vessels was not regarded as altogether visionary. Sir John Jellicoe, when Commander-in-Chief of the Grand Fleet, stated that it would be difficult to go to the Baltic, but not impossible, and he hoped the day might come when the two navies would fight a common foe. That day never arrived. Submarines alone represented the might and majesty of the British Navy; and excellent representatives they made. These underseas craft, which threaded their way through the tortuous channels of the Cattegat and the Sound, or were conveyed in sections from Archangel by inland water transport, rendered yeoman service.

Some of the boats put in three long years of hard and hazardous work before the signature of the fatuous Brest-Litovsk Treaty negatived further effort and the ice-bound condition of the frozen waters made escape impossible. Their tasks accomplished, they were blown up by their own crews. The battered plates of seven worthy successors of the gallant little *Revenge* lie buried deep in the Gulf of Finland. Not every British victory is perpetuated to an apathetic posterity by such visible tokens as a sail-of-the-line or a gun at the United Service Museum. There are other and grimmer relics which will never meet the public eye.

Scouting for months in conditions bordering on life in the Arctic, eternally on the prowl for the High Sea Fleet, sinking men-of-war and German cargoes, holding the enemy at bay while the Russian Fleet secured safety in the Gulf of Finland and the Huns sought to corner it at Reval—these and other things must be put to the credit of British submarines in the 160,000 odd square miles of waterway which constitute the changeful northern sea. Flat and sandy coast, rocky and precipitous cliff, treacherous shallows, weather as fitful as the temper of a fractious child, added to the anxieties of the watchers. If ever there existed a legitimate excuse for jumpy nerves, surely it was here. Yet throughout their long vigil officers and men upheld the worthy tradition of the British sea game.

Not one enemy merchant ship was sunk without warning, or before ample time had been afforded every member of the crew to secure safety in the boats. No shot was fired until they had pulled away from the danger zone. If the distance from land was great, the submarine stood by until a neutral took charge of the refugees. "*That bloody wild beast that slumbers in man*" of whom Robert Louis Stevenson makes mention was never allowed to awake, though often enough there was sufficient of insolence and bitter hate on the part of the enemy to arouse it.

The case of the s.s. *Nicomedia*, of Hamburg, is typical of British methods in the Baltic. This big steamer was laden with 6700 tons of valuable ore for the hungry melting-pots of Essen. E19 hauled her up, gave her complement 'fain'its' to gather their belongings and stow them into the boats, patiently waited for them to clear out, and then sent the ship to the bottom with the assistance of a dynamite cartridge. No cold-blooded-murder tricks sullied the fair fame of the English-speaking seafarers, who thus gave the lie direct to the Teutonic assertion that submarine warfare could only be carried on if it set at nought the common decencies of humanity.

The sportsmanlike behaviour of the British was entirely unappreciated by the enemy. They deliberately falsified the accounts which they sent broadcast throughout the world as part of their propaganda work. For instance, neutrals were informed that the commander of a British submarine had blown up the s.s. *Germania* in Swedish territorial waters by placing a bomb in her hold. When sighted off the Swedish coast the vessel was bound for Stettin with a cargo of 2750 tons of concentrated iron ore. Shots were fired as a signal to her captain to stop, and also to warn him that he was making straight for a dangerous sandbank. They were disregarded, with the inevitable result that the *Germania* ran ashore.

Then, and not till then, the British boat entered Swedish waters, intent only on saving the crew and helping to salve the vessel. Not a soul was found on board. After spending an hour in a useless endeavour to move the steamer, the ship's papers and some fresh meat were removed to the submarine. When the British officers and men left the *Germania* the engine-room was already partly submerged. On the water reaching the boilers they quite naturally blew up. No attempt was made to destroy the vessel.

After the high seas had been swept of much Teutonic baggage, the Baltic alone remained to the German merchant service as a field for possible operations with surface vessels. Westward of the Skager-Rack the way was barred by the British Grand Fleet; eastward, the German High Sea Fleet felt more or less confident of supremacy, though not positively sure. The Russian Baltic Fleet, consisting of four pre-Dreadnought battleships, six armoured cruisers, four protected cruisers, over a hundred destroyers, twenty or more submarines, and four Dreadnoughts in the making, (duly put in commission), was obviously numerically weaker than that of the second naval Power in the world. It was not in a position to undertake a vigorous offensive. The strategy adopted, to quote Admiral Kanin, was that of regarding the Baltic Fleet as "a continuation of the extreme flank of the Army."

Its task was "as far as possible to support the movements of the army, protecting it against envelopment by the German Fleet." The element of uncertainty, from the enemy's point of view, was introduced by England as usual. Had the latter not declared war, Germany could have swamped the Russian Fleet and landed troops for the invasion of Russia without fear of molestation from the sea. As it was she had to keep both eyes open, for on each flank she had maritime enemies. It was scarcely likely that any of Britain's battleships would venture to render assistance, but what of her submarines? The machines in which Germany placed so much faith were not her secret. They represented no new departure. Britain might attempt to get a squadron or two through the narrow passageway. When the devil gets among tailors, complications are more than likely.

Evidence that the Germans anticipated inroads from hostile underwater craft is afforded by the vigilance of their guard at the doors affording entry and exit. Three E boats once tried to make the passage in company. Two of them got through unscathed, though trawlers were busily hunting for poachers at the time. No. 3 got into difficulties with a sweep slung between two of the afore-mentioned watch-dogs. She ran smack into the hawser, seeing nothing, got entangled, and gave her commander furiously to think on ways and means of possible extrication. By the 'feel' of it the officer knew approximately where the cable had caught, so he went astern, cocked the boat's nose up a little, and attempted to 'step' over it. The manoeuvre was executed with celerity. Rapidity of movement is the soul of underwater warfare. Once let the watchers above become aware that they had a 'bite,' and an explosive charge would come rattling down the line with the ease of a load of bricks on an aerial railway.

Then goodbye to the Baltic and all deeps. They must have felt the tug, but it was so momentary that it is more than likely it was put down to jetsam, and one does not waste good material on lumps of sunken wreckage. The string of death rasped along the keel of the submarine, slipped over the bow, and freed itself. If the commander of E— failed to mutter an audible exclamation of thankfulness, he at least breathed a little more freely as a sign of relieved tension. He had lived an hour in less than sixty seconds, and for aught I know added a grey hair or two to his head as outward and visible indications of inward perturbation.

On another occasion a squadron of the High Sea Fleet left the sheltering shores of Kiel Bay for a trip in the Baltic. Three additional British submarines were detailed to pass through the Sound. No patrol work this; their orders were to attack. They left their base in company, intending to make the passage of fifty miles together on the first favourable night. During the voyage one of the craft developed a minor malady, to which submarines are subject. As she could not keep up with the others, and instructions were not to be disregarded, the lame duck had perforce to limp her way alone. Her consorts aroused no suspicion until they had actually entered the Baltic. Then the enemy became aware of their presence. While trawlers and torpedo-boats hunted for them, four merchantmen in line abreast, supported by warships, swept the entrance to prevent others from following suit.

The third submarine, restored to health, arrived twenty-four hours late. The commander fully appreciated what was happening. He sought salvation in bluff. As the sweepers were showing navigation lights he quite reasonably argued that if he made a similar display he might possibly get through. He came to the surface, lamps were placed in position, the operation began. For a time it looked as if the artful little ruse would be successful. Then from out the surrounding darkness a torpedo-boat was felt rather than seen coming full tilt at the submarine. It took the latter three minutes to submerge, according to the log-book; the surface craft occupied a little longer in reaching the spot. Even then it was a mighty close shave. There were not many feet of blue water between the enemy's keel and the submarine's conning-tower.

After an interval the British commander thought he would try his luck again, minus lights. He waited his opportunity, riding quietly on the waves in the meantime, and keeping a pair of keen eyes to his night-glasses. Presently a ship came along, seemingly intent on navigating the difficult passage through the Sound. The low-lying craft awakened into life, and followed at a respectful distance. There was just a chance that she would not be detected. The blackness of the night prevented the officer from being certain of the nature of his pilot, otherwise he would scarcely have used her as a screen. A mouse does not creep behind a cat. Meantime she was making no great speed, and looked like some old tub loaded to the Plimsoll mark with merchandise.

Then for no apparent reason the vessel suddenly developed marked eccentricity, went dead slow, then put on full speed, altered course, and made in the direction of her follower. The submarine again sought refuge in the chilly and inhospitable waters, and her company listened to the threshing of propellers racing above. She returned home, "prior to making a further attempt." Thus the commander in his official communication to My Lords of the Admiralty.

In October 1914 it was announced that the cruiser *Prinz Adalbert* had been sunk by two shots from a submarine off Libau, with the loss of most of her crew. According to a Petrograd report, her demise "was effected after much skilful manoeuvring" by a British submarine. The cruiser was not actually the *Prinz Adalbert*, but a vessel of the same class. The warship bearing that name fell a victim to a British torpedo in the autumn of the following year.

A light cruiser—name unknown—and a torpedo-boat were taking an airing when a certain British submarine of the celebrated 'E' class met them. The larger vessel was torpedoed forward, apparently set on fire, and showed signs of sinking by the head. As the torpedo-boat sought to pounce on the enemy the submarine passed under her stern and struck the cruiser in or near the after-magazine. There was a double explosion. The torpedo-boat and her tornado of shell were dodged a second time. Three minutes later the periscope showed no cruiser.

On the 10th October, 1914, an attempt was made by enemy submarines to sink the Russian *Admiral Makaroff*, at the moment busily engaged in searching a suspicious fishing-boat flying the Dutch commercial flag. Several torpedoes were fired, but missed, and the armoured cruiser beat off the enemy. On the next day, however, the German craft atoned for previous bad marksmanship by sinking the *Pallada*, a sister ship of the *Admiral Makaroff*, while she was scouting in company with the *Bayan*. This success was achieved through the 'neutral flag' trick. The submarine lay in waiting behind a vessel displaying Dutch colours. The ruse was discovered too late. Although subjected to a heavy fire, the submarine got a shot home which apparently exploded the magazines.

This vessel, armed with two 8-in., eight 6-in., and many smaller guns, had a normal complement of 568 men. Not a soul was saved. An interesting sequel to this disaster was furnished by the announcement of the Russian Naval Headquarters Staff that during the course of their predatory operations on the 10th and 11th a German submersible had been sunk by the fire of the *Bayan*, a second foundered through striking a mine, and a third was put to flight by a torpedo-boat. Admiral von Essen, Commander-in-Chief of the Russian Baltic Fleet, told the *tsar* that twenty unsuccessful submarine attacks had been made within two months previous to the sinking of the *Pallada*.

Early in 1915 the German cruiser *Gazelle* was attacked off the Danish coast by a submarine whose nationality was not disclosed, although rumour had it that she was Russian, but commanded by a British officer. Despite a big hole in her side made by the explosion, the cruiser was able to keep afloat and reach Sassnitz with the assistance of a ferry steamer. As a withering fire was kept up by the enemy, and floating mines were flung out indiscriminately as a further means of protection, a second shot was impracticable.

A lonely Russian submarine boldly attacked an enemy squadron of ten battleships and a swarm of torpedo-boats in the following summer. One evening, when far out in the Baltic, the commander picked up dense black clouds of smoke on the horizon. Then the funnels of warships and their massive hulls rose out of the sea. They were proceeding in two columns, the smaller vessels on the flanks of the larger ones.

An hour or more passed before the squadron was sufficiently near for action. As the vessels approached, the commander concluded that his best position would be on the port side of the oncoming ships, between the enemy and the light. He raised his periscope, and believing he had ample time to change his position before the torpedo-boat in the van of the right column came abreast of him, proceeded to carry out the manoeuvre. The submarine rose a matter of fifteen feet to bring her periscope again into use. The 'eye' revealed the distance between her and the first of the oncoming battleships as certainly not more than sixty yards. The officer fired a torpedo, dived immediately, and struck the ram of the object at which he had aimed. As no German battleship draws less than twenty-six feet of water, the boat had evidently not submerged sufficiently rapidly.

Everybody on board firmly believed that their craft would founder. Only those who have been in a similar occurrence or a railway collision can appreciate the appalling suddenness of such a crash. The electric light bulbs burst, the boat assumed a list to starboard, something in the superstructure snapped, water came in. Apparently the engines had sustained no damage from the shock, for they continued to work without any appreciable loss of speed. The boat descended seventy-five feet. Then the sound of a great tumult penetrated her steel plates. The commander afterward declared that when he heard the explosion he was perfectly convinced that the boat in her damaged state could not withstand the pressure of the water.

He tried to reach the surface several times, but on each occasion was compelled to descend because the thud of screws above told only too plainly that the enemy vessels were still in the same area, some doubtless assisting the wounded battleship, others zigzagging about in the hope that the assailant might be made to pay the full penalty. When the officer tried to use the periscope he found it to be irretrievably damaged, and about as useless as a broken cowl on a chimney-stack. It revealed a blank. At 11.30 the commander, hearing nothing to suggest the presence of the enemy, rose to the surface after having been below four hours. The submarine reached port without further incident, and was docked for repairs. To this day the commander does not know whether the vessel he aimed at was put *hors de combat*.

Late in June 1915 a number of enemy warships bombarded Windau with 9.4-in. guns, and also tried to effect a descent on the coast with a view to co-operating with the German Army in Courland. The invasion project was entirely unsuccessful, and the naval forces were compelled to retire. The defence seems mainly to have been the work of torpedo-boats; no mention was made on either side of the presence of submarines. A similar attempt made three weeks before had robbed the Russians of the *Yenissei*, which fell a victim to a U-boat. According to reports furnished by commanders of Russian submarines, three of the enemy vessels were sunk or damaged by mines previously dropped by the wrecked vessel.

Early in the following month Russian naval forces came across two enemy light cruisers and destroyers on outpost duty between Gothland and Windau. On this occasion the tables were turned, and the Germans lost a minelayer. The *Albatross*, the ship in question, was so severely handled that she ran aground near Oestergarn, and became a total wreck, her consort, the *Augsburg*, managing to escape in the fog. While the Russian squadron continued its course northward, two cruisers, four destroyers, and a flotilla of U-boats joined battle, but speedily retreated after the armoured cruiser *Roon* had been badly damaged. On being reinforced by a battle squadron, another attempt was made against the Russian vessels, including a spirited submarine attack on the *Rurik*. The latter was saved by a destroyer, which was reported to have sunk one of the hostile underwater craft.

The 2nd July was a disastrous day for Germany in the Baltic. In addition to the *Albatross* she lost a battleship of the *Pommern* type at the hands of Commander Max K. Horton. On the 30th, E1 sank a large transport, despite a determined effort on the part of the latter to run down the attacking party.

The next happening of importance from the point of view of the submarine war was a dramatic series of actions at the entrance of the Gulf of Riga in the succeeding August. These were carried out with the object of assisting Hindenburg's land offensive in the direction of the great seaport of Riga, whose fall would open the road to Petrograd. The weather, mostly calm and foggy, was entirely favourable to the enemy, who slipped past the patrols and were able to sweep up many mines that barred further progress. In this dangerous operation it would have been nothing short of miraculous had the enemy escaped scot-free, and one or two vessels were destroyed. The Russian warships put up an excellent defence, with the result that the attempt to capture the old city of the Merchant-Venturers completely failed and the Gulf was evacuated.

Again British submarines were to the fore. Commander Noel F. Laurence in E1 torpedoed the Dreadnought cruiser *Moltke* in thick weather on the 19th. This great vessel of 23,000 tons, a sister-ship of the more romantic *Goeben*, mounting ten 11-in. guns, was believed to have taken part in the infamous raid on Scarborough. Although the *Moltke* did not sink, she was sufficiently damaged to be placed temporarily out of commission, thereby easing the situation for a time by denuding Germany of a very formidable fighting machine. Laurence, whose boat had been the first British submarine to penetrate the Baltic, narrowly escaped having E1 rammed on this occasion. A torpedo-boat missed her by a few feet only. The *tsar* acknowledged the officer's services by decorating him with the St George's Cross of the Fourth Class.

In this month of August 1915, so big with events in the Baltic, the enemy committed a flagrant breach of international law by firing on the British submarine E13 while she was ashore in Danish territorial waters. The outrage was intensified by the attacking torpedo-boat firing shrapnel and bringing machine-guns to bear on the members of the crew struggling in the water.

E13, in charge of Lieutenant-Commander Layton, grounded on the island of Saltholm, and was given the usual twenty-four hours' grace to get off. Long before the time-limit had expired a German torpedo-boat let off a torpedo at a range of about 300 yards, and opened fire with all her other available weapons. The torpedo exploded on hitting the bottom, close to E13. Within a few seconds the submarine was a mass of flame. Unable to offer any defence, the officer ordered the crew to abandon the ship. Had it not been for the intervention of a Danish man-of-war, which lowered her boats and steamed between the attacker and the attacked, probably not a soul would have been saved.

Fishermen who witnessed the tragedy avowed they had never seen any bravery to equal that of the helpless crew. When E13 was refloated by the Danish authorities the hull was found to be riddled with shells, but her colours were still on the charred staff. Fifteen bluejackets lost their lives in an attack which Sweden's leading newspaper characterized as "wilful murder."

Acting under the orders of the Russian commander-in-chief, the British boats in the Baltic carried on as before. They rendered valuable support to the Allies by cutting off supplies of timber, ore, and coal consigned to the Fatherland, and sinking transports and merchantmen whenever bigger prey was undiscoverable. As Mr David Hannay has so well said:

> The capture of an enemy's merchant ship is the maritime equivalent for the occupation of territory.

This active warfare was carried out despite vigorous search on the part of Zeppelins and seaplanes.

E— was treated with three bombs from an enemy aircraft. Then the latter, apparently not satisfied with the result, dropped seven more. Sixty minutes later the submarine came up to have a look round, and was obliged to retreat hurriedly on account of a biplane coming toward her at great speed. Five bombs followed her passage below. After a lapse of forty-five minutes E—again rose to the surface. Subsequent events are best related by reference to the commander's log:

> Decided to rise and get the gun into action. Got under way on a north course at 10 knots with the upper deck awash. The biplane was sighted on the starboard bow at 6.20 p.m., and we opened fire at 3000 yards. The biplane immediately sheered off, and got out of range after the eighth round, and then kept three miles astern of us. I decided to run north till dark or till the aeroplane retired, and then to return under water to —— position. At 7.30 we lost sight of the aeroplane, and at 8.30 decided to turn and dive south. Just then the aeroplane was sighted. Dived. Heard nine distant explosions. Decided to remain down till dark.

For a month business was bad in the 'big event' line, but things brightened in October, although E19, sighting a German cruiser and two escorts outside Danish territorial waters off Klintholm Moen, had rather an unpleasant ten minutes in trying to hit one of them. The large warship opened fire with great promptitude, while the smaller fry cruised about trailing high-explosive charges. E19 dodged, got in a neat shot at one of the torpedo-boats, and was rewarded by the knowledge that she sank.

On the 23rd October the cruiser *Prinz Adalbert*, although escorted by a couple of destroyers, one on each bow, was sent to the bottom by a British submarine near Libau. Regarding the manner of her death, the commander of the boat which wrought her destruction has this to say:

> Fired bow tube at enemy's fore-bridge. Observed very vivid flash of explosion along water-line at point of aim. This was immediately followed by very large concussion, and entire ship was immediately hidden in huge columns of thick grey smoke, fore magazine having evidently been exploded by torpedo.

For some unknown reason a newspaper correspondent's account of the loss of this ship was allowed to be sent by the German official wireless to New York. The writer asserted that the affair took place in hazy weather—"ideal conditions for an attack," according to the British commander—and that the vessel was struck by two torpedoes almost simultaneously. According to him the *Prinz Adalbert* went down "immediately, like a piece of iron." How the following paragraph came to be passed by the censor is a greater mystery:

> The enemy submarines in the Baltic offer a difficult problem. The Admiralty is confronted with the practically impossible task of keeping them out. The Admiralty can mine or set barrier nets in the Sound between Denmark and Sweden only up to the three-mile limit, where the neutral waters of the two countries begin. The problem is causing the Admiralty serious thought.

The range was some 1300 yards, and the "very large concussion" so great that it upset the working of the torpedo mechanism of the submarine and necessitated the craft's burying herself in deep water to avoid injury from the great masses of debris that were falling over a wide area. The *Prinz Adalbert* was not wrecked, but annihilated.

The light cruiser *Undine* was dispatched by two torpedoes in three minutes, while convoying the steam ferry *Preussen* from Trelleborg to Sassnitz on the 7th November, 1915. The first missile missed, and merely put a couple of attendant torpedo-boats on the *qui vive*. In attempting to ram the assailant, one of them uncovered her charge, with the result that the second weapon struck the *Undine* full amidships. The underwater craft, uninjured by the withering fire of the disconcerted cruiser, ducked and was seen no more. As a neutral captain remarked:

> The submarines pop up everywhere, and disappear again with an alertness which only an intimate knowledge of the waters would allow. Several times they have been seen in close proximity to the minefield, but they seem to be as much at home as in the North Sea.

A little later the *Preussen* played into the enemy's hands by ramming and sinking her escorting torpedo-boat, of whose company only five were picked up.

The *Flying Dutchman* of the Great War was surely the German light cruiser *Bremen*, completed in 1904 at the port whose name she bore. This little 3200-ton warship, mounting ten 4.1-in. guns and fourteen smaller weapons, was reported from time to time as having been seen in the Atlantic, the North Sea, and the Pacific. Then she appeared—and disappeared—in the Baltic. On the 18th December, 1915, Berlin admitted her loss, together with a torpedo-boat escorting her. This double event of the previous day was due to a British submarine.

In May 1916, when the eastern and southern parts of the Baltic were once more free from ice, British submarines lost no time in renewing their activity, to the utter discomfiture of traders who did not mind running big risks for big money. A German convoy was also intercepted off the coast of Sweden by Russian torpedo-boats, destroyers, and submarines. The squadron sank the auxiliary cruiser *König von Sachsen*, and set fire to another auxiliary ship, the *Hermann*. The latter was afterward blown up by her crew.

The raid in the Gulf of Finland in November 1916, again under cover of a fog, showed the efficiency of the Russian Baltic Fleet to be still unimpaired, but the Revolution achieved what the enemy failed to do. "Confusion and mistrust prevailed": in these words Admiral Koltchak summed up the whole unhappy situation. In October 1917 the German High Sea Fleet held the mastery of the Gulf of Riga. The most belligerent representative of the London Press went frantic because the enemy's object had been carried out "without any interference from the British Fleet, which, as we are accustomed to say, commands the sea." Presumably it would have had battleships and vessels of Sir David Beatty's celebrated 'Cat Class' forging ahead through the entrance, disregarding the imminent likelihood of their being sent to the bottom by U-boats and mine-fields. The difficulties surmounted by underwater craft in penetrating the Baltic, to which I have already drawn attention, is surely sufficient answer to the most amateur of amateur strategists, who, indeed, were somewhat roughly handled by Sir Eric Geddes in the House of Commons. What it was possible for the British Navy to do it achieved.

On the 23rd it was announced that a British submarine had fired two torpedoes at an enemy Dreadnought of the *Markgraf* class mounting ten 12-in. guns, with what result was unknown. The Germans made it somewhat too hot with shells from ships and bombs from seaplanes for her commanding officer to wait and see. She certainly succeeded in blowing up a big transport.

Opportunity is four-fifths of the battle where underwater craft are concerned. As the war progressed and Britain learned how to tackle those of the enemy, so the Germans gained experience in dodging our boats. Three Dreadnoughts, a light cruiser, and several torpedo-craft hailing from Kiel were chased for four hours by one of our submarines. Every ounce of energy was got out of the motors, but never once did she succeed in getting closer than eight miles. A decent-sized gun would have reached readily enough, but no torpedo has ever achieved so distant a range. The squadron covered a wide area of sea, frequently changed course, and manoeuvred in such a way that the British skipper candidly confessed that his German rival "made use of very confusing and successful anti-submarine tactics."

This chapter cannot be other than a faint and incomplete outline of happenings in the Baltic between 1914 and 1917. The British campaign ended in April 1918. When the German naval forces and transports approached Hangö, South-west Finland, four 'E' and three 'C' boats were taken outside the harbour of Helsingfors and blown up. The crews made their way, not without difficulty and danger, to Petrograd. Sir William Temple said over two centuries ago: "Whether it be wise in men to do such actions or no, I am sure it is so in States to honour them."

Russia had gone into 'Committee.' The Baltic had ceased to be a battle area. A chapter in which the names of Horton, Laurence, Goodhart, and Crombie afforded something more than a tinge of romance had been added to the history books. To quote Admiral Kanin, successor to the hard-working and reforming von Essen, Russia had been "helped extraordinarily by the English submarines." The boats were "magnificent," the officers "fine young fellows." Their bearing was "wonderful—and their coolness!"

CHAPTER 14

Blockading the Blockade

This blockade is a complete avowal of Germany's weakness.—
Lord Robert Cecil.

Shelling an enemy is merely a scientific way of throwing stones. When a schoolboy in God's open air is not quite sure of the nature of an object, his primitive ancestors prompt him to fling something at it; middle age, having the full advantage of civilization, pokes it with a stick.

In naval warfare 'throwing things' is perfectly legitimate cricket, but mining, which is invisible poking, is scarcely recognised as a worthy substitute for football. Two or three years passed before the last mine was swept from the waters that formed the theatre of the maritime drama of the Russo-Japanese War; it may take thrice that time to clear up the aftermath of the World Conflict. The prospect is not pleasant to contemplate. The belligerents sowed these murderous canisters in many latitudes.

Germany, to her lasting shame, did not always provide the necessary apparatus to render them innocuous when they broke loose, or for those of the unanchored variety to become worthless "one hour at most after the person who laid them shall have lost control over them," according to Article 1 of the Eighth Convention of The Hague Conference of 1907. Her favourite trick after a naval engagement was to fling floating mines overboard in the hope that the pursuing fleet would blunder into them. Many thousands were scattered along the trade routes. Let me hasten to add that in the use of mines Germany was well in advance of every other belligerent in 1914. It was weeks before the British Navy took advantage of what most salt-water sailors regard as a device associated with the dirty, low-down trick of hitting below the belt.

Mines, like their cousin the depth charge, played a very important part in combating the submarine menace. As Germany showed a partiality for them, we did our best to oblige her. The most extensive mine-field ever planted was sown by Great Britain. It stretched from the Orkney Islands to the fringe of the territorial waters of Norway, and covered an area of not less than 22,000 square miles. Access to the Atlantic, rigidly guarded by the naval police of the patrol, was provided on the Scottish side. Other British mine-fields existed at the farther end of the North Sea, guarded by a hundred or more surface craft, and in the neighbourhood of Flanders, Heligoland, and Denmark.

The object of these vast prohibited areas was to prevent U-boats from gaining easy access to the great ocean routes. Germany early laid a mine-field inside the Skager-Rack to prevent British submarines from entering the Baltic—which it did not do—and afterward violated international law by taking similar steps in the Cattegat. While the latter operation was proceeding, certain of our naval forces came across a batch of enemy minelayers at their nefarious task, sank ten of them, and rescued their crews. The men ought to have been ordered to walk the plank, *pour encourager les autres*, as Voltaire said of Admiral Byng's execution.

Britain's bold bid to foil the U-boats was undertaken, in the words of the official explanation, "In view of the unrestricted warfare carried on by Germany at sea by means of mines and submarines, not only against the Allied Powers, but also against neutral shipping," and because merchant ships were "constantly sunk without regard to the ultimate safety of their crews." The big northern mine-field proved very useful. That was why the enemy immediately started a loud-mouthed campaign in neutral countries in the hope of inciting their Governments to protest against an effective method of warfare decidedly prejudicial to the German cause.

A word or two about the surface barrage maintained across the Channel. Every day and night, ceaselessly and relentlessly, in fair weather and foul, over a hundred armed patrolling craft of various sorts and sizes kept sentinel at the great southern gateway, and enabled troops and munitions to cross the drawbridge from England to France. It was not so difficult a task during the day as at night. When darkness fell the guard burned flares that made the passage of a submarine travelling on the surface an exceedingly dangerous undertaking.

If a U-boat tried the underwater route, there were other means of obstruction quite as deadly as the methods of the fire-breathing trawlers. There is no truth in the yarn that a steel net stretched across the Straits of Dover, thereby guaranteeing with more or less certainty the immunity of transports from attack by underwater vessels.

The fisherman's device for catching members of the finny tribe was, of course, applied to submarines. Long nets with meshes ten or fifteen feet square proved of great service when the war was young. Dropped in the course of an approaching U-boat, the probability was that she would poke her nose into it and find extreme difficulty in getting out. Subsequently cutters were fitted to the enemy's craft, but nothing could eliminate the movement of the net, which was supported on the surface by small buoys or planks. Moored nets with mines attached boded no good to the submarine that was unfortunate enough to encounter the obstacle.

An enemy commander found that his boat was towing a red buoy, and shortly afterward that she was entangled in wire-netting, he relates:

> For an hour and a half the netting carried us with it, and although I made every effort to get clear of it, rising and then sinking with the object of getting to the bottom of the netting, it was all in vain, for we were always dragged back, sometimes to the right and sometimes to the left.

By increasing the weight of water in the tanks the U-boat managed to tear the netting. She remained under water for eighteen hours, came up and found patrol craft in the vicinity, and was compelled to descend for another six hours. After a further look round, the officer adds:

> I remained submerged for two hours, then slowly turned outward, and at a distance of some fifty yards from the leading enemy craft passed toward the open sea. At nine o'clock in the evening we were able to rise to the surface in safety.

The arming of traders gave the Central Powers furiously to think, especially as the policy was a perfectly natural sequel to their own misdoings. Details of the calibre of guns mounted by ships of the British Mercantile Marine were withheld from Parliament as "not in the public interest." The French Minister of Marine was more communicative. At the end of 1917 every French merchantman was armed with two 3.7-in. guns. International law held that trading vessels during war-time must be stopped and searched before further action could be taken. Exceptional circumstances alone justified the sinking even of an enemy vessel, the usual practice being to conduct the captive to port, the final disposal being settled in the Prize Court. Neutral ships could in no circumstances be destroyed. Germany's difficulty was that it was next to impossible for a submarine to follow this programme, which she herself had recognized previous to the advent of the U-boat. While the process of search was going on, a necessarily slow and tedious task, ten to one a patrol boat would appear on the scene and show an untoward amount of inquisitiveness. The natural development of blockade by submarine was *via* the line of least resistance. Rules and rights, obligations and understandings must go by the board. The word illegitimate was wiped out. From naval virtue to piracy is but a step; the enemy took it. She would sink at sight.

As a direct consequence of the arming of merchantmen there was an increase in the number of submerged attacks and a decrease in the use of the gun on the part of the submarine. This was entirely to the good, because it necessitated more frequent visits to the base to replenish depleted magazines.

Elsewhere I have dealt at length with the wonderful way in which the men of the Merchant Service settled down to the altered condition of affairs. (*Daring Deeds of Merchant Seamen in the Great War*, Harrap, 1918). The crews showed as much faith in their solitary weapon mounted in the stern as a gun-layer of the *Queen Elizabeth* believed in the giant organs of destruction housed in the fore turret. They achieved wonders with the little spitfires, though sometimes their confidence was misplaced. Uncertainty is the only certainty in war.

Lest I should be accused of being a devotee of mere drum and trumpet history, let me relate the story of a failure. At a few minutes to 3 a.m., in squally and heavy weather, the captain of a merchantman made out the form of a U-boat right ahead. His attempt to ram missed by a few feet. Putting the helm hard over to bring the submarine astern, he ordered the gun to be brought into action. The first shot looked as though it had struck the evil thing. But the bursting shell failed to check the enemy, despite what the master called "a big, bright flare-up." A little later he observed what he presumed to be the wake of a torpedo, followed by the appearance of the U-boat travelling parallel to the steamer.

Again the gun was fired, and again achieved nothing. As the darkness made range-finding exceedingly difficult, and the flash of the cordite betrayed the position of the steamer, the captain gave orders to cease fire, and sent every available man to the stokehold. What the trusted gun had failed to do the engines might achieve. He then told the steward to get coffee. What a delightful human touch! It reminds one of Nelson writing a prayer when within sight of the Combined Fleet, and of Sturdee shaving before giving battle to von Spee.

At 6.20 a.m. a torpedo struck the port side of the steamer, the boilers burst, and ship and gun disappeared in a welter of steam, smoke, and flame. The survivors were picked up a few hours later. But don't think for one moment that they blamed their armament. They attributed their failure to unfortunate weather conditions.

Now for a more pleasing picture. A U-boat tried to torpedo the *Nyanza*, an American steamer with an Imperial name, at a range of approximately 1000 yards. By quick manipulation of the helm the tin fish was skilfully dodged, and the ship's gun opened fire. The submarine thereupon brought two guns to bear on the vessel. The running fight continued for two and a half hours, and was ended by four shots from the *Nyanza*. The enemy visibly staggered, slowly heeled over, and is now gathering rust and barnacles on the ocean floor.

The first of all anti-submarine appliances is the human eye. "It is seven to three on the ship if the submarine is sighted, and four to one against it if it is not," says Sir Eric Geddes.

In every British merchant vessel of 2500 gross tonnage and upward, four men possessing the special Board of Trade certificate as to eyesight were required to act as look-outs at the masthead or elsewhere in areas in which U-boats were likely to be encountered. They kept watch in turn for not more than two hours, and although not necessarily additional members of the crew, were specially engaged and received extra pay.

The necessity for keeping a keen look-out was early recognised. The Admiralty offered a reward not exceeding £1000 for information leading to the capture or destruction of an enemy vessel, including a mine-layer or submarine, and a sum up to £200 for information leading to the craft being sighted and chased. Prominent shipowners and other patriotic citizens aided and abetted these rewards by offering various sums to the captain and crew of the first British merchantman who sank a U-boat.

In due course the idea of 'camouflage' was borrowed from the army. In military campaigns the ingenious daubing of guns with paint that harmonised with the colours of the surrounding scenery became, if not high art, a most skilful artistic device. It was found impossible to make ships invisible at sea, but much was done to render them considerably less conspicuous. The constantly changing light defeated every plan that had invisibility for its aim.

While it is a wise thing to consume one's own smoke, steamers are unable to do so. Smoke is an excellent tell-tale. On the other hand it was not always a friend of the enemy. Destroyers in battle often put up a smokescreen sufficiently dense to cover battleships and cruisers—it was a marked device of the German fleet at Jutland—and many a 'black gang' in the stokehold have saved their ship by its means. Boxes filled with smoke-making powder that burnt slowly and gave off black clouds when flung in the sea have enabled many a vessel to escape behind a dense pall. They played their part in the daring raids on Ostend and Zeebrugge. Special smoke-funnels for use on board were also introduced with success. The Compagnie Transatlantique liner *Le Gard* escaped from two U-boats by means of this system.

On those rare occasions when an unsuspecting U-boat popped up under the very nose of a patrol boat the lance-bomb proved a thoroughly efficient weapon. It consisted of a 14-lb. bomb that exploded on contact, placed on the end of a shaft some 6 feet in length. An expert thrower could hurl this naval hand-grenade quite a fair distance and with splendid precision. A destroyer or chaser towing explosive charges at breakneck speed was a sure and certain harbinger of death should a marauder happen to be in the way.

Armed yachts and fast motor-boats displayed their sea-keeping qualities as never before, and to these were added capacities as auxiliary righting vessels. One of the former picked up an S.O.S. signal. The sender proved to be a trader, and at no great distance from her was a periscope. The enemy was just a little too late in getting under, for the 'eye' had scarcely disappeared when the yacht cut right across her back. A couple of depth charges were thrown out to complete the business, and the yacht was swung round to cross the spot again after the explosion had subsided, when a peculiar disturbance was noticed in another direction. A third depth charge added considerably to the turmoil. As the sailors watched a human form came to the surface. The 'peculiar disturbance' was doubtless the death-rattle of the U-boat, and as she broke in halves the solitary survivor was flung up. He did not live to relate his terrible experience.

The celebrated submarine-chasers, while they varied in design, were usually stubby craft mounting a remarkably serviceable quick-firer on a high forecastle and carrying a liberal supply of 'pills' in the stern. As the range of the former was about three and a half miles, and the engines were capable of attaining a speed of thirty or more knots an hour in calm weather, a submarine was at considerable disadvantage unless she managed to deliver the first blow. Should a U-boat consider it worthwhile to risk a fight on the surface or attempt to torpedo the 'weasel' from below, the speed of the chaser was obviously her greatest asset. Italian chasers, by the way, resembled small submarines, minus the conning-tower; those of France were very similar to our own. When the United States entered the war one of President Wilson's first measures was to order the construction of a large number of these vessels.

Many of the motor launches in the Service were commanded by former amateur yachtsmen, who soon became hardy seafarers. Pluck, energy, and resource characterized their hazardous work. As a senior naval officer reports:

> Day after day, year after year, they have kept the sea in the worst weather when other craft have had to run for shelter.
>
> One story must suffice as typical of many others.

Three motor launches of the Auxiliary Patrol were forging ahead one morning when a lookout saw certain movements known as 'white feathers,' sure indications of the presence of a U-boat. The Germans led them many miles afield in their effort to escape. The launches hung on, and gradually worked themselves into a position which cornered the submersible. Overboard went several depth charges, followed by convulsions and the end of the 'spasm'—naval for submarine chase.

Several ingenious inventions having sound as their basis were introduced. Of these the microphone, enabling the listener to detect the rhythm of submarine motors when submerged, is undoubtedly the most important. The *télémétriste* and the hydrophone, somewhat similar contrivances, were fitted on certain ships of the French Navy.

The convoy system of gathering together a group of merchantmen and conducting them through the danger zone was merely the revival of a venerable institution. Its modern application met with considerably greater success than was often evident in the past. The First Dutch War of 1652-4, for instance, consisted very largely, so far as England was concerned, of attacks on convoys. The necessity for protecting them was responsible for four of the seven battles fought.

Beginning in a comparatively small way, the idea of shepherding merchant shipping was gradually enlarged until few vessels sailed overseas unattended. The system was extraordinarily successful. Before it was introduced nearly 10 per cent, of Britain's food ships were sent to the bottom by an enemy bent on starving England into submission. When the vessels were assembled and protected only 1 *per cent*, was lost, and 26,000,000 tons of foodstuffs were brought over from different parts of the world, in addition to 35,000,000 tons of munitions of various kinds. The whole of the Argentine wheat crop was transported to Great Britain, France, and Italy in 307 ships, of which only one was lost through enemy action.

The celebrated 'Q' ships are mystery ships no longer. The idea of these decoy vessels was obviously suggested by the raider *Möwe*, which resembled a tramp and was really a powerfully armed righting unit of the German Navy, as many a captain of the Mercantile Marine found to his cost. Officered and manned by volunteers, the avowal of Sir Eric Geddes that the crews were made up of "the very bravest that our sea service can produce" was more than a mere figure of speech. No fewer than eight of their commanders won the V.C.

Some of the Q class were sailing ships, others looked like colliers or aged cargo boats; all resembled slow-going, nondescript tubs likely to attract the fond attention of the Germans. When a submarine appeared and called upon the captain to surrender, a special 'panic party' would abandon ship in a terrible state of consternation. They showed beyond doubt that the U-boat campaign had put the fear of the Hun in their hearts. Sometimes the poor fools of Englishmen were not given an opportunity to get away. Fire was opened on the innocent babe without palaver.

The panic party would then go frantic with terror, try to launch the boats, occasionally upsetting one in their haste to get away, or leaving it dangling like a skeleton on a gibbet. Not until the submersible popped up alongside or presented a 'dead certain' target was the true nature of the vessel revealed. Sometimes the ship was torpedoed, shelled, set on fire, and sunk almost to the water's edge before the captain deemed that the psychological moment had arrived. Then flaps dropped that uncovered guns guaranteed by Woolwich to sink the stoutest submersible afloat, bullets spat from chicken coops, and hell was let loose on the surprised enemy. The story of the Q ships is full of dramatic incidents, but words fail to describe the agony of waiting for action or the cool courage of the men who went through strange performances to order when under fire.

H.M.S. *Stock Force* was a steam mystery ship of only 360 tons. What she lacked in size she more than made up for in impudence. On the 30th July, 1918, at 5 p.m. by the captain's chronometer, a torpedo struck her abreast No. 1 hatch. Her stubby nose was blown off, its component parts and contents hurled sky-high, and the bridge completely wrecked. This was a bad beginning, particularly as several of the crew of the foremost guns were wounded. One poor fellow was pinned under the weapon it was his duty to serve when occasion arose, and there he remained throughout the action.

A few seconds later lumps of iron, planks, and unexploded shells flung up from the fore part of the ship by the force of the explosion fell on deck and added to the injuries already sustained by the ratings, at the same time wounding the first lieutenant and the navigating officer. As the vessel began to settle down forward the panic party pushed off. Although the lower deck was flooded, the surgeon got to work standing up to his waist in water, and the engine-room staff went on with their labours. The captain and two guns' crews alone had nothing to do at the moment beyond keeping themselves out of sight. Sometimes waiting is the hardest of all tasks.

The attacking U-boat behaved in a most irritating way. She came to the surface straight ahead, and showed no immediate intention of approaching nearer. Meanwhile the *Stock Force* was going down. There was not the slightest doubt about that. It was then that the panic party played their second act. They began to row back to the ship, hoping to entice the enemy nearer. The U-boat swallowed the bait, approaching slowly. When she was abeam, up went the White Ensign, the contraptions fell away, and two guns crashed out. Three rounds smashed the conning-tower, felled a periscope, and tore a great rent in the hull on the water-line. Several Germans were blown out through the hole, while the officer on watch got a sudden rise in the world.

As the water rushed into the stricken U-boat her bows rose, to be instantly subjected to a terrific bombardment. Then she disappeared. Her assailant kept afloat until 9.25 p.m. Officers and men were taken off by torpedo-boats and a trawler.

For nearly half an hour after the panic party had pulled away from H.M.S. *Prize*, another Q ship, the guns' crews were lying face downward on the deck subjected to heavy fire from a U-boat. When the enemy came abeam the schooner's weapons were revealed in no uncertain fashion. The action was over in four minutes. One shell shattered the foremost gun of the U-boat, killing everybody near it. Another wrecked the conning-tower, and the interior of the craft became a mass of flame. Three survivors were rescued, though how they escaped passes understanding. The *Prize* had been so badly holed that she looked like following her victim. Q boats, however, were built to stand a lot of knocking about. More often than not they were severely handled before they got an opportunity to retaliate. On this particular occasion every available man turned carpenter or lent a hand with the pumps. The nearest port was 120 miles off. The Q ship sailed to within five miles of the 'haven where she would be' before accepting assistance. She was then given a friendly tow by a nimble little motor-launch.

The following is the official account of what happened to H.M.S. Q 5 on the 17th February 1917, after she had been torpedoed abreast of No. 3 hold. The chief hero of the exploit was Commander Gordon Campbell, who had been awarded the D.S.O. for sinking a U-boat when in command of H.M.S. *Farnborough* nearly a year before.

> Action stations were sounded and the 'panic party' abandoned ship. The engineer officer reported that the engine-room was flooding, and was ordered to remain at his post as long as possible, which he and his staff, several of whom were severely wounded, most gallantly did. The submarine was observed on the starboard quarter 200 yards distant, watching the proceedings through his periscope. He ran past the ship on the starboard side so closely that the whole hull was visible beneath the surface, finally emerging about 300 yards off on the port bow. The enemy came down the port side of the ship, and fire was withheld until all guns could bear at point-blank range.
> The first shot beheaded the captain of the submarine as he was climbing out of the conning-tower, and the submarine finally sank with conning-tower open and crew pouring out. One officer and one man were rescued on the surface and taken prisoner, after which the boats were recalled, and all hands proceeded to do their utmost to keep the ship afloat. A wireless signal for assistance had been sent out when (but not until) the fate of the submarine was assured, and a destroyer and sloop arrived a couple of hours later, and took Q5 in tow. She was finally beached in safety the following evening.
> The action may be regarded as the supreme test of naval discipline. The chief engineer and engine-room watch remained at their posts to keep the dynamo working until driven out by the

water, then remaining concealed on top of the cylinders. The guns' crews had to remain concealed in their gun-houses for nearly half an hour, while the ship slowly sank lower in the water.

One such adventure would suffice most men. Not so Commander Gordon Campbell. He was 'at it again' in August 1917, when in command of another Q ship, the *Dunraven*. This particular vessel was ostensibly an armed British trader. On the U-boat beginning the action, the undisguised stern gun was brought into play, the speed of the ship reduced so that the submarine might overtake her, and wireless calls for help were sent out. She caught fire aft, in the vicinity of a magazine, above which was a concealed gun with its crew ready for immediate service. Shortly after the panic party left the vessel the magazine exploded, starting the electric gongs that signalled 'Action' at the other gun positions. This was unfortunate, for only one weapon could be brought to bear on the enemy, then in the act of submerging. Although the *Dunraven* was on fire, a wireless code message was sent to warn approaching traffic not to intervene.

After two torpedoes had struck the vessel a second panic party abandoned ship, leaving the guns unmasked. Apparently not a soul remained on board, but the commander of the submarine was evidently not quite sure. For nearly an hour he regarded discretion as the better part of valour. He merely watched and waited for the ship to blow up or go down. As the mystery ship did neither, the U-boat pounded her for twenty minutes, then slowly passed at a distance of about 150 yards. A torpedo fired by the *Dunraven* missed by a hair-breadth, but was apparently unperceived. A second torpedo was tried as the enemy returned on the other side. That likewise failed. Uncertain as to the next proceeding of her astonishing antagonist, the U-boat made off. When destroyers arrived on the scene the fire on the gallant little ship was got under, and a valiant attempt made to keep her afloat. She eventually succumbed to bad weather. But what a career, and what superb courage! You will not meet the like in fiction.

These wonderful mystery ships, that took such a lot of sinking, that purposely courted trouble to entice their aggressors into the same, were no ordinary vessels. Externally, as I have said, they resembled rusty old tramps; internally they were built for battering. Iron girders gave them additional strength, and bales of cork served to check the shock of a torpedo and keep them afloat. No wonder Fritz got scared and threw up the game!

Chapter 15

Bottling up Zeebrugge and Ostend

Their Lordships desire to express to all ranks and ratings concerned in the recent gallant and successful enterprise on the Belgian coast their high admiration of the perfect co-operation displayed, and of the single-minded determination of all to achieve their object. The disciplined daring and singular contempt of death exhibited by those who were assigned the posts of greatest danger places this exploit high in the annals of the Royal Navy and Royal Marines, and will be a proud memory for the relatives of those who fell.—General Order to the Fleet.

Prevention is better than cure, even in the Navy. To bottle up the U-boats was obviously a far quicker way of ridding the sea of the vermin than scouring the ocean highway for them. It required no effort of genius to come to that conclusion. But how? Many minds had puzzled over the problem and evolved all kinds of devices for the purpose, most of them more ingenious than practical. Zeebrugge and Ostend were within a comparatively few miles of the Essex coast, and from these ports there issued U-boats that played the part of maritime highwaymen every hour of the twenty-four, and surface craft that stole along in the darkness of night and raided the Straits. The importance attached by the enemy to Zeebrugge and Ostend was so great that they said they would never give them up. That defiant attitude, suggestive of a rude little boy putting his fingers to his nose in token of profound disrespect, was calculated to make every British son all the more determined that the Germans should be compelled to clear out.

Napoleon I quite rightly regarded Antwerp as a pistol held at the heart of England; when William II ravished Belgium he brought his

C3 AT ZEEBRUGGE MOLE
An old British submarine, loaded with explosives, was run into the piles of the jetty at the shore end of Zeebrugge Mole and blown up, to the amazement and destruction of the defenders.

weapons nearer still. Under German domination Zeebrugge and Ostend became vastly important bases for submarines and torpedo-boats. Together they formed a veritable pirates' lair. From time to time since August 1914 they had been heavily bombarded by the navy and from the air, but always with surprisingly little effect on their fiendish activities. Warships came and warships went, tons of high explosive shells and bombs were rained on them, until one dismally surmised that they must be invulnerable.

Zeebrugge was the more important because it was directly connected by canal with medieval Bruges. Previous to the outbreak of hostilities the City of the Golden Fleece was a sort of Sleepy Hollow kept awake by its carillon and tourists. The German invaders transformed the place into a naval arsenal. Torpedo-boats and submarines found shelter in the port, making their entry and exit *via* Zeebrugge Harbour, with its broad mole extending about a mile and a half seaward. The latter was connected with the shore by a wooden jetty of enormous strength. This arrangement prevented the harbour from silting up, which otherwise it would have done. The long concrete arm sheltering the canal was something more than a mere breakwater. It had been converted into a fort, with batteries and machine-guns, seaplane hangars and stores, and was strongly garrisoned. No fewer than 120 guns guarded the littoral of Zeebrugge and Ostend.

Could the ports be sealed, despite the difficulties presented by the treacherous nature of the coast, the mine-fields that shielded them, the batteries that bristled on the sand-dunes, the aircraft that kept watch and ward, the warships that lay in hiding? The question was entertained seriously by Rear-Admiral Sir Reginald Tyrwhitt. There seemed to be little likelihood at that date that the army would achieve the result by military means, and so if these places were to be rendered useless as sea bases the task, it was clear, must be accomplished by the Navy.

The scheme was laid before Sir John Jellicoe, at that time First Sea Lord, and given to Vice-Admiral Roger Keyes, in command at Dover, to carry out. We have already met the latter as Commodore of Submarines in August 1914; he now returned to a task he had undertaken on a much smaller scale in 1900, during the Boxer Rebellion in China. With a dozen men he stormed a fort and blew it up, despite the opinion of some of his seniors that the attempt was little more than a forlorn hope. While he and his associates were planning the multitudinous details of the Zeebrugge-Ostend expedition, the memory of the former 'impossible' task must have crossed his mind more than Zeebrugge and Ostend once. Here was an operation ten thousand times more difficult, requiring the most minute calculations, an efficient fighting force, a considerable fleet, and an exact time-table. Chinamen can fight, and fight desperately, but the garrison Keyes purposed to attack was officered and manned by the German Army, and the place defended by the most modern weapons.

The resources that Keyes asked for were a covering force, half a dozen obsolete cruisers—there is sometimes a good deal of 'kick' in a ship marked for the scrap-heap—a couple of ferry-boats, and a number of auxiliary vessels. Of the six old-timers, five were to be filled with concrete and sunk in such a position that navigation would be blocked (hence the term block-ships) and one was to land the main storming party; the ferry-boats were to convey additional fighting men, and the auxiliaries were to pick up any survivors there might be. For mark this: the desperate nature of the enterprise made annihilation possible. None expected to get back, but all had made up their minds to dam up the raiders. That was the sole and sufficient object of the expedition. It formed part of no invasion project.

There was urgency but no hurry, a naval paradox which meant that while the Service fully realised the importance of bottling up the U-boats, it also understood that delay in executing the operation was preferable to a tragic anti-climax. Twice the armada set out and returned without having accomplished its purpose. On St George's Day 1918 Keyes and his men showed their mettle in the most dashing naval exploit of the Great Conflict.

The cruiser *Vindictive*, accompanied by the *Daffodil* and the *Iris*, both Mersey ferry-boats, carried storming and demolition parties of bluejackets and 'jollies,' all picked men. The *Vindictive*, armed with various species of things Satanic, was to focus the attention of the enemy. The *Intrepid*, the *Iphigenia*, and the *Thetis*, cargoed with concrete, were to be sunk by explosives detonated from their respective bridges in the channels and entrances to Zeebrugge; the *Brilliant* and the *Sirius* were to perform similar operations at Ostend.

The night was hazy and overcast. Navigation in mined waters is not easy, but there were no casualties. As the *Vindictive* and her consorts headed for Zeebrugge Harbour they shrouded themselves in a smoke-screen so dense that the strongest search-light could not penetrate it. Everything went splendidly until the old cruiser and the ferry-boats were just off the mole. Then the wind turned Hun. The star-shells and search-lights that suddenly awakened, lighting up the harbour almost as though it were day, revealed the visitors to the enemy. Batteries thundered, machineguns on the mole awoke to life, shells burst above, about, and on the incoming cruiser. In addition to the immediate din the boom of the guns of the supporting monitors and of siege guns in Flanders could be heard. The *Vindictive* held on her way through the inferno as though the reception was nothing more formidable than fireworks sent up to welcome her.

Commander Alfred F. B. Carpenter, standing on the exposed bridge of the cruiser, brought the bows of his ship alongside the mole, while the *Daffodil* ran a grave risk of bursting her boilers in a giant effort to shove her stern in. As the parapet of the mole was thirty feet high the *Vindictive* had been fitted with a temporary deck, from whence eighteen gangways were speedily run out. Before they had ordered their men to land both Colonel Elliot, of the Marines, and Captain H. C. Halahan, who was to lead the sailors, were lying dead. When the word was given the fighters moved down the brows in face of a withering fire, an operation made more difficult by the rolling of the ship in a heavy swell. Many were killed and wounded as they attempted to land. Lieutenant H. T. C. Walker, with one arm blown off, was trodden under before he could be dragged away. "Good luck!" he yelled, "good luck!"

The howitzer mounted forward in the *Vindictive* was fed and fought with uncanny precision, though two crews were wiped out. In the foretop a solitary man alone remained to work one of the Lewis guns, and he was grievously wounded. Near by, sitting in a little cabin, a mere landsman fired rockets for the guidance of the block-ships with as little concern as if he were managing a benefit performance at the Crystal Palace. Commander Carpenter's coolness was infectious. There was no 'panic party,' real or fancied, on this mystery ship. The *Daffodil*, still holding the cruiser in position, was ordered to maintain her station and withhold landing her storming party. The *Iris*, owing to the failure of her grapnels to grip the parapet, fell astern of the cruiser, though Lieutenant-Commander Bradford and Lieutenant Hawkins clambered up and tried to fix them, sitting at work on the wall until they were shot dead.

The *Thetis*, with a nucleus crew—the others had been taken off by motor-boats—approached the mole, but failed to reach it. One of her propellers got entangled in a steel defence net. Becoming unmanageable, she struck the edge of a shoal and refused to budge. Shell after shell crashed against her old sides, but it was not until she was virtually a wreck that Commander R. S. Sneyd, D.S.O., exploded the charges in her hold and sank her. Then he signalled the course to the other ships.

The *Intrepid* and the *Iphigenia* came bowling along, sorry for their consort's ill-luck but anxious only to get on with the immediate task in hand. Lieutenant S. Bonham-Carter beached the *Intrepid* on the muddy spot marked as her grave, blew a great hole in her side, and was smilingly told by the chief engineer, who had remained below, that the performance was eminently satisfactory. Surely that engineer was the embodiment of dignity and impudence, that peculiar combination that marks the true Briton. Lieutenant E. W. Billyard-Leake, in command of the *Iphigenia*, also entered the canal and carried out his task with splendid efficiency. Both ships were sunk about 200 yards up the fairway.

The officers and men of the block-ships were picked up with conspicuous gallantry by perky little motor-launches that were all the while subjected to the attention of land batteries as they bustled about their business. Lieutenant Bonham-Carter sent away his boats before leaving the ship, trusting to a Carley float for his own salvation. The calcium flare, which is an integral part of this apparatus, showed him up to the Germans, who kindly turned on a machine-gun for his special benefit. Probably the smoke from his own vessel saved him. He was subsequently picked up by a launch.

The most dramatic incident was yet to come. Suddenly the shore end of the mole was lit up by a sheet of livid flame that seemed to sear the sky. C3, an old submarine commanded by Lieutenant R. D. Sandford, R.N., had been jammed into the great piles that supported the jetty. No ordinary submarine this, but one loaded with several tons of high explosive. Her little crew of heroes got away in a boat before the charge was fired, but not before the craft had been driven right home. The explosion severed the communications of the mole with the shore, a break 60 feet wide being effected. The Germans crowding the wooden structure were blown to bits.

The landing parties, working under a galling fire, blew up buildings, destroyed gun-emplacements, and did as much damage as was possible before being recalled. Not a few of the enemy felt the cold steel of British bayonets, and at least two of their guns were captured and turned on them. Fifty minutes elapsed before the siren of the *Vindictive* sounded for the men to return.

The operation against Ostend was not so successful. Owing to the change of wind the *Sirius* and the *Brilliant* were revealed by means of the calcium flares lit to guide them, which had previously been hidden by the smoke-cloud. These lights were promptly extinguished by the enemy's gunners. Unable to find the entrance, the two ships grounded east of the piers, and were there sunk.

Taking all things into consideration, the casualties in these two dare-devil actions were small, although they totalled over 600. Vice-Admiral Keyes, who was present in the destroyer Warwick, was knighted in recognition of his distinguished service, and Commander Alfred F. B. Carpenter was promoted to Captain and received the V.C. Sandford, of C3, Lieutenant P. T. Dean, R.N.V.R., who performed wonders in rescuing men from the *Intrepid* and the *Iphigenia*, Captain E. Bamford, D.S.O., who landed three platoons of the Marines on the mole, Sergeant N. A. Finch, who fought in the foretop of the *Vindictive*, and Able Seaman A. E. Mackenzie, who worked a machine-gun in an exposed position, were also decorated with the Victoria Cross.

Battle-scarred and holed in many places, the *Vindictive* was patched up at Dover for a final exploit. The British Navy does not like leaving things half done. The affair at Ostend had miscarried through sheer bad luck. It must be completed. In the early hours of the morning of the 10th May, 1918, the brave old cruiser, now rigged up as a blockship, faced 15-in. guns and found the entrance, though twice she lost her way. She got a terrible pasting from the defenders of the port. The after-control was wiped out, the conning-tower struck by a heavy shell. On reaching the eastern pier she swung round to an angle of about forty degrees to the structure, the charges were fired, and she settled down. The casualties reached 136 officers and men.

That these stirring episodes in the War in the Underseas aided and abetted in the final surrender of the U-boats in November 1918 cannot be doubted.

CHAPTER 16

The Great Collapse

The Board of Admiralty desire to express to the officers and men of the Royal Navy and Royal Marines on the completion of their great work their congratulations on a triumph to which history knows no parallel.

They came in flying the White Ensign, which was the cleanest thing about them. Only a few weeks before the commanders of these same bedraggled U-boats had boasted of defying the world; now they had been brought to heel like a pack of whipped curs. German officers and men were taking part in the biggest collapse in naval history; their conquerors in the greatest triumph. At Beatty's bidding they meekly surrendered their piratical craft at the rate of a score a day for a week or more. The bluejackets at Harwich rechristened the Stour "U-boat Avenue "when the captives were given floating-room in its sluggish waters.

On the 9th November, 1918, Sir Eric Geddes gave it as his opinion that the High Sea Fleet had "gone mad" because it "dared not fight" and because it "had not got a good cause." That is the psychological explanation, true to fact and experience. Its morale broke down, which is another way of saying that it lost its nerve. When ordered to put to sea on the 28th October, 1918, ostensibly for manoeuvres, but in reality as a gambler's last hazardous throw of the dice, the German Fleet mutinied in a far more thorough manner than had obtained a few months previously.

At Wilhelmshaven about one thousand sailors were imprisoned for taking part in the mutiny; Kiel, on the other hand, went wholly 'red,' as did also the commercial ports of Hamburg, Bremen, and Lübeck. Soviets came into being, a Workers' and Soldiers' Council was formed,

Entry of the surrendered U-boats into Harwich, November 20, 1918

Bolshevism was openly preached, fireworks were let off at Wilhelmshaven in honour of the German Republic.

Apart from the moral issue, three main causes led to the defection of the German Navy. It did not fight because the Battle of Jutland had proved the vast superiority of the Grand Fleet; it did not want to fight because the complements of the vessels were mainly landsmen by upbringing and inclination; it had no heart to fight because the U-boat campaign had failed to win the war according to promise, or even to shake Britain's resolution by one iota. Probably the ultimate and determining factor was the frightful mortality among the submersibles. When the High Sea Fleet failed at Jutland the U-boat campaign was undertaken in real earnest; when that failed the. mutiny took place. The death-rate toward the end was frightful. Of 360 submarines launched during 1914-18, 200 were sunk or captured.

That Germany made a bold bid for triumph cannot be gainsaid. There were times when the Allied Admiralties regarded the situation as critical. The statistics of the matter are instructive, though not pleasing. From first to last Great Britain lost 9,000,000 tons of shipping, while Allies and neutrals suffered to the extent of a further 6,000,000 tons. In addition there were eighty British vessels, with an aggregate tonnage of 172,554, held up in German ports during hostilities, an amount by no means to be despised, although it is small compared with the enemy tonnage captured and brought into Allied service. The latter reached the respectable figure of 2,392,675. British naval casualties totalled 39,766 in killed, wounded, interned, and captured. In the Merchant Service 14,661 lost their lives, and 3,295 were taken prisoners.

War in the Underseas was waged at frightful cost to all belligerents, both vanquished and victors. Taking British losses by enemy action and marine risks during the war, the worst quarters were in this order: second quarter of 1917, third, first, and last quarters of the same year, and first quarter of 1918 and last quarter of 1916. In April 1917, 555,000 tons of British shipping were sent to the bottom. Had things gone on at that rate, "we were in deadly danger; had it gone on for nine months we were ruined," (Sir L. Chiozza Money in the House of Commons, 14th November, 1918). In September 1918 the depletion had been reduced to 151,000 tons.

Captain Persius asserts that, following the action off the Danish coast, twenty-three battle-ships were disarmed for the purpose of obtaining metal for constructing U-boats—excellent proof of the grip of the blockade and of the British victory at Jutland. His figures regarding undersea craft are a little difficult to follow, because he only deals with what he calls ' front submarines,' presumably those definitely on active service and not merely patrolling in home waters. In April 1917, he says, Germany had 126 U-boats, in the following October 146; in February 1918 she possessed 136; in June of the same year, 113. In January 1917 only 12 *per cent*, were at sea, 30 *per cent*, in harbour, 38 *per cent*, under repair, and 20 *per cent*, incapacitated.

His most important admission is that the ill-trained crews had no confidence in their craft, and that toward the end of the campaign it was difficult to get men to work them. He flatly contradicts the assertion that losses were made up by new construction. Apart from the offensive operations of the navy proper, the defensive equipment of traders and the introduction of the convoy system in the summer of 1917 were of enormous importance in thwarting the submarine. In addition to merchant shipping and munitions 16,000,000 fighting men were escorted, and of these less than 5000 met with disaster.

Sea-power worked miracles in other directions. "The blockade," says Sir Eric Geddes, (Speech at the Grosvenor Galleries, 4th December, 1918), "is what crushed the life out of the Central Empires." That was the work of the 10th Cruiser Squadron. From 1914 to 1917 the ships of that squadron:

> Held the 800 miles stretch of grey sea from the Orkneys to Iceland. In those waters they intercepted 15,000 ships taking succour to our enemies, and they did that under almost Arctic conditions, and mainly in the teeth of storm and blizzard; out of that 15,000 they missed just 4 *per cent.*, a most remarkable achievement under impossible conditions. Behind the blockade was the Grand Fleet, the fulcrum of the whole of the sea-power of the Allies. If ever testimony were needed of the value of sea-power, I can give it. In every individual case when an armistice was signed by our enemies, and in one, if not two, cases before, the one cry that went up was, 'Release the blockade.'

Admiral Sir Percy Scott holds that four years of U-boat warfare have "tragically demonstrated the truth" of his neglected warning, but he also acknowledges that the navy did not fail us. To quote the apostle of the submarines:

> From the first Great Britain kept command of the seas.

His prophecy of 1914 that the day of the big surface ship was over has not been fulfilled, though the submarine may become the capital ship of the future. He contends that if Germany could have placed 200 U-boats on the ocean trade routes at the outbreak of war she would have defeated the Allies. She might have done so, but the important fact is that she did not possess the requisite number. At that time we were lamentably short of light craft, German cruisers and raiders were running amok in various parts of the world, and the Grand Fleet was fully occupied 'containing' the main German squadrons. Given the hypothetical conditions mentioned by the admiral, it is not improbable that the enemy would "have defeated the Allies and practically conquered the world," but it is not "certain," as Sir Percy asserts.

Germany regarded the intensified U-boat campaign as a sure thing; we know the result. In his now famous letter to the *Times*, one of the eminent correspondent's contentions was that "the introduction of vessels that swim underwater has already done away with the utility of ships that swim on the top of the water," that "as the motor vehicle has driven the horse from the road, so has the submarine driven the battleship from the sea." The Great War of 1914-18 disproved this very definite statement, and witnessed the introduction of mighty 'hush' ships which lived and moved and had their being on the surface of great waters.

On the other hand we should be crass fools if we neglected the lessons of the war as regards the latest naval arm. The records of British submarines are eloquent of their effectiveness. Summed up they amount to this: Two battleships sunk and three badly damaged; two armoured cruisers destroyed; two light cruisers sunk and one badly damaged. The long obituary list also included seven torpedo-boats, five gunboats, twenty submarines, five armed auxiliaries, fourteen transports, two store ships, half a dozen ammunition and supply ships, fifty-three steamships, 197 sailing vessels, and one Zeppelin, making a grand total of 315 vessels dead and buried. As to the sea-going qualities of the craft, one British commander made twenty-four cruises, covering 22,000 miles, in a year, while in a single month British submarines navigated 105,768 sea miles, one mile in every ten being in the submerged position.

We have seen in previous chapters that the Allied naval losses, while they made no appreciable difference to the situation, were not negligible. Approximately 230 fighting ships were lost from all causes by Great Britain during the war. Without going so far as Mr Arthur Pollen, whose opinion regarding the submarine is that, "viewed strictly as a form of sea force, it is the feeblest and least effective that has ever been seen," all available facts show that warships travelling at a good speed are comparatively immune from attack. There is also little danger when they are going slowly, provided they have a covering screen of destroyers. The majority of battleships and cruisers that fell victims to U-boats were taking life easy, as for instance the *Aboukir*, the *Cressy*, and the *Hogue* in the North Sea, and the *Formidable* in the Channel.

The Great Collapse revealed no new wonders, though the cargo-carrying *Deutschland*, converted into a 'front submarine' and mounting 5.9-in. guns, was a sight for the gods as she lay floating on the bosom of old Father Thames. Another former commercial cruiser, U139, had just returned to the Fatherland after a voyage of sixty-four days with a company of ninety-one, fifteen of whom were specially detailed for manning prizes. One ugly brute, believed to have been responsible for the sinking of 47,000 tons of shipping, carried forty-two mines and twenty-two torpedoes. Perhaps the most interesting discovery was a cat-o'-nine-tails stained with blood, extracted from under the bunk of a certain U-boat commander.

Two sailors were so enamoured of their own country that they had to be persuaded to go on board the transport at the point of a revolver. One commander, in handing over his signed declaration, was good enough to remark, "We shall be coming over again for them soon." Another officer explained that his periscope was missing and his compass gave an incorrect reading because a steamer had 'sat' on his boat, while a British lieutenant-commander had the satisfaction of piloting a submarine he had once attacked in German waters. Another boat was brand-new from the shipbuilding yard. Nearly all were camouflaged. The majority of the submarines surrendered were certainly not of the cruiser type, about which one heard so much during the war, although in the first batch to reach Harwich was a monster 340 ft. long, with a displacement of 2300 tons and accommodation for a crew of seventy. The remainder were mostly of 800 tons displacement, 225 ft. long, and 22 ft. beam.

It has taken ten centuries to make the British Navy; it took four and a quarter years for the Senior Service to secure the surrender of its most formidable rival in the greatest Sea Conquest of all time.

Submarines, Mines and Torpedoes in the War

The British Submarine "E.2."

Displacement, 800 tons; Speed 16.10 knots; Armament, 4 torpedo tubes, and 2 q.f. guns. There are 17 vessels of this class, completed between 1912-14

Contents

Preface	169
Introduction	171
The Modern Submarine Torpedo-boat	188
British Submarines	196
French Submarines	206
Russian Submarines	215
Japanese Submarines	220
German Submarines	222
Austrian Submarines	226
Submarines in Action	229
Anti-Submarine Tactics	241
The Submarine Torpedo	247
Submarine Mines	251
Mine-Laying Fleets	256
Mine-Sweeping Fleets	259
Comparative Fighting Value of the Submarine Fleets at War	261

Preface

Warfare has become so largely a matter of science that in order to arrive at an intelligent understanding of the *naval situation* or of the *military campaigns* in the Great European War, a knowledge of the scientific factors contributing to victory or defeat is essential. And in this volume it has been my aim not only to review the actual fighting underseas, but also to present a compendium of information relative to the submarine fleets and arms of the great Naval Powers engaged; which I venture to hope will prove of present interest on account of the prominent part played by the underwater fighting ships and appliances, and of permanent historic value as being the first work to describe the vast preparations and curious events leading to the new "Submarine Phase" in naval warfare.

C.W. D-F.

Introduction

THE SUBMARINE PHASE OF THE NAVAL WAR

In the mist of war which envelops over half the entire world, no less than 264 underwater fighting ships are engaged. They form the submarine fleets of England, France, Russia, Japan, Germany and Austria; and the highly-trained crews of these modern additions to the fighting navies comprise nearly 20,000 men. But the conduct of submarine warfare on the grand scale requires far more than flotillas of submergible warships and their daring crews. This new branch of naval science is ever widening in its scope, its means of offence, and in its attendant ramifications.

Every important naval base has its curious submarine floating docks, ready for crippled members of Its attached flotilla; every naval construction department has its corps of submarine experts; each of the 1,500 surface warships engaged in this titanic struggle for the dominion of Europe and the mastery of the seas carries the means for delivering submarine attacks in its torpedoes and surface and submerged discharging tubes. The oceans in the theatres of war have been strewn with German and Austrian mines; then they have been either counter-mined or swept clear and mined again. British seaplanes, with specially trained observers, are continually searching from high in the air for the *dark patches in the semi-transparent sea-green* which denote the presence of mines and submarines. Within signal-range or wireless call of the aerial scouts and their attendant ships are destroyer flotillas to give battle to the hostile submarines, while hundreds of trawlers and small steamers, fitted with special apparatus, are continually sweeping up the hundreds of submarine mines kid by the enemy's vessels which are fitted to enable them to sow like seeds over the pathways of the sea these deadly perils to navigation.

Submerged wire entanglements in conjunction with boom-defences and observation and contact submarine mines protect the seaward approaches to harbours in the same way as similar appliances are used to protect the approaches to land fortifications; and every harbour, waterway and channel of strategic importance is protected by elaborate submarine mine defences. All this is part of the new warfare underseas—that science which is daily rendering hazardous the life of the greatest battleship and the smallest merchantman afloat in the zone of war.

Before placing in review order the vast preparations made for submarine attack and defence in the years which preceded the outbreak of war and describing in detail the powerful submarine fleets engaged, it is necessary to make clear to the reader the wonderful change which this new mode of attack has made in all branches of naval warfare and its influence on sea power. As indicative of this change we have only to survey *in their submarine aspect* the naval operations in the opening phase of this, the greatest war in history.

In the domain of naval strategy we find reflected the altered conditions caused by these invisibly arms. Every battle on land and sea teaches its lesson of concealment and sudden stealthy attack; and even as the huge siege guns and devastating artillery fire of the land forces is causing the extension of the battle-front and the rapid burrowing under earth or entrenching of positions dearly won or with difficulty retained—"approximating to siege warfare"—so are the powerful 12 and 13.5-inch naval guns (weight of projectile 850 lbs. and 1,400 lbs. respectively), combined with the rapidity and accuracy of the modern warships secondary armament, necessitating the reduction in numbers of the big surface ships of the opposing fleets by frequent submarine and torpedo attacks prior to the decisive engagements between the battle fleets.

Hence we find, in the opening phase of the naval war, the German and Austrian fleets, inferior in numbers and gun power, skulking behind fortifications and waiting for their submarine and surface torpedo-boats and light cruisers, in conjunction with the hundreds of submerged mines strewn over the North Sea, Baltic, Adriatic and elsewhere to reduce the number and power of the British, French, Russian and Japanese fleets before the decisive actions are fought; and in order that these tactics might be frustrated, and the big British ships, as well as those of her allies, costing several millions sterling each, should not be exposed to these grave risks when no good could result, they have been compelled to delay initiative, and meanwhile all their operations had to be screened by smaller and faster vessels of the cruiser and destroyer types, while they waited within call should the German Battle Fleet—in the case of the North Sea—dare to come out to fight.

The British submarines of the large sea-going type were in the meantime employed in watching the Frisian coast with the object of attacking any of the enemy's ships which ventured from behind the elaborate coast fortifications. Not content with this role, however, several British submarines made their way unseen through the dangerous waters of the Heligoland Bight and succeeded in getting within reconnoitring distance of the German submerged harbour defences, behind which lurk their big ships.

With what degree of success this new opening or *submarine phase* in naval warfare has been attended is shown by the sinking, during the first few weeks of the war, of the British cruiser *Amphion*, a vessel of 3,440 tons displacement, completed in 1912, and carrying ten 4-inch guns, with a loss of 131 men, by contact with a German mine; the destruction of the German submarine U.15 by the British cruiser *Birmingham*; the sinking of an Austrian torpedo-boat by a mine off Pola; the torpedoing of H.M.S. *Pathfinder*, a fleet scout of about 3,000 tons displacement, completed in 1905-6, by a German submarine; the destruction of the Wilson liner *Runo* by a mine; the sinking of the German cruiser *Hela*, a vessel of 2,000 tons displacement, built in 1896, by the British submarine E.9, and the torpedoing of the British armoured cruisers *Aboukir*, *Hogue* and *Cressy*—vessels of 12,000 tons displacement, carrying two 9.2-inch and twelve 6-inch guns besides twelve 12-pounder quick-firing guns and two torpedo tubes—by German submarines concealed behind a trawler engaged in laying mines, over which the Dutch flag had been hoisted as a blind.

This is in addition to the lamentable destruction of much life and property belonging to neutral powers caused by the laying of German floating mines on the trade-routes.

To the Allies this *submarine phase* did not come unexpected. The British Naval yards in conjunction with the big shipbuilding and engineering firms, such as Messrs. Vickers Ltd., Barrow-in-Furness; Messrs. Armstrong, Whitworth and Co. Ltd., Newcastle-on-Tyne; the Whitehead Torpedo Company Ltd., Weymouth; Messrs. Siebe, Gorman and Co. Ltd., London; and Messrs. Scotts' Shipbuilding and Engineering Co. Ltd., as well as many other firms and individual submarine experts had been engaged for many years in solving one after another the problems continually arising in the practical application

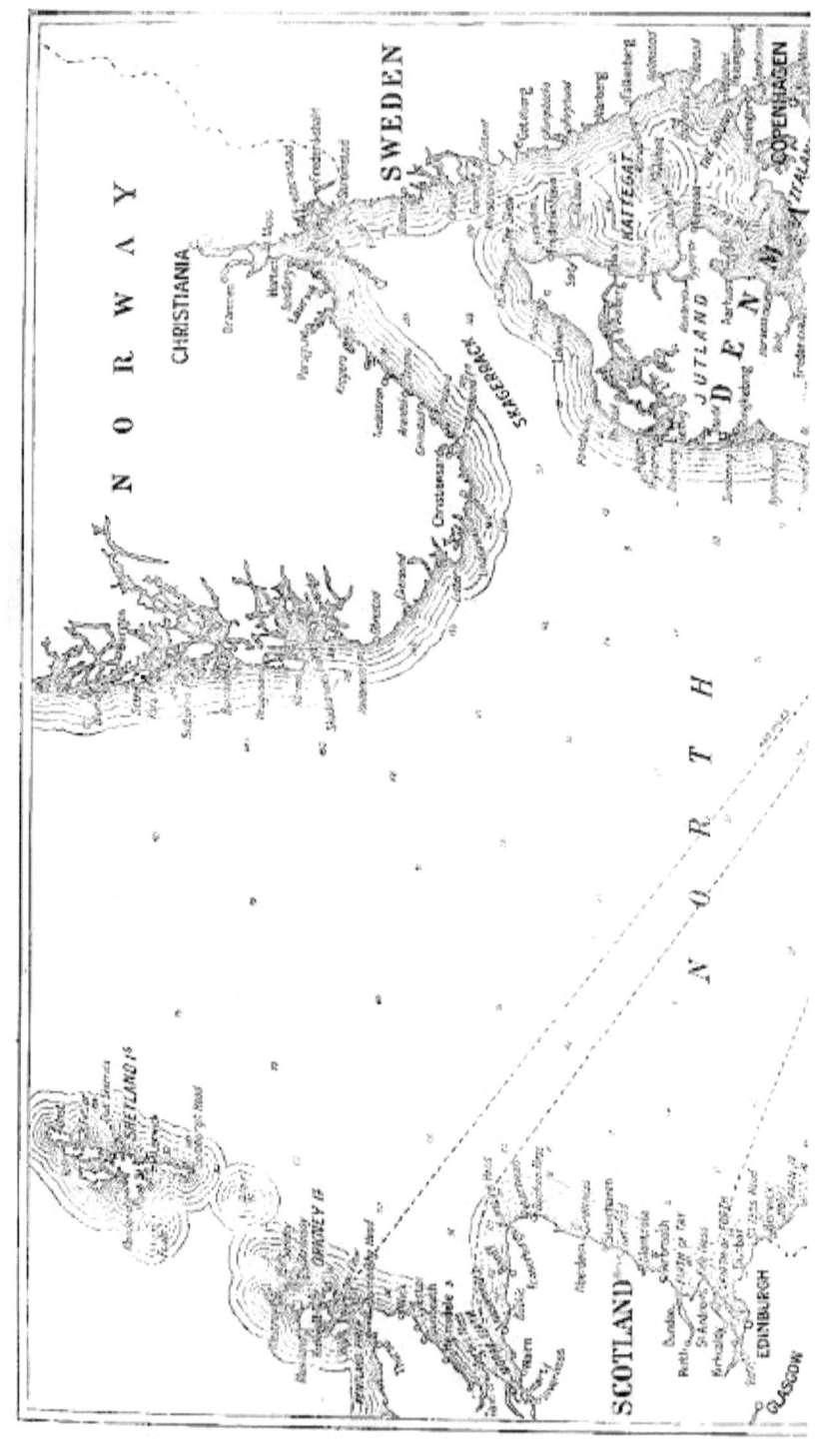

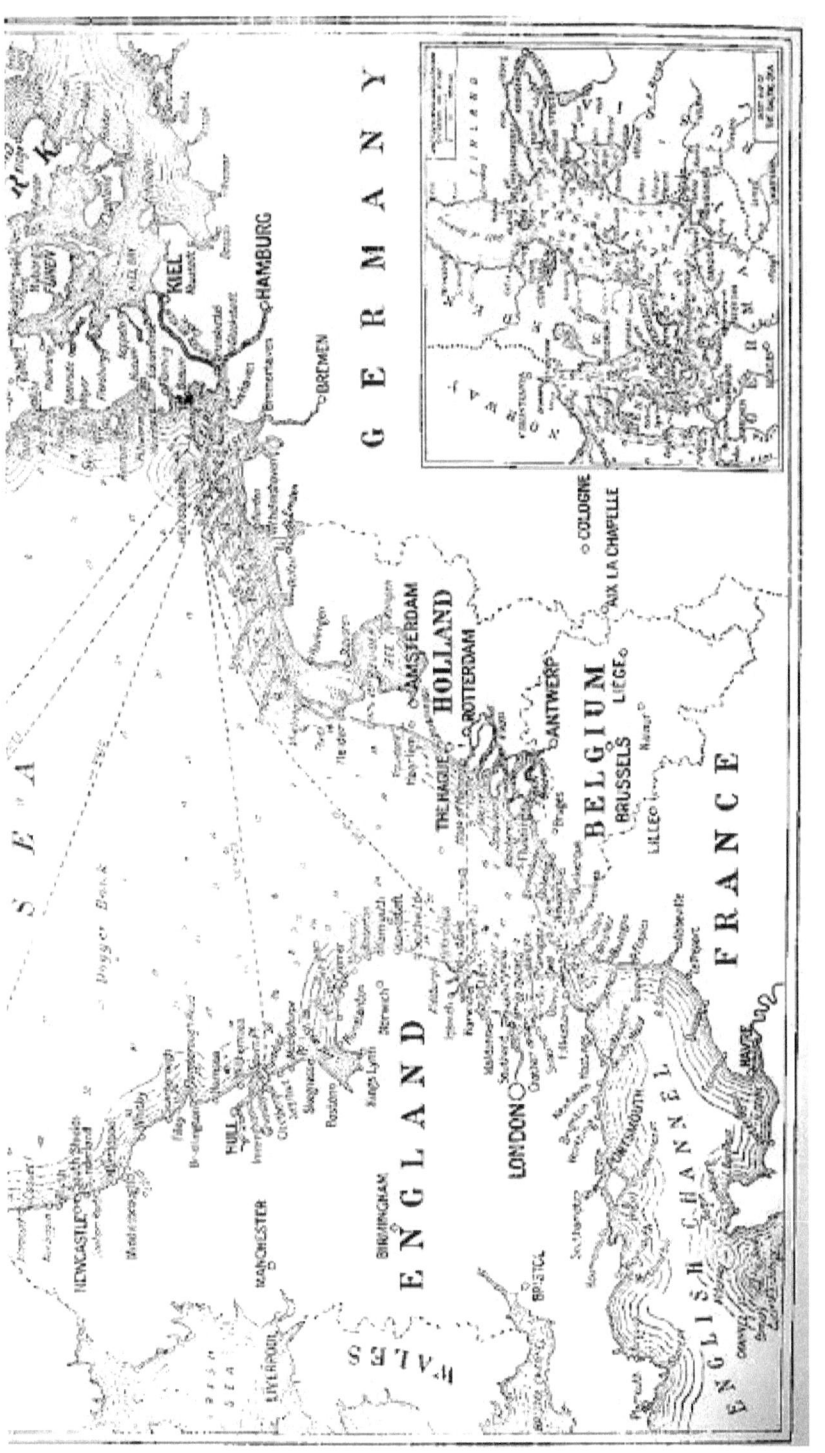

of all forms of submarine warfare. The first British naval submarines were launched in 1901-2 from Messrs. Vickers' works at Barrow, and the subsequent growth of our submarine flotillas has been rapid both in number of vessels and in size and armament. The British submarine fleet now numbers 82 vessels. The original boats from which the British type has since been evolved were built from the designs of Mr. John P. Holland, an American inventor.

To France belongs the honour of being the first naval power to adopt the submarine torpedo-boat as a vessel of war; and the first vessel, the *Gymnôte*, was launched in 1888, but it was not until 1893 that the Republic commenced the construction of her now powerful submarine flotilla, numbering 92 vessels.

The first Russian submarine was launched at Kronstadt in 1902, and since that date the Russian flotilla has steadily increased until it now numbers 37 vessels.

Japan commenced the construction of what is now a powerful and up-to-date flotilla of seventeen vessels by the acquisition of a British-Holland boat in 1904. Turning to Germany we find at first a great reluctance on the part of the Ministry of Marine to provide for the construction of submarines, but in 1905-6 this initial hesitation was overcome and the two vessels U.1 and U.2 were launched. Since then the belief in a powerful submarine flotilla steadily grew until at the moment when war was declared Germany possessed no less than 30 to 36 submarines of a very efficient type. The Austro-Hungarian Navy did not adopt submarines as units of the Fleet until 1909, and now possess only six small vessels.

From this brief *resumé* of the growth of the submarine fleets of the six great naval Powers at war, it will be seen that in point of numbers as well as in priority, bringing with it practical experience, Great Britain and France have a very appreciable superiority. It must, however, be left for succeeding chapters to describe in detail the steady growth and present size and capabilities of the submarine fleets at war.

The lessons taught by the Russo-Japanese war were not lost on the British Admiralty, and special methods had been prepared to deal with submarine attack in its various forms. Having in mind the destruction caused to both Russian and Japanese warships by submarine mines—especially those of the "offensive contact" type, which are moored to the bottom, float just under the surface and explode immediately on contact; and in the Russo-Japanese War were responsible for the sinking of the Japanese battleships *Hatsuse* and *Yashima* as well as the

Russian battleship *Petropavlavsk* and the cruiser *Boyarin*—the British Admiralty foresaw the danger to which both warships and merchantmen would be exposed in time of war if the seas strewn with these mines could not be quickly cleared, and a new type of auxiliary came into being. (For further details see *The Russo-Japanese War at Sea* 1904-05: Volumes 1 & 2 by Vladimir Semenoff and *Naval Conflict—North Pacific* 1904-5 by Nicolas Klado, Leonaur 2014).

This was the mine-sweeper, and eight vessels of the old torpedo-gunboat type were fitted out for the work. In addition to these, however, the Admiralty purchased a considerable number of steam fishing trawlers, and fitted them with mine-sweeping appliances, and made arrangements for a large fleet of similar vessels to be placed at the disposal of the navy in the event of war. In order to man this new minesweeping fleet with experienced sailors on the outbreak of war, a new section of the Royal Naval Reserve was created in 1911. This is known as the "Trawler Section," and consists of 142 *skippers* and 1,136 men taken from the fishing fleet. (See *Fishermen in Wartime* by Walter Wood, Leonaur, 2012).

Realising the value of the submarine mine in certain cases, the British Admiralty went further and created a small mine-laying fleet from seven old second-class cruisers, which had their aft-decks cleared and provided with rails for a large number of mines to be run down and slid over the stern into the water as the vessels steamed along, thus quickly laying a mine-field. But as the laying of mines, speaking generally, is a defensive mode of warfare and the policy of the British Navy—owing to its supremacy—is attack and not defence, the mine-laying fleet is of second importance to the sweeping fleet, the work of which, although much augmented by additional small steamers pressed into service, was, during the first few weeks of the war, of a nature more arduous and dangerous than will ever be realised. Hundreds of German mines were swept up, and hundreds more were exploded by being dragged into contact with each other during the progress of sweeping operations.

What the clearance of these vast fields of floating and anchored mines in the North Sea meant to the British Navy, engaged in blockading the German Fleet, and to the Mercantile Marine not only of England, France, Russia and Belgium, but also to that of the neutral countries, it is perhaps a little difficult to realise until one remembers that several hundred British and French warships were patrolling the North Sea and Channel, and, at the opening of hostilities, there were hundreds of merchantmen homeward bound whose course lay across this mine-infested sea. Many of these vessels had on board not only valuable cargoes of food, raw material for manufacture and gold and silver bullion, but also officers and men returning from various parts of the world to rejoin their regiments. Again, the Expeditionary Force had to be transported across the Channel to France. This could not be attempted until a guarantee had been given by the navy that the seas were clear of hostile warships, submarines and mines.

The fleet blockading the Frisian coast had to be supplied with coal and fresh food; and last but by no means least it was of vital importance to the Allied Armies in the Field that the whole coast-line from Bordeaux to Antwerp, forming the rear and left-flank, should be accessible to friendly shipping. It is not difficult to realise what would have been the effect had thousands of these deadly German contact mines been allowed to float unhindered in these narrow seas, for, notwithstanding the magnificent effort made by thousands of seamen in hundreds of mine sweepers assisted by seaplanes, many vessels—some belonging to neutral powers and others to the enemy themselves—were destroyed before the seas could be effectively swept clear, the hostile mine-layers destroyed or chased into port and there blockaded with their cowardly fleet.

The torpedo has long been recognised as one of the most effective of naval arms. It is carried by every modern warship afloat, but it is essentially the arm of the submarine and of the small and fast surface vessel. For a torpedo attack to be successful it is absolutely necessary for the vessel carrying the weapon to get within about 1,000 yards of the object of attack. The difficulty of accomplishing this manoeuvre with an enemy on the alert is easily apparent, but if the attacking vessel can creep up to within torpedo range unobserved her chances of sinking the enemy are decidedly good, and it is the quality possessed by the submarine of making herself invisible by sinking beneath the surface and approaching her enemy "seeing but unseen" that makes this type of vessel the ideal torpedo-boat.

But, like everything else, there are limits to its use, for a submarine, although it can navigate on the surface like an ordinary torpedo-boat, cannot deliver a submerged attack at night owing to the periscopes, which are the "eyes" of these underwater fighting ships, being useless in the dark. When night covers the sea, however, the chances of the fast grey-painted surface torpedo-boat or destroyer being able to approach the enemy unseen are more than doubled, and in this way fleets become exposed to submarine torpedo attack by day and surface torpedo attack by night. Further, a submarine will often attack while a seaplane hovers over the enemy in order to draw attention. It is this constant exposure to sudden and unseen submarine attack which is primarily responsible for the terrible nerve strain imposed on the crews of modern surface warships in time of war. Owing to the ability of submarines to deliver stealthy attacks by day, naval tacticians have designated this type of craft "Daylight torpedo-boats," but they are rapidly passing beyond the purely torpedo and coastal defensive stage and are taking on to themselves the role of the ocean cruiser.

The size of these vessels has increased from 50 to 1,000 tons displacement in ten years. They now, (1914), carry not only a considerable number of the largest size torpedo but also quick-firing guns for repelling attacks by small surface vessels, and are capable of accompanying fleets to sea. The Australian naval submarines A.E.1 and A.E.2 both made the voyage from Barrow to Sydney under their own power and without convoy.

The radius of action of the latest vessels both of the British and French Navies amounts to several thousand miles. In the case of the British "F" class the displacement has risen to 1,500 tons, the speed to 20 knots and the armament to six torpedo tubes and four 12-pounder quick-firing guns, thus making them in every sense ocean cruisers capable of keeping the sea in almost any weather and possessing wide range of action and considerable offensive power. Hitherto British submarines, like the ordinary surface torpedo-boats, have been known by numbers only, but the latest vessels are to receive names which indicates the increase in size and importance of these craft. They may be termed the advance guards of the submarine battleships of the future.

The torpedo, which is the principal arm of the submarine boat, is itself a submarine projectile. After being discharged from the firing tube it sinks a short distance below the surface and is propelled by its own engines at a high rate of speed in a straight line towards its object of attack. Great improvements have been made during the past ten years in the construction of these delicate weapons. The extreme effective range and speed has risen from 4,000 yards at 18 knots to 7,000 yards at 45 knots or 11,000 yards at 30 knots. The "war-head" or front section of the torpedo contains a charge of about 200 pounds of damp gun-cotton which is fired by a detonator on the torpedo striking an object. This very powerful explosive charge is capable of tearing open an enormous hole in the unprotected under-water skin of the surface warship. The type of weapon used in the British, French, Russian and Japanese Navies is the Whitehead torpedo (18-inch and 21-inch). The German Navy uses the Schwartzkopf torpedo (18-inch and 21-inch), which is very similar to the Whitehead and is a very powerful weapon.

In the first phase of the naval war no less than eight warships have been sunk by submarine torpedoes.

The activity of the British submarines *in the theatre of war*, from the beginning of hostilities, is admirably set forth in the following dispatch from Commodore Roger B. Keyes, C.B., which is the first dispatch in the history of naval warfare to describe in detail submarine attack and reconnaissance:—

H.M.S. *Maidstone*,
17th October, 1914.

Sir,—In compliance with Their Lordships' directions, I have the honour to report as follows upon the services performed by the Submarines since the commencement of hostilities:—

Three hours after the outbreak of war, Submarines E.6 (Lieutenant-Commander Cecil P. Talbot), and E.8 (Lieutenant-Commander Francis H. H. Goodhart), proceeded unaccompanied to carry out a reconnaissance in the Heligoland Bight. These two vessels returned with useful information, and had the privilege of being the pioneers on a service which is attended by some risk.

During the transportation of the Expeditionary Force the *Lurcher* and *Firedrake* and all the Submarines of the Eighth Submarine Flotilla occupied positions from which they could have attacked the High Sea Fleet, had it emerged to dispute the passage of our transports. This patrol was maintained day and night without relief, until the personnel of our army had been transported and all chance of effective interference had disappeared. These submarines have since been incessantly employed on the enemy's coast in the Heligoland Bight and elsewhere, and have obtained much valuable information regarding the composition and movement of his patrols. They have occupied his waters and reconnoitred his anchorages, and, while so engaged, have been subjected to skilful and well executed anti-submarine tactics; hunted for hours at a time by Torpedo Craft and attacked by gunfire and torpedoes.

At midnight on August 26th, I embarked in the *Lurcher*, and, in company with *Firedrake* and Submarines D.2, D.8, E.4, E.5, E.6, E.7, E.8, and E.9 of the Eighth Submarine Flotilla, proceeded to take part in the operations in the Heligoland Bight arranged for August 28th. The destroyers scouted for the submarines until nightfall on the 27th, when the latter proceeded independently to take up various positions from which they could co-operate with the destroyer flotillas on the following morning.

At daylight on August 28th the *Lurcher* and *Firedrake* searched the area, through which the battle cruisers were to advance, for hostile submarines, and then proceeded towards Heligoland in the wake of Submarines E.6, E.7, and E.8, which were exposing themselves with the object of inducing the enemy to chase them to the westward.

On approaching Heligoland, the visibility, which had been very good to seaward, reduced to 5,000 to 6,000 yards, and this added considerably to the anxieties and responsibilities of the commanding officers of submarines, who handled their vessels with coolness and judgment in an area which was necessarily occupied by friends as well as foes.

Low visibility and calm sea are the most unfavourable conditions under which submarines can operate, and no opportunity occurred of closing with the enemy's cruisers to within torpedo range.

Lieutenant-Commander Ernest W. Leir, Commanding Submarine E.4, witnessed the sinking of the German Torpedo-Boat Destroyer V.187 through his periscope, and, observing a cruiser of the *Stettin* class close, and open fire on the British destroyers which had lowered their boats to pick up the survivors, he proceeded to attack the cruiser, but she altered course before he could get within range. After covering the retirement of our destroyers, which had had to abandon their boats, he returned to the latter, and embarked a lieutenant and nine men of *Defender*, who had been left behind.

The boats also contained two officers and eight men of V.187, who were unwounded, and eighteen men who were badly wounded. As he could not embark the latter, Lieutenant-Commander Leir left one of the officers and six unwounded men to navigate the British boats to Heligoland. Before leaving he saw that they were provided with water, biscuit, and a compass. One German officer and two men were made prisoners of war.

Lieutenant-Commander Leir's action in remaining on the surface in the vicinity of the enemy and in a visibility which would have placed his vessel within easy gun range of an enemy appearing out of the mist, was altogether admirable.

This enterprising and gallant officer took part in the reconnaissance which supplied the information on which these operations were based, and I beg to submit his name, and that of Lieutenant-Commander Talbot, the commanding officer of E.6, who exercised patience, judgment, and skill in a dangerous position, for the favourable consideration of Their Lordships.

On September 13th, E.9 (Lieutenant-Commander Max K. Horton) torpedoed and sank the German Light Cruiser *Hela* six miles South of Heligoland.

A number of destroyers were evidently called to the scene after E.9 had delivered her attack, and these hunted her for several hours.

On September 14th, in accordance with his orders, Lieutenant-Commander Horton examined the outer anchorage of Heligoland, a service attended by considerable risk.

On September 25th, Submarine E.6 (Lieutenant-Commander C. P. Talbot), while diving, fouled the moorings of a mine laid by the enemy. On rising to the surface she weighed the mine and sinker; the former was securely fixed between the hydroplane and its guard; fortunately, however, the horns of the mine were pointed outboard. The weight of the sinker made it a difficult and dangerous matter to lift the mine clear without exploding it. After half an hour's patient work this was effected by Lieutenant Frederick A. P. Williams-Freeman and Able Seaman Ernest Randall Cremer, Official Number 214235, and the released mine descended to its original depths.

On October 6th, E.9 (Lieutenant-Commander Max K. Horton), when patrolling off the Ems, torpedoed and sank the enemy's destroyer S.126.

The enemy's torpedo craft pursue tactics which, in connection with their shallow draft, make them exceedingly difficult to attack with torpedo, and Lieutenant-Commander Horton's success was the result of much patient and skilful zeal. He is a most enterprising submarine officer, and I beg to submit his name for favourable consideration.

Lieutenant Charles M. S. Chapman, the second in command of

E.9, is also deserving of credit.

Against an enemy whose capital vessels have never, and light cruisers have seldom, emerged from their fortified harbours, opportunities of delivering submarine attacks have necessarily been few, and on one occasion only, prior to the 13th September, has one of our sSubmarines been within torpedo range of a cruiser during daylight hours.

During the exceptionally heavy westerly gales which prevailed between the 14th and 21st September the position of the submarines on a lee shore, within a few miles of the enemy's coast, was an unpleasant one.

The short steep seas which accompany westerly gales in the Heligoland Bight make it difficult to keep the conning tower hatches open. There was no rest to be obtained, and even when cruising at a depth of 60 feet, the submarines were rolling considerably, and pumping—*i.e.* vertically moving about twenty feet.

I submit that it was creditable to the commanding officers that they should have maintained their stations under such conditions.

Service in the Heligoland Bight is keenly sought after by the commanding officers of the Eighth Submarine Flotilla, and they have all shown daring and enterprise in the execution of their duties. These officers have unanimously expressed to me their admiration of the cool and gallant behaviour of the officers and men under their command. They are however, of the opinion that it is impossible to single out individuals when all have performed their duties so admirably, and in this I concur.

The following submarines have been in contact with the enemy during these operations:—

D.I (Lieutenant-Commander Archibald D. Cochrane).
D.2 (Lieutenant-Commander Arthur G. Jameson).
D.3 (Lieutenant-Commander Edward C. Boyle).
D.5 (Lieutenant-Commander Godfrey Herbert).
E.4 (Lieutenant-Commander Ernest W. Leir).
E.5 (Lieutenant-Commander Charles S. Benning).
E.6 (Lieutenant-Commander. Cecil P. Talbot).
E.7 (Lieutenant-Commander Ferdinand E. B. Feilmann),
E.9 (Lieutenant-Commander Max K. Horton).

                I have the honour to be, Sir,
                    Your obedient servant,
        (Signed)   Roger Keyes.
                                                    Commodore (S).

In conclusion, it must therefore be set on record that the opening phase in the greatest naval war in history has been one of submarine attack and counterattack, mine-laying and destroying, warships and merchantmen sunk in a few minutes by submarine torpedoes and mines, with sharp engagements between the cruisers and destroyers acting in conjunction with the under-water craft. The much-vaunted German Fleet, like that of its ally Austria-Hungary, has not dared to show itself from behind the forts and carefully-screened anchorages of the naval bases. suffering rather the everlasting disgrace of having stood in cowardly idleness while the 5,000 merchant ships it was built to protect hauled down the flag of the "Fatherland," and German maritime commerce was swept from the seas while the Allied fleets hold undisputed command of every ocean.

The First Lord of the British Admiralty has said that if the German Fleet will not come out to fight it must be "dug out like rats in a hole." This, then, may be the second phase in the naval war, and out in the grey mist of the North Sea, ready and eager for the work, lies the great battle fleets of England.

CHAPTER 1

The Modern Submarine Torpedo-boat

The submarine torpedo-boat is to most people a complete mystery, and before describing the composition and strength of the submarine fleets at war it may therefore be of interest to say something of the principal features common to all types of submarine craft.

METHOD OF SUBMERGENCE

It may sound ridiculous, in face of the many accidents which have occurred, to say that one of the greatest difficulties is to make a submarine sink sufficiently quickly, and one of the easiest of operations to make her rise, and yet such is undeniably the case. (*Submarine Engineering of Today*).

It will be readily understood that any delay in disappearing beneath the surface when attacking would be a great danger to a submarine in action. For example, a number of hostile torpedo-boat destroyers are scouring the sea in advance of a fleet, and are discovered at daybreak by the submarines, which are waiting to attack the fleet behind, approaching at a speed of 30 knots an hour. A hurried dive beneath the surface is necessary if the waiting submarines would avoid detection, which would, in all probability, mean destruction by the quick-firing guns of the destroyers.

When a submarine is travelling on the surface she is in what is technically called the *light condition*, that is to say, with her water ballast tanks empty, but when it is required to sink her so that only the tiny platform, or deck, and conning-tower are above the surface, water is let into these ballast tanks, and the additional weight causes her to sink into the sea until her back is almost flush with the surface—this is known as the *awash condition*.

It is not difficult to perceive that when travelling awash, a wave might at any moment roll along the tiny unprotected deck of the submarine, break over the mouth of the conning-tower, and descend like a waterspout into the interior. Were this to happen a terrible disaster might result, for it must be remembered that when travelling awash, a very little additional weight would cause the submarine to plunge beneath the surface. In order to obviate this risk it has become a rule that when proceeding with this small margin of buoyancy, the hatch covering the mouth of the conning-tower should be screwed down and the submarine hermetically closed, ready to sink.

To many it may appear strange that total submergence is not accomplished by letting still more water into the ballast tanks, but entirely with the aid of the propellers and rudders, A submarine has two, and sometimes three, pairs of rudders; one pair of ordinary vertical ones to guide her to port or starboard, and a horizontal pair to cause her to dive and rise. Two additional *fins* are frequently placed on each side of the forepart of the vessel to assist the diving and rising.

In order to make the submarine dive beneath the surface, the horizontal rudders are deflected when the boat is proceeding at full speed. The action of the water against the rudders is such that the bows are forced down and the whole vessel slides under the surface; The principle is much the same as that of steering an ordinary surface vessel, where the force of the water against the rudder causes the vessel to swing to right or left.

From this it will be seen that a submarine is only held below the surface by the action of her rudders on the passing water; should the propellers driving her along cease to revolve and the vessel slow down, she automatically rises to the surface because the rudders have no longer any effect.

Although the steering both on the vertical and horizontal plane is controlled by hand, it would be quite beyond the strength of a man to move the various rudders as required, so electric motors are installed to perform the actual work. In fact, almost everything in a submarine is operated by electricity.

In the earlier types of submarine boats, a considerable time was required to open the valves and allow sufficient water to enter the ballast tanks to make them sink to the awash condition. Some of the now obsolete French naval boats took as long as fifteen to twenty minutes to carry out this simple operation. The main reason for this was, that they were designed with too much surface buoyancy, that is to say, they rode too high in the water when floating in the light condition compared with the inadequate means then employed for the inlet of water into the ballast tanks, and were thus forced to let in an enormous quantity of water at a very slow rate before they settled down sufficiently to enable total submergence to be accomplished by the use of the horizontal fins and rudders. This great drawback has now been completely overcome, and the modern submarine can sink below the surface in about three minutes.

When water is pumped into the ballast tanks in order to make the submarine settle down, the air which normally fills these tanks is compressed into a fraction of its proper space, and is therefore always exerting a downward pressure which increases as more water is pumped in. Therefore, when it is desired to bring the submarine to the surface again, all that is necessary is to open the valves and allow the compressed air to force the water out. It should, however, be remembered that there is really no need to "blow out" the ballast tanks in order to bring the submarine to the surface, for this can be much quicker accomplished by simply elevating the horizontal rudders; but in this case the submarine only rises just above the surface—to the awash condition—whereas if the tanks are emptied of water she rises to the light or cruising condition. This substantiates the assertion made at the beginning of this chapter—that it is far more difficult to make a submarine sink than it is to make her rise.

It has been said that a man walking from one end of a submarine to the other would, in all probability, cause her to plunge dangerously, so delicate is the state of equipoise when totally submerged. Whatever may have been the case in the early types it is certainly not so now. So steady are modem submarines when running below the surface, especially those of the British, Russian, French, and Japanese and German Navies, that the long up and down hill glides, which, with some boats, used to amount to yaws of from 20 to 30 feet, have now been reduced to a few feet in so many hundreds of yards. In fact, this switchback motion is almost unnoticeable except when the submarine is being swung round at a sharp angle. In no case, however, is it sufficient materially to affect the firing of the torpedoes.

The reserve buoyancy of a submarine in the awash condition—or *diving-trim*, as it is called in the British flotillas—is necessarily very small, amounting to little more than two or three pounds in a thousand, which in a 300-ton vessel means a difference of only about 100 gallons of sea-water between the ability to float and the inevitability of sinking. Any material increase in the small margin of what is known as *positive-buoyancy* must be accompanied by a corresponding increase in the power of propulsion, otherwise it would be quite impossible to drive her under, or, in other words, to overcome the vessel's natural tendency to float on the surface.

For these and other reasons, a submarine when running submerged is in such a delicate state of equipoise that any sudden increase or loss of weight would upset the balance and so cause the vessel to either dive or rise with dangerous rapidity.

This would be the effect produced when a torpedo was discharged were provision not made to counter-balance this sudden loss of weight by means of *compensating-tanks*, into which sufficient water is pumped to compensate for the loss of weight incurred by the discharge of *each* torpedo.

Many submarines are also fitted with bow and stern trimming-tanks, into which water can be pumped in such a manner as to correct any tendency of the vessel to float too high or low at either extremity.

Propulsion

Of the many complicated problems surrounding submarine boat construction the motive power and propelling engines have been in the past, and are still, the most profound puzzles. Steam, compressed air, electricity, petrol, and heavy oil have all been used with varying results since first this type of vessel came into being; and many curious engines for using these *prime movers* in conjunction with each other and with chemical compounds have been evolved by ingenious inventors.

About steam and compressed air little need be said, for although given a good trial, especially by the French naval authorities, they were abandoned some years ago in favour of a combination of petrol and electric engines, which in turn have given place to more powerful machines using heavy oil and electricity. Steam is, however, again being used in conjunction with turbine engines for surface propulsion.

The carrying of large quantities of petrol, or heavy oil, is under all circumstances attended with a certain amount of risk, and when many tons have to be carried in a confined as in a submarine, this risk is more than doubled, as the slightest leakage when the vessel is submerged would mean that a powerful explosive mixture of petrol and air would be made.

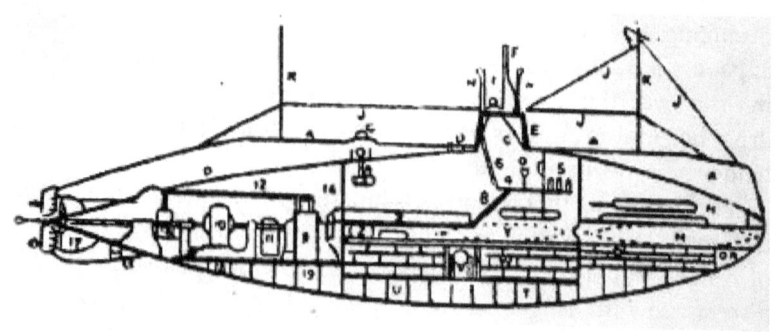

A modern submarine torpedo-boat (British type). *A*. Deck superstructure. *B*. Scuppers for filling superstructure. *D*. External connections. *E*. Conning-tower (4-inch armour). *F*. Periscope. *G*. Periscope motor (for turning, &c.). *H*. Air cowls. *I*. Conning-tower cap (opening sideways). *J*. Mast stays. *K*. Mast (not part of service equipment). *L*. Torpedo-tube cap. *M*. Torpedo-tubes (twin), torpedoes in. *N*. Air-flask (for expelling torpedoes). *O*. Hydroplane engines. *X*. Double casing, with special vent for accumulators. *Y*. Spare torpedoes. *Z*. Petrol storage tanks (2). 1. Air flasks. 2. Centrifugal pumps. 3. Air-lock, with submarine escape dresses. 4. Commander's platform. 5. Ladders. 6. Depth and deflection indicator, registering submarine's deflection from horizontal. 7. Speed dials. 9. Petrol engines. 10. Electric engines. 11. Dynamo, for recharging batteries. 12. Petrol engines—exhaust.

It being also quite impossible, for obvious reasons, to use a petrol engine when running submerged, a second motive power, an engine, with its additional space and weight, has to be carried to drive the submarine when under water. For this purpose electricity is used in almost all types. But electricity, again, has many drawbacks. It costs in weight nearly thirty times more than other motive powers, and is extremely dangerous, for should salt water in any way gain access to the storage batteries, chlorine gas would be given off in large quantities, although in the more recent vessels of the British, American, and French Navies this danger has been minimised by enclosing the batteries in air-tight cases. On account of the weight and the space required, it is impossible to install a very powerful electric engine in a submarine (compared with the size of the boat), and thus both the speed and radius of action are curtailed.

If this division of power between the surface and submerged engines could be overcome, and the whole space made available for one powerful set of engines suitable for driving the vessel both on the surface and when submerged, not only would the mechanism of submarines be simplified, but a very considerable increase in both speed and range of action would naturally result.

In the "D," "E" and "F" classes of British submarines, and in the more modern vessels of the French, Russian and German Navies, heavy oil is being used in place of petrol on account of the increase in power obtained with greater safety.

Arrangements are made in almost all modern submarines so that when the vessel is using the oil engines for running on the surface the electricity for use when submerged is being made by a dynamo and stored in batteries. From this it will be seen that/there are really three separate engines in a submarine:—

(1) the oil or petrol motor, which drives the vessel when on the surface, and, at the same time, by a suitable arrangement of gearing, operates a dynamo, (2) which makes the electric current for storage, and (3) an electric engine which drives the vessel when submerged, obtaining the necessary power from the batteries.

It is, however, technically incorrect to say that there are two sources of power in a submarine, for electricity is not, in itself, a source of power, but merely a handy method of storing and transmitting it. The only actual source being the oil or petrol.

There are also numerous small engines to add to the complexity of machinery in a submarine, such as the air compressors used for charging the torpedo tubes with compressed air for expelling the torpedoes and for other purposes, and electric motors for operating the pumps, steering mechanism, and periscopes. In addition to all this, hand-mechanism is provided for use in case of a breakdown to operate most of these important appliances. Then again there is. of course, the armament mechanism for working the torpedo tubes and semi-automatic quick-firing-guns.

From the foregoing it may appear that the interior of a submarine presents a picture of mechanical complexity utterly incomprehensible. Yet such is not the case. The fanciful belief that the crew stand boxed up in these vessels, sweating with the heat, struggling for breath, and with crank-shafts whirling uncomfortably dose to the small of their backs, electric motors buzzing within a few inches of their ears, and nervous hands grasping one or other of the levers ranged in rows in front of them, is, doubtless, most romantic, but quite unreal. Much of the undoubtedly complicated machinery in a submarine is tucked away in the conical extremities, under the interior decking, and fixed to the arched steel sides. The centre is left almost entirely clear, so that trestle-tables may be erected for meals, hammocks swung for sleeping, and sufficient space allowed to make these small vessels as habitable as possible. Not the least difficulty of the submarine designer is to create order and leave space among the chaos of machinery which has to be installed in these peculiar and deadly little torpedo craft.

Vision when Submerged

Perhaps the greatest difficulty which has beset both submarine construction and navigation is the puzzle how to see when submerged. This is now accomplished by means of periscopes, or tubes extending up from the roof of the submarine to a height of several feet above the surface—not unlike hollow masts. By a series of lenses and reflectors a picture of the surface is thrown down these tubes on to reflectors inside the submarine. A man with his eyes at the bottom of a periscope can see the surface clearly. Although it projects above the surface when the whole submarine is submerged, it is far too small an object to be easily seen moving through the water, and extremely difficult to hit by gun-fire.

The latest panoramic periscope—two of which are fitted in modern submarines—has a field of vision of about 60 degrees. The range of vision is, however, very short, owing to the periscopic tube projecting only a few feet above the surface. On a moderately smooth and fairly clear day steering by periscope is not altogether difficult, but at night or in fog this instrument is useless, and for this reason it would be almost impossible for a submarine to effect a submerged attack on an enemy at night. Hence the name given to this type of craft—daylight torpedo-boats—for in the brilliant light of day, when any attempt by ordinary torpedo craft to get sufficiently close to hostile warships to discharge a torpedo with reasonable hope of success would be foredoomed to failure, there is every possibility that submarines would effect a surprise attack.

Armament

The chief armament of all naval submarines is the torpedo, which is expelled by a blast of compressed air from one of the tubes fitted in the bow and stern. Several torpedoes are usually carried by each boat, so that if one failed to strike the object of attack further attempts can be made.

About the efficiency of torpedoes nothing need be said here, for they now form an important weapon in every navy, and to this subject a future chapter is devoted.

The latest submarines built are also fitted with quick-firing guns for use when these vessels are cruising on the surface. The guns are arranged so that when it is desired to sink they can be made to disappear beneath the narrow deck of the submarine. The provision of guns has been made with the object of giving these vessels a means of defence should they be discovered by prowling hostile torpedo-boat destroyers, or by air-craft.

Habitability

Many people imagine the interior of a submarine to resemble a stokehold, hot, stifling, and semi-dark, whereas the exact contrary is the truth. The temperature is but little above the normal for a ship's engine-room, the air-supply is amply sufficient, and the whole interior is well illuminated by electric lamps.

The necessary supply of pure air is derived either from large steel cylinders containing the air in a highly compressed state or from flasks of oxylithe. The carbonic acid gas of the rehired air being at the same time chemically absorbed.

Food is cooked for the crew by electricity, and drinking water obtained from special tanks. Notwithstanding these arrangements, however, it is almost impossible for the crew to live on board for many weeks at a time, owing to the small free space in the interior and to the cramped deck; but as the size and radius of action of these boats increase, so also does the space available for exercise, and thus the habitability.

Chapter 2

British Submarines

The British Fleet at the moment when war was declared possessed 82 submarine torpedo-boats built and 22 building. Some of these were, however, stationed at the oversea naval bases. The composition and distribution of the submarine flotillas at the outbreak of hostilities were as follows:—

SUBMARINES IN HOME WATERS.
PATROL FLOTILLAS.

1st Flotilla. Devonport.
    Depot ship: *Onyx*.
    Submarines: A.8 and A.9.
2nd Flotilla. Portsmouth.
    Depot ship: *Dolphin*.
    Submarines: A.5, A.6, A. 13 and B.1.
3rd Flotilla. *Devonport*.
    Depot ship: *Forth*.
    Submarines B.3, B.4, B.5, C.14, C.15 and C.16.
4th Flotilla. Portsmouth.
    Depot ships: *Arrogant* and *Hazard*.
    Submarines: C.17, C.18, C.31, C.32, C.33, C.34, C.35.
5th Flotilla. Chatham.
    Depot ship: *Thames*.
    Submarines: C.1, C.2, C.3, C.4, C.5, C.6.
6th Flotilla. Chatham.
    Depot ships: *Bonaventure* and *Hebe*.
    Submarines: C.7, C.8, C.9, C.10, C.12, C.13.
7th Flotilla. Chatham.
    Depot ships: *Vulcan* and *Alecto*.

The British Submarine "D.7."
Displacement, 620 tons; Speed 16.10 knots; Armament, 2 bow and 1 stern torpedo tube.
There are 8 vessels of this class, completed between 1908-12

Submarines: C.19, C.20, C.21, C.22, C.23, C.24, C.25, C.26, C.27, C.28, C.29, C.30.

8th Flotilla. Portsmouth.
Depot ships: *Maidstone* and *Adamant*.
Submarines: D.1, D-2, D.3, D.4, D.5, D.6, D.7, D.8, E.I, E.2, E.3, E.4, E.5, E.6, E.7, E.8, E.9.

9th Flotilla. Devonport.
Depot ship: *Pactolus*.
Submarines: A. 10, A.11, A.12.

SUBMARINES ON FOREIGN STATIONS.

Attached to Mediterranean Fleet.—Submarines B.9, B.10, and B.11.
At Gibraltar.—Submarines B.6, B.7, and B.8.
Attached to China Squadron.—Submarines C.36, C.37, and C.38.
With Australian Fleet.—Submarines A.E.1, (sunk October, 1914), and A.E. 2.

The statement that the headquarters of the various submarine flotillas in home waters are at Chatham, Portsmouth, and Devonport, must not be taken as indicating that these are the only points along the coast protected by submarines. These places are merely the chief bases of the Patrol Flotillas. The wide range of action of modern submarines enables them to operate several hundred miles from any base or depot, and consequently Chatham becomes merely the general store, or head-depot, of what should be termed the North Sea Flotillas, which not only patrol the whole East, North-East and South-East Coasts of England and Scotland, but also have their floating secondary bases in the form of Depot Ships, which, with their attached submarines, are often at Harwich, Newcastle, Rosyth, etc.

In the same way Portsmouth is merely the headquarters of the submarines patrolling the Channel; and Dover, Portland, etc., are seldom without strong flotillas of submarines with their Depot ships. The Devonport Flotillas have the longest coast-line to patrol, for their area covers not only the West Coast of England, Wales and Scotland, but also the Irish Coast. They are, however, furthest removed from the zone of war.

Considerable alterations have taken place in the composition and distribution of the British submarine flotillas since the outbreak of war, with the object of materially strengthening the Fleet in the main theatre of operations, but the addition to the flotillas of new vessels of the latest "E" type—nearly completed when war broke out—has made this rearrangement possible without materially weakening the flotillas guarding the more distant coasts of Great Britain or recalling vessels from overseas.

The first submarine torpedo-boat built for the British Navy was launched from the yard of Messrs. Vickers Ltd., Barrow-in-Furness in 1901, and was designated the No. 1. It was constructed from the designs of the famous American inventor, Mr. John P. Holland, and was one of the most successful boats afloat at that time. A series of exhaustive trials with this and the succeeding five vessels, all of the same type and launched during 1901-2, proved conclusively the fighting value of this type of craft, and a further order was given by the British Admiralty for four new vessels embodying the improvements suggested by the trials of the first five. These vessels were the first of the "A" class, and were designated the "A's 1, 2, 3, and 4." They had a submerged displacement of 180 tons, a length of 100 feet and a beam of 10 feet. They were propelled by petrol motors of 190 h.-p. on the surface and by electric motors of about 80 h.-p. when submerged. Their speed ranged from 8 knots an hour on the surface to 5 knots when travelling submerged, and their maximum surface endurance (or fuel capacity) was only 400 knots at 8 knots. Their armament consisted of three 18-inch Whitehead torpedoes and one bow tube.

All these vessels were, however, obsolete and therefore scrapped before the opening of hostilities, hence information concerning them is only of interest as showing the rapid growth in size, power and armament of British submarines. The next batch of vessels were the A's 5 to 13, launched at Barrow in 1904, but these, as will have been seen from the table lowing the composition and distribution of. the submarine flotillas at the outbreak of war, are still on the effective list. All the following British submarines are now in the fighting line.

"A" CLASS.

(Completed 1904.)

A's 5, 6, 8, 9, 10, 11, 12, 13.

These vessels are the oldest British submarines in commission. They were built at Messrs. Vickers' works at Barrow, and have a submerged displacement of 204 tons. Their length is 150 feet. They are propelled on the surface by petrol motors of 600 h.-p. and by electric engines of 100 h.-p. when submerged. Their surface and submerged speed is 11 knots and 7 knots respectively. The cruising range, or maximum surface endurance on the fuel carried, is 400 knots at 10 knots an hour, and the endurance submerged three hours at full speed. Their armament consists of two bow tubes with four 18-inch Whitehead torpedoes. Complement: Eleven officers and men.

These vessels, which are now used almost entirely for harbour defence, can be distinguished from later types by their high conning-towers and single short periscopes. The A.7 was lost off Plymouth early in 1914, and was never raised.

"B" Class.
(Completed 1904-6.)
B's 1, 3, 4, 5, 6, 7, 8, 9, 10, 11.

These are submarines of the improved Holland type, and are in every way superior to their predecessors. They may be considered the first of the seagoing type. Their submerged displacement is 316 tons; length 135 feet, and beam 13½ feet. The motive power is the same as in the "A's"—petrol for surface propulsion and electricity for use when submerged. The horse-power of the petrol engines is 600, and that of the electric engines 189. As in most submarines the supply of current for driving the electric engines is derived from storage batteries charged by dynamos driven from the petrol engines while the vessels are running on the surface. In the "B" class a special system of encasing these storage batteries was introduced. Their speed averages 12 knots on the surface and 8 knots when submerged. The surface cruising range is 1,300 knots at 10 knots per hour, and the maximum submerged endurance 80-100 knots at 5 knots per hour. Their armament consists of two bow tubes with 4-6 18-inch Whitehead torpedoes. Complement: Sixteen officers and men.

The "B" type are vessels about 50 *per cent,* larger than the "A" type which preceded them. The "B's" have superstructures extending from the bow to the conning-tower, forming a narrow deck which tends to disperse the wave which heaped around the blunt noses of the "A's" and original Hollands. Vision when submerged is obtained by two panoramic periscopes, each having an arc of vision of 60 degrees. In the more modern vessels three periscopes are fitted. The twin screws of the "B's" are placed below the centre line of the vessel and consequently operate in deeper water when the vessels are cruising on the surface. This gives them better surface cruising qualities, as in a seaway the propellers are liable to race if worked too near the surface.

The increase in the speed of these vessels over that of the "A's" was of great importance, as in this respect lies the weakness of the submarine. The tactical advantages derived from high speed in actual warfare cannot be overestimated. The speed of a fleet is governed by that of its slowest unit.

The distinguishing feature of the "B" type is the straight bow, the forward superstructure, and the *two* periscopes. The B.2 was run down by the liner *Amerika* in the Straits of Dover in October, 1912, and was never recovered.

"C" Class.

(Completed 1906-10.)
C's 1, 2, 3, 4, 5, 6, 7, 8, 9, 10, 12, 13, 14,
15, 16, 17, 18, 19, 20, 21, 22, 23, 24, 25, 26, 27, 28,
29, 30, 31, 32, 33, 34, 35, 36, 37, 38.

This class of submarines is composed of vessels of the improved "B" type. They have a submerged displacement of 320 tons and are 135 feet long and 13½ feet broad. The petrol motors develop 600 H.-p. and give to these vessels a speed of 14 knots an hour on the surface. The power of the electric engines was increased to 300 h.-p., giving a submerged speed of just over 9 knots an hour. The surface cruising range is 2,000 knots at the most economical speed, and the submerged endurance 100 knots at 5 knots an hour. Their armament consists of two bow tubes with six 18-inch Whitehead torpedoes; and their complement sixteen officers and men.

In the later vessels of the "C" class heavy oil is used instead of petrol, giving a great increase in power without the comparative additional weight; enabling a wider radius of action. The vessels of both the "B" and "C" classes are fitted with air-traps and safety-helmets, giving the crew a possible means of escape in the event of disaster while submerged.

The distinguishing feature of the "C" class is the sloping bow. The C.11 collided with the steamer *Eddystone* in the North Sea in 1909 and was irretrievably lost.

"D" Class.

(Completed 1908-11.)
D's 1, 2, 3, 4, 5, 6, 7, 8.

These are all modern vessels of the sea-going type, and are of considerable fighting value. They, however, differ slightly from each other:

THE BRITISH SUBMARINE "C.34."
Displacement, 320 tons; Speed 14.9 knots; Armament, 2 bow torpedo tubes.
There are 37 vessels of this class, completed between 1906–12

D. 1 has a submerged displacement of 595 tons; D.2 of 600 tons; and the remaining vessels of this class of 620 tons. They have an approximate length of 150 feet and a beam of 15 feet. Heavy-oil engines of 1,200 h.-p. drive them at a maximum speed of 16 knots an hour on the surface, and electric motors of 550 h.-p. give them a submerged speed of just over 10 knots an hour. All these vessels have twin-screws situated below the centre line. Their cruising range on the surface is 4,000 miles, and when submerged 120 knots at 7 knots an hour.

These vessels were the first to be fitted with a special and more efficient pattern of electric storage battery and a safer type of electric motor. The armament of the "D's" consists of two bow and one stern tube with six 18-inch Whitehead torpedoes. D's 4, 5, 6, 7, and 8 are also fitted with a small quick-firing, high-angle gun for defence against aircraft. This gun is fixed on a disappearing mounting, enabling it to be quickly and almost automatically lowered into a watertight cavity in the superstructure before the submarine dives below the surface. The complement of these vessels is twenty-one officers and men.

"E" Class.
(Completed 1912-14.)
E's 1, 2, 3, 4, 5, 6, 7, 8, 9, 10, 11, 12, 13, 14, 15, 16, 17, 18.

These fine ocean-going submarines are the latest additions to the British Flotillas. They have a submerged displacement of 800 tons, are 176 feet long and 22½ feet in beam. The heavy-oil engines of nearly 2,000 h.-p. give them a surface speed of over 16 knots, while the electric engines of 800 h.-p. drive them at a maximum speed of 10 knots an hour when submerged. Their surface cruising range is 5,000 miles at economical speed, and the submerged endurance 140 knots at 8 knots an hour. In point of armament the "E's" are far more powerful than their predecessors, being fitted with four tubes and carrying six of the largest and most powerful Whitehead torpedoes.

They are also equipped with two 3-inch quick-firing guns on high-angle disappearing mountings for defence against air-craft and hostile torpedo-boats and destroyers. They have wireless telegraphic apparatus; and, like the vessels of the "B," "C" and "D" classes, have armoured conning towers and decks. Three tall panoramic periscopes are fitted, and their high superstructures and increased buoyancy when travelling on the surface enable them to keep the sea in almost any weather.

Australian Submarines:
A.E.1 and A.E.2.

These vessels are exactly the same as the "E" class. The fact that they both accomplished the 13,000-mile voyage from Barrow to Sydney under their own power and without convoy is practical proof of the wide range, seaworthiness and general efficiency of the latest British Naval Submarines. The A.E.1 mysteriously disappeared in Australian waters in October, 1914, and has not been recovered.

British Submarines Building:

At the commencement of the great war there were 22 British submarines in course of construction at the various shipbuilding works and naval dockyards. Up to 1909 Messrs. Vickers Ltd., had constructed all the British submarines, but in that year the vessels C.17 and C.18 were laid down at Chatham Dockyard. Since then several other boats have been constructed there, and of those now in hand some are being built by Messrs. Vickers Ltd. at Barrow, others at Messrs. Scott's shipbuilding yards at Greenock, and a few by Messrs. Armstrong, Whitworth and Co. Ltd. at Newcastle-on-Tyne, and at H.M. Dockyard at Chatham.

Hitherto, British submarines, although divided into classes—each of which has shown a marked improvement on the preceding class—have been all of one type—the "Improved Holland." Among the vessels being constructed at the opening of hostilities they were, however, no less than three different types. Those being built at Barrow and Chatham were of the original design with modern improvements, but the submarines under construction at Greenock were of the *Laurenti*, or Italian type, and those at Newcastle-on-Tyne of the *Laubeuf*, or French type. In addition to this wise departure from previous practice, two of the new vessels have been given the names of *Nautilus* and *Swordfish*.

The haze of war has obscured these vessels, and it is impossible to say definitely which of them have taken their place in the active flotillas, and further the necessity for observing the very strictest secrecy regarding new types of warships at a time like the present makes it advisable to give here only the briefest particulars and not to discuss too freely the peculiarities of their design or their probable capabilities.

"F" Class.

There are several vessels of this class now being constructed. They are the latest improvement of the original Holland design and are sea-going submarines of wide range, high speed and great fighting power. The F.1, which was built at Chatham Dockyard, has a submerged displacement of 1,500 tons. Heavy-oil engines of about 5,000 h.-p. give her a maximum speed of 20 knots an hour on the surface, and electric motors of 2,000 h.-p. drive her at 12 knots when submerged. The armament consists of six torpedo tubes, ten torpedoes, and two quick-firing, high-angle guns.

"V" Class. "W" Class. "S" Class.
Nautilus and *Swordfish*.

These three classes include the vessels of entirely different design to those now forming the British flotillas. The "V," or Vickers' type, of which four were under construction at the beginning of the war, are large seagoing submarines with a submerged displacement of over 1,000 tons, and a probable surface speed of 20 knots. The "W" Class, of which four are being built at Elswick, comprise vessels of the French *Laubeuf* type. The "S" Class, building at Greenock, and four in number, are of the Italian, or F.I.A.T.—*Laurenti* type. The two named vessels—*Nautilus* and *Swordfish*—are large sea-going submarines of wide range and high speed. Their submerged displacement is about 1,000 tons, and their speed 20 knots on the surface and 12 knots when submerged. The armament is six tubes, with eight torpedoes, and two quick-firing guns. The complement of all these large submarines is about 25 officers and men.

CHAPTER 3

French Submarines

France possessed 92 submarines in active service when war was declared. In addition to these, nine large and powerful vessels were in various stages of construction. The flotillas of the French Navy are composed of two different types of vessels: *Submarines Defensive* and *Submersibles*. The former are intended, as their name implies, solely for coast and harbour defence; their radii of action is very small, and they are incapable of action independent of a naval base. The submersibles are like the large sea-going submarines of England and Germany, and have a wide radius of action, high speed, and great offensive power.

The first naval submarine (*Gymnôte*) was launched in 1888, giving to France the honour of being the first Naval Power to adopt the submarine torpedo-boat as a vessel of war. The pioneers of submarine construction in France were Captain Burgeoise, Engineer Brun, M. Dupuy de Lome, M. Gustave Zédé, and Admiral Aube. The second submarine ordered for the French Navy was the *Gustave Zédé*, launched in 1893. So successful did this vessel prove that another of the same type, and named the *Morse*, was launched at Cherbourg Dockyard in 1899. In the same year four vessels of a new type were laid down in the dockyard at Rochefort, and named *Lutin*, *Farfâdet* (re-named *Follet*), *Korrigan*, and *Gnôme*. These, with the exception of the ill-fated *Lutiun*, are still in the active flotillas.

LUTIN CLASS.

(Completed 1901-2.)
Follet. Korrigan. Gnôme.

These are the oldest submarines in the French Navy, and are all of the defensive type. They have a displacement of about 185 tons,

A French submarine of the Harbour Defence Type.

A French submarine of the Coast Defence Type.

with electric engines for propulsion both on the surface and when submerged. Their speed is 12 knots on the surface and 8 knots when submerged. Their range of action is about 200 miles at 7 knots. The armament consists of one bow tube and two holders, with four 18-inch Whitehead torpedoes. The complement is nine officers and men.

Française Class.
(Completed 1901-2.)
Française. Algérien.

These two vessels are of the improved *Morse* type, and are intended solely for coast and harbour defence. Their surface displacement is 146 tons, and they have electric engines of 350 h.-p. for both surface and submerged propulsion, giving them a speed of 12 knots and 8 knots an hour, respectively. Their surface radius is about 80 miles at 8 knots. They have one bow tube and two holders, with four torpedoes. The complement is nine officers and men.

Triton Class.
(The *Narval*, the first of this type, has been removed from the effective list).
(Completed 1901-2.)
Triton. Sirene. Espadon. Silure.

These four vessels were the first of the submersible type and were designed by M. Laubeuf, who has since designed many vessels for both France and other countries (*Laubeuf* type). They have a submerged displacement of 200 tons, and are in feet long and 12½ feet in beam. Steam is used for surface propulsion (217 h.-p.) and electricity when submerged. Their speed is 11 knots on the surface and 8 knots when submerged, with a cruising radius of 600 miles at 8 knots. They are armed with four holders fitted with 18-inch Whitehead torpedoes, and have a complement of ten officers and men.

Naiade Class.
(Completed 1902-4.)

Naiade. Loutre. Protée.
Lynx, Perle. Truite.
Castor, Oursin. Meduse.
Otarie. Phoque. Ludion.
Alose. Anguille. Grondin,

Dorade. Souffleur. Thon.
Bonite. Esturgeon.

Twenty small harbour defence submarines, having a displacement of about 67 tons. They have petrol and electric motors, giving them a speed of 8½ knots on the surface and 5 knots when submerged. Their armament consists of one bow tube and two holders; four torpedoes are carried. Their complement is six officers and men.

AIGRETTE CLASS.
(Completed 1904.)

Aigrette. Cicogne.

These two vessels are submersibles of the *Laubeuf* type, and were great improvements on their predecessors, the Triton Class. Their submerged displacement is 351 tons, and their dimensions 118 x 12 x 12 feet. A triple expansion steam engine of 200 h.-p. is used for surface propulsion and an electric motor of 150 h.-p. when submerged. Their speed is 10 knots and 8½ knots. Their maximum surface endurance is 700 miles at 8 knots, and submerged 60 miles at 6 knots. Their armament consists of one bow tube with four 18-inch torpedoes. Their complement is about fifteen officers and men.

ARGONAUTE.
(Completed 1905.)

A submersible designed by M. Bertin (late Chief Constructor French Navy). This vessel, which was first named *Omega*, has a displacement of about 300 tons. She is driven by steam and electricity, and has a speed of 11 knots and 9 knots. Her armament consists of two bow tubes and two holders, with six 18-inch Whitehead torpedoes. The complement is about seventeen officers and men.

EMERAUDE CLASS.
(Completed 1906-8.)

Emeraude. Saphir. Opale.
Topaz. Rubis. Turquoise.

These six vessels are of the *Maugas* type and are sea-going submarines with a submerged displacement of over 400 tons. They have petrol and electric motors of 600 h.-p. and 450 h.-p., reflectively. Their surface speed is 12 knots and submerged 8½ knots. Their surface cruising radius is just over 1,000 miles at economical speed. Their

A French submarine of the sea-going type

armament consists of two tubes and four holders with 8 torpedoes of the usual pattern. Their complement is seventeen officers and men.

CIRCE CLASS.
(Completed 1907.)
Circe. Calypso.

These two vessels are of the *Laubeuf* type, and are improvements on the *Aigrette* class. They have a submerged displacement of about 450 tons and are 160 feet in length. They are driven by a steam engine of 440 h.-p. (flash boiler and oil fuel) when on the surface, and by electric motors when submerged. Their speed is 11 knots and 8 knots; and the range of action 1,000 miles. Their armament comprises two tubes and four holders with eight torpedoes. The complement is 21 officers and men.

PLUVIÔSE CLASS.
(Completed 1907-12.)
Pluviôse. Nivôse. Ventôse.
Messidor. Thermidor, Fructidor.
Brumaire. Frimaire. Florèal.
Prairial. Germinal.

Submarines of the *Laubeuf* type with a submerged displacement of nearly 600 tons. All built at Cherbourg. The *Brumaire* and *Frimaire* are driven by petrol motors of 700 h.-p. when cruising on the surface, but all the others have small steam turbines with a special type of flash-boiler. Electric motors are used for submerged propulsion. Their speed is 12 knots above and 9 knots below. The armament is seven 18-inch torpedoes. Their complement is 22 officers and men.

FRESNEL CLASS.
(Completed 1908-12.)
Fresnel. Berthelot. Papin.
Monge. Ampère. Gay-Lussac.
Cagnot. Faraday. Giffard.
Montgolfier. Newton. Volta.
Watt. Euler. Faucault.
Franklin. Arago. Permouilli.
Joule. Coulomb. Curie.
Le Verrier.

Twenty-two submarines of the largest sea-going *Laubeuf* type. Only three of these are steam driven, the others using heavy-oil engines for surface propulsion. They are in all respects similar to vessels of the *Pluviôse* class, and have a displacement of about 600 tons. Their speed is 12 knots above, and 9 knots below, and the armament seven 18-inch torpedoes. These vessels are fitted with stern as well as bow tubes. Their surface cruising range is over 2,000 miles.

AMIRAL BOURGEOISE.
(Completed 1912.)

An experimental boat of the *Bourdelle* type, built at Cherbourg. The submerged displacement is just under 800 tons and the length 190 feet. She is driven on the surface by heavy-oil engines of 1,600 h.-p., which give a speed of 15 knots. The electric motors for submerged propulsion are of 700 h.-p., giving a speed of 10 knots. The armament consists of seven 18-inch torpedoes, and the cruising range is 3,500 miles.

ARCHIMÈDE.
(Completed 1912.)

Another experimental boat built at Cherbourg. The submerged displacement is about 810 tons, and the length and beam 212 feet and 22 feet respectively. Steam turbines are used for surface propulsion and electric motors when submerged. Her speed is 15 knots above and 10 knots below. The armament is seven 18-inch torpedoes, and the complement 24 officers and men.

MARIOTTE.
(Completed 1912.)

The third experimental boat, of the *Rodiquet* type, built at Cherbourg. The displacement when submerged is 650 tons and the length about 200 feet. Petrol motors of 1,500 h.-p. drive her at 15 knots an hour on the surface and electric motors of 550 h.-p. at 10 knots when submerged. Her radius of action is 3,000 miles, and her armament seven 18-inch torpedoes, which can be fired from both bow and stern tubes. The complement is about 25 officers and men.

CHARLES BRUN.
(Completed 1912.)

The fourth experimental vessel, built at Cherbourg during 1909-12.

The submerged displacement is 450 tons and the length 145 feet. Steam turbines of 1,300 h.-p. drive her at 15½ knots an hour on the surface, and electric motors of 500 h.-p. at 10 knots when submerged. Her armament consists of six 18-inch torpedoes. The complement is 22 officers and men.

Clorinde Class.
(Completed 1913-14.)
Clorinde. Comélie. Amphritrite.
Astree. Artémis. Aréthuse.
Atalante. Amaranthe. Ariane.
Andromaque.

These ten vessels are the very latest additions to the French Submarine flotillas. They have a submerged displacement of about 550 tons, a length of 177 feet and a beam of 16 feet. Heavy-oil engines of 1,300 h.-p. give them a speed of 15 knots on the surface, and electric motors of 550 h.-p. enable them to travel at 9½ knots an hour when submerged. They carry eight torpedoes, and have a complement of 25 officers and men.

Gustave Zédé Class.
(Completed 1913-14.)
Gustave Zédé. Néréide.

These two vessels are the largest submarines in the French flotillas. They have a submerged displacement of 1,000 tons, a length of 240 feet, and a beam of 20 feet. Heavy-oil engines give them a surface speed of 16 knots and electric motors a submerged speed of 10 knots. Their armament consists of two bow and two stern tubes with eight 18-inch torpedoes. They are also equipped with two 14-pdr. quick-firing guns on high-angle, disappearing mountings. The cruising range is 4,000 miles, and the complement 27 officers and men.

Bellone Class.
(Completed 1914.)
Bellone. Hermione. Gorgone.

Fast sea-going submarines with a submerged displacement of 610 tons. They have heavy-oil engines of about 2,000 h.-p., which give them a surface speed of 17½ knots. Electric motors of 950 h.-p. drive them at 12 knots when submerged. Their surface cruising range is 4,000 miles. Their armament consists of eight 18-inch torpedoes and two 14-pdr. quick-firing, high-angle guns. The complement is 30 officers and men.

FRENCH SUBMARINES BUILDING.

On the day when war was declared nine submarines were in the early stages of construction. The two most advanced of these were the *Diane* and *Daphne*. These vessels have a submerged displacement of about 800 tons, and the anticipated speed is 18 knots and 10 knots. Their armament will consist of ten torpedoes and four 9-pdr. guns. The complement will be 30 officers and men.

The other seven vessels are of the improved *Gustave Zédé* Class. They will have a submerged displacement of over 1,000 tons and a speed of 20 knots on the surface and 12 knots when submerged. Their armament will consist of ten torpedoes and four 9-pdr. guns. The complement will be about 35 officers and men.

CHAPTER 4

Russian Submarines

The Imperial Russian Navy at the commencement of hostilities included 37 submarines in active service, and 19 in various stages of construction. The composition and distribution of the submarine flotillas was as follows:—

Baltic Flotilla: 14 Submarines with depot ships in commission, and 12 vessels building. Bases: Kronstadt, Port Peter the Great (Reval) and Port Alexander III. (Libau) (ice free).

Black Sea Flotilla: 11 Submarines with depot ships in commission, and several new vessels building. Bases: Sevastopol and Nikolaieff.

Siberian Flotilla: 12 Submarines with depot ships in commission, and 6 vessels building. Base: Vladivostok.

The first Russian naval submarine was completed at Kronstadt in 1902, and named the *Petr Kochka*. She was built in sections to facilitate transport over the Siberian Railway, being intended for the defence of Port Arthur, and had a surface displacement of only 20 tons. Her armament consisted of two holders, or Darzewiecki launching apparatus, containing two small Whitehead torpedoes. The maximum speed was 8 knots on the surface and 4 knots when submerged. The second submarine ordered for the Russian Navy was the *Delphin*, which foundered off Kronstadt, but was subsequently raised and is now used as a training ship for the submarine service. These two vessels have been removed from the active flotillas, but the third vessel to be built for the Russian Navy—the *Graf Cheremetieve*—is still in commission, (1914).

Graf Cheremetieve Class.
(Completed 1904-5.)
Graf Cheremetieve. Kasatka. Nalim. Skat.

These are the oldest submarines in the Russian Navy, and are small vessels of the Holland-Bubnoff type. They have a submerged displacement of 200 tons. Petrol and electric engines drive them at 9 knots on the surface and 6 knots when submerged. Their armament consists of one bow torpedo tube and two exterior holders, with four 18-inch Whitehead torpedoes.

Ostr Class.
(Completed 1904-6.)
Ostr. Byts-chok. Kefal. Platus. Plotva.

These five submarines are of the American Lake type. The *Ostr* was originally the American Lake Co.'s boat *Protector*. They have a submerged displacement of 175 tons, are 65 feet in length and 11 feet in breadth. Have petrol engines of 250 h.-p. for surface propulsion and electric motors for use when submerged. Their speed is 11 knots above and 7 knots below. The surface cruising radius is 450 knots at full speed. The armament consists of two bow and one stern tube with four 18-inch Whitehead torpedoes. The *special* characteristics of the American Lake type will be seen further on in chapter 7.

Som Class.
(Completed 1904-6.)
Som. Shtshuka.

These two vessels, which are of the Holland-Bubnoff type, have a submerged displacement of about 150 tons. Petrol and electric motors are used for surface and submerged propulsion, and the speed is 9½ knots and 7 knots, above and below, respectively. Their armament consists of two bow tubes with four 18-inch Whitehead torpedoes. Their complement is about fifteen officers and men.

Sterliad Class.
(Completed 1905-6.)
Sterliad. Bialuga. Peskar.

These three vessels are also of the Holland-Bubnoff type. They have a submerged displacement of 150 tons. The petrol motors for surface propulsion are of 160 h.-p. The speed is 9½ knots and 7 knots, above and below, respectively. Their armament consist of two bow tubes with four 18-inch Whitehead torpedoes. Their complement is eleven to fifteen officers and men.

SIG.
(Completed 1906.)

A submarine of the Lake type; similar in almost every respect to vessels of the *Ostr* class.

MAKREL CLASS.
(Completed 1907.)
Makrel. Okun.

Two vessels of the *Improved* Holland-Bubnoff type. They have a submerged displacement of about 200 tons. The petrol motors are of 300 h.-p., and the electric engines of 150 h.-p. Their speed is 10 knots on the surface and 8 knots when submerged. They are fitted with two bow tubes and two stern *holders*, and carry six 18-inch Whitehead torpedoes. Their complement is fifteen officers and men.

LOSSOS CLASS.
(Completed 1907.)
Lossos. Ludak.

Two somewhat smaller submarines of the Holland type. Intended either for the Black Sea or Far Eastern Flotilla. Similar to those of the *Sterliad* class.

KARP CLASS.
(Completed 1907-8.)
Karp, Karas.

These two submarines are of the Germania, or Krupp type, and have a submerged displacement of 250 tons. They have Krupp-Nuremburg heavy-oil engines of 400 h.-p., and electric motors of 160 h.-p. Their speed on the surface is 12 knots, and 8 knots when submerged.

The surface range of action is about 1,000 miles, and the submerged endurance about three hours at full speed. Their armament consists of two bow torpedo tubes and four torpedoes are carried. Their complement is fifteen officers and men.

ALLIGATOR CLASS.
(Completed 1908-9.)
Alligator. Kaiman. Drakon. Krokodil.

Four submarines of the improved Lake type. They have a submerged displacement of 500 tons. Their speed is 15 knots on the surface and 10 knots when submerged. They are fitted with two bow and two stern tubes, and carry six 18-inch Whitehead torpedoes. Their complement is seventeen officers and men. (See also chapter 4).

MINOGA CLASS.
(Completed 1908.)
Minoga. Potschovy.

Two small submarines of the Holland-Bubnoff type, which were built in sections to facilitate transport by rail. They have a submerged displacement of about 150 tons, and a speed of 12 knots and 9 knots, above and below, respectively. Their complement is eleven officers and men.

AKULA.
(Completed 1909.)

A large submarine of the Holland-Bubnoff type. Her displacement is about 570 tons, and her speed 16 knots on the surface and 10 knots when submerged. The armament consists of two bow and one stern tube, with six 18-inch Whitehead torpedoes. The complement is 20 officers and men.

KASCHALOT CLASS.
(Completed 1909-12.)
Kaschalot. Kit. Krab.
Morsk. Narval. Nerpa. Tinlen.

These seven vessels are among the most modern submarines in the Russian flotillas. They are of the Holland-Bubnoff type, and have a submerged displacement of about 500 tons. Heavy-oil engines of over 1,000 h.-p. drive them at a maximum surface speed of 16 knots, and electric motors of 550 h.-p. give them a submerged speed of just over 10 knots an hour. Their surface cruising range is about 3,000 miles. Their armament consists of two bow and one stern tube with six 18-inch Whitehead torpedoes. They are also fitted with a small, quick-firing, high-angle gun for defence against aircraft. Their complement is 21 officers and men.

Russian Submarines Building.

At the commencement of the war there were nineteen Russian submarines in course of construction. Very little information concerning these boats can be obtained, except that their submerged displacement ranges from 800 to 1,500 tons, and their *anticipated* surface speed is 20 knots. Some of the 800-ton vessels have already been completed, and the first twelve will be named: *Svitza, Leopard, Pantera, Ruisy Kaguar, Tiqr, Yaguar, Vepr, Wolky Baro, Gepard,* and *Tur*. These vessels have a speed of 16 knots on the surface and 10 knots when submerged. Their complement is 25 officers and men.

CHAPTER 5

Japanese Submarines

The Imperial Japanese Navy includes a submarine flotilla of seventeen vessels, all except two of which are of the British Holland or Vickers type. Japan commenced the construction of what is now a rapidly increasing and powerful flotilla in 1904 by the purchase of five elementary Holland boats. These, however, are still in the active flotilla and are designated Nos. 1-5. They have a submerged displacement of 120 tons, and are 65 feet in length and 12 feet in beam. Petrol motors of 160 h.-p. drive them at 9 knots on the surface and electric motors of 70 h.-p. at 7 knots when submerged. Their armament consists of one bow expulsion tube with three 18-inch Whitehead torpedoes.

Nos. 6 and 7.
(Completed 1906.)

These two vessels were the first submarine boats to be built in Japan, but are of the same type as Nos. 1-5, only larger and faster. They have a submerged displacement of 180 tons, a length of 100 feet and a beam of 10 feet. The petrol engines are of 300 h,-p. and the electric motors of 100 h.-p. The surface and submerged speed is 10 knots and 8 knots an hour, respectively. Their armament consists of one torpedo tube with three 18-inch Whitehead torpedoes.

Nos. 8 and 9.
(Completed 1907-8.)

These two vessels are very similar to the British "C" class, and were built by Messrs. Vickers Ltd. They have a submerged displacement of 320 tons; petrol motors of 600 h.-p., and a surface and submerged speed of 13 knots and 8 knots an hour, respectively. Their armament consists of two bow tubes with four to six 18-inch Whitehead torpedoes. Their complement is sixteen officers and men.

Nos. 10—15.

(Completed 1909-12.)

These six vessels are the same in almost every respect as the later "C" class of British submarines (chapter 2).

Nos. 16—17.

(It is very doubtful if these two boats were delivered before the outbreak of war).
(Completed 1912-14.)

These two vessels are of the *Schneider-Laubeuf* or French type. (British "W" class.) Their submerged displacement is about 500 tons, and the horse-power of their surface engines 2,500. The surface and submerged speed is 18 knots and 9 knots respectively. Their armament consists of six torpedo tubes with eight Schneider torpedoes. The complement is about 30 officers and men.

The natural adroitness with which Japanese sailors manipulate complicated machinery, combined with their absolute fearlessness, make them ideal for torpedo work.

CHAPTER 6

German Submarines

On "The Day"—August 4th, 1914—Germany possessed 30 submarine torpedo-boats These were divided into three flotillas, with their headquarters at Kiel, the largest and most modern vessels being attached to the Heligoland or North Sea Flotilla, During 1913, although 24 submarines were stated as being in commission, only about 15 were actively employed, and these mostly in training reserves, the older boats being docked and modernised where possible. But during the year six new vessels were added to the flotilla and the personnel of the submarine service was largely increased.

At the same time the inspection of submarines was separated from that of the other torpedo-boats and a flag-officer was appointed as head of the submarine branch of the Naval Service, with headquarters at Kiel. Thus when the hour came for the great struggle which was to decide the mastery of the seas the whole German Flotilla of 30 vessels, *with a reserve of six new boats which had been secretly hurried forward and were rapidly nearing completion*, was ready to put to sea.

The German Naval Law provided for the construction of 72 submarines by the end of 1917. All the vessels built up to the present time have been known as the "U" class and numbered in rotation. They are painted a brownish-grey colour and have high collier-like bows with massive armoured conning-towers and long superstructures amounting to narrow decks. They have all been built at either Kiel or Dantzig.

Although the first submarine boats built for the German Navy were two vessels of the Nordenfeldt type, launched in 1890, they were never actively employed with the fleet and have long since been reduced to scrap-iron, and the first vessel which can now be reckoned as a fighting unit of the German torpedo-boat flotilla was a vessel designated the "U.1." This was built at the Germania Shipyard, Kiel, and launched on August 30th, 1905. This was the forerunner of the "U" class, which in most of the essential features resembles the British Improved Holland type.

U.1.
(Completed 1905.)

This U.1 was built as an experimental boat by the famous firm of Krupps. She has a surface displacement of 197 tons, a submerged displacement of 236 tons, and her heavy-oil surface engines are of 250 h.-p. The electric motors for submerged use develop just over 100 h.-p. The speed ranges from 10 knots an hour on the surface to 7 knots when submerged, and her surface range of action is about 700 to 800 miles. The armament consists of one bow torpedo tube and three (17.7) Schwartzkopf torpedoes are carried. The complement is nine officers and men.

The trials of the U.1 extended over a period of a year and a half, and all proved remarkably satisfactory. During the tests which took place in Eckernforder Bay she succeeded, twice in succession, in torpedoing a moving target while travelling submerged at full speed.

The uncertainty displayed for some years previous by the German Naval Authorities regarding the value of submarine boats gave place to a thorough sense of the important part these "mighty atoms" would play in future naval warfare, and to a strong determination that the German Navy should include a powerful submarine flotilla,

U.2—U.8.
(Completed 1907-10.)

These seven vessels were great improvements on the U.1. Their displacement is 210 tons on the surface and about 250 tons when submerged. They are fitted with Krupp-Nuremburg heavy-oil engines of 400 h.-p, and electric motors of 160 h.-p. Their speed on the surface is 12 knots and 8 knots when submerged. The surface range of action is 1,000 miles and the submerged endurance about three hours at full speed. Their armament consists of two bow torpedo tubes and four torpedoes are carried. The complement is eleven officers and men.

U.9—U.18.
(The U.18 was sunk by a British patrol in November, 1914).
(Completed 1910-12.)

These ten vessels are of increased size and power, their submerged displacement being 300 tons, and the horsepower of their heavy oil surface engines is 600. The electric motors develop 200 h.-p. The surface and submerged speeds are 13 knots and 8 knots respectively. The surface range of action is 1,500 miles, and the armament consists of two bow and one stern torpedo tube with five torpedoes. The U.13 and subsequent vessels of this class are provided with a quick-firing, high-angle gun for defence against aircraft, and have sleeping accommodation for the crew. They may be termed the first German sea-going submarines. Their complement is twenty officers and men.

U.19 AND U.20.
(Completed 1912-13.)

There are only two vessels in this class owing to the adoption of certain improvements with the aid of which a partly new type has been evolved. These two vessels have a displacement when submerged of 450 tons. Their oil engines of 650 h.-p. give a speed of 13½ knots an hour on the surface, and their electric motors of 300 h.-p. give 8 knots an hour when submerged. Their surface range of action is 2,000 miles, and their armament, consists of two bow and one stern torpedo tube with six torpedoes, and two 14-pdr. quick-firing, high-angle guns on disappearing mountings. The complement is seventeen officers and men.

U.21—U.24.
(Completed 1912-13.)

These four vessels are the first of the new type of large sea-going submarines for the German Navy. Their submerged displacement is 800 tons. They are propelled on the surface by heavy-oil engines of 1,200 h.-p., and when submerged by electric motors of 500 h.-p. Their speed above water is 14 knots an hour and below the surface 9 knots. The surface range of action is 3,000 miles and the submerged endurance 120 miles at economical speed. Their armament consists of two bow and two stern torpedo tubes with eight torpedoes, and one 14-pdr. quick-firing gun and two 1-pdr. high-angle guns, all on disappearing mountings, for defence against hostile destroyers and aircraft. Their complement is twenty-five officers and men.

U.25—U.30.
(Completed 1913-14.)

These six vessels are the latest additions to the German submarine flotilla. They are vessels of 900 tons submerged displacement with heavy-oil engines of 2,000 h.-p., and electric motors of 900 h.-p. Their surface and submerged speed is 18 knots and 10 knots, respectively. The surface cruising range is 4,000 miles. Their armament consists of two bow and two stern torpedo tubes, with eight large size torpedoes, and, in addition, two 14-pdr. quick-firing guns and two 1-pdr. high-angle guns. They have wireless telegraphic apparatus on board, and are specially constructed with long superstructures and high *collier-like* bows to enable them to keep at sea in almost any weather. They are fitted with two or three periscopes, and also possess a small *look-out* cap on the top of the lofty conning-tower to facilitate an "awash" attack in the half-lights of dawn and dusk, when the periscope is almost useless. The conning-towers and decks are armoured. Their complement is 30 to 35 officers and men.

U.31—U.36.
(Building.)

These are the six vessels which are rapidly nearing completion, (1914), and which were in a much more advanced state, at the opening of hostilities, than was generally known in foreign naval circles. They are the same in almost every respect as the vessels U.25 to U.30. There is, however, another submarine being built for Germany of a totally different design. This is the F.I.A.T. or *Laurenti* boat (Italian), laid down at the beginning of 1914. This vessel is very similar to the four "S" boats being built at Greenock for the British Navy.

No German submarines have in the past been sent to any Colonial or oversea station. Therefore, the whole flotilla of 30 to 36 vessels was immediately available for operations in the North Sea and Baltic when war began. The personnel of the whole torpedo service is very efficient, great attention having been paid to this branch of the navy. The three German Submarine flotillas have their headquarters at Kiel, Wilhelmshaven, and Heligoland.

CHAPTER 7

Austrian Submarines

At the commencement of the war the Austro-Hungarian Navy included six submarines in the active flotilla and five others were being *completed* at the Germania Yard, Kiel, but it is doubtful if they had been delivered. In which event they must be added to the strength of the German flotilla. In addition to these, several larger vessels, mostly of the latest "U" or Krupp design, had been ordered, but were not expected to take their place in the active flotillas before the end of 1915.

Austria commenced the formation of a submarine flotilla in 1908 by the acquisition of two vessels of the *Improved Holland type* from Messrs. Vickers Ltd., and two others of the American *Lake type*. In the following year two more submarines were ordered, this time from Krupp's Germania Yard, All these vessels were delivered during 1910, and Austria's first submarine flotilla came into being.

U.1 AND U.2.
(Completed 1910.)

These two vessels are of the American Lake type. They have a submerged displacement of 250 tons and petrol surface motors of 720 h.-p. Their speed is 12 knots on the surface and 8 knots when submerged. The armament consists of two bow and one stern torpedo tube. This type of submarine has three special features which distinguish it from all others. It is fitted with a kind of underframe and wheels, and is designed to travel in four different positions: (1) on the surface; (2) semi-submerged, with only a look-out cowl above water; (3) submerged, with nothing but the periscope showing; (4) totally submerged and running along the sea-bed on wheels, like a submarine motor car. It is drawn down from the surface to the sea-bed by an ingenious system of wire-hawsers and drop-weights, which can be released in the event of accident. A "diving chamber" enables members of the crew to don diving-dresses and leave the submarine when on the sea-bed, for the purpose of laying or destroying submerged mines. The Lake type of submarine is also used in the Russian Navy. (*Submarine Engineering of Today*).

U.3 AND U.4.
(Completed 1910.)

These two vessels are of the Krupp design, and have a submerged displacement of 300 tons. The horse-power of their heavy-oil surface engines is 600. The electric motors develop 200 h.-p. The surface and submerged speeds are 13 knots and 8 knots respectively. The surface range of action is 1,500 miles, and the armament consists of two bow and one stern tube with five 18-inch torpedoes. Their complement is fifteen officers and men.

U.5 AND U.6.
(Completed 1910.)

These are submarines of the Improved Holland type. Their submerged displacement is about 316 tons; length 135 feet, and beam 13½ feet. The horse-power of the petrol engines is 600 and that of the electric engines 189. The speed averages 12 knots on the surface and 8 knots when submerged. The surface cruising range is 1,300 knots at 10 knots an hour. Their armament consists of two bow tubes with four to six 18-inch Whitehead torpedoes. Their complement is sixteen officers and men.

U.7—U.11.
(Completed 1914. Delivery doubtful.)

These five vessels are of the Krupp-Germania type, and are similar to those completed for the German Navy in 1912-13. They are large sea-going submarines with a submerged displacement of 800 tons. They are propelled on the surface by heavy-oil engines of 1,200 h.-p., and when submerged, by electric motors of 500 h.-p. Their speed is 14 knots and 9 knots, above and below, respectively. The surface range of action is 3,000 miles, and the submerged endurance 1 20 miles at economical speed.

Their armament consists of two bow and two stern torpedo tubes, with eight torpedoes, and one 14-pdr. quick-firing gun and two

1-pdr. high-angle guns, for defence against hostile destroyers and aircraft. Their complement is twenty-five officers and men.

One or two Austrian submarines are supposed to have been sunk by the Allied Fleet during the first few weeks of the war, but exactly which vessels they were is not known.

Several other submarines have been ordered in foreign countries for the Austrian Navy, but cannot be delivered while the war lasts.

SUBMARINE FLOTILLAS OF NEUTRAL EUROPEAN POWERS.

COUNTRY.	VESSELS BUILT.	VESSELS BUILDING.
Italy	20 (100-300 tons)	8 (large size)
Denmark	9 (100-300 tons)	several
Holland	6 (100-300 tons)	4 (large)
Sweden	7 (150-300 tons)	3 (large)
Greece	2 (Laubeuf)	—
Norway	1 —	4 (Germania)
Portugal	1 —	3 —
Turkey	—	3 —
Spain	—	3 —

CHAPTER 8

Submarines in Action

Submarines have two great advantages over all types of surface warships; they can become invisible at will—or sufficiently invisible to make gun or torpedo-practice, except at very close quarters, almost entirely useless—and they can, by sinking, cover themselves with armour-plate of sufficient thickness to be absolutely shell-proof. These are the two main points in favour of the submarine. There are, however, many minor features. Although submarines are known in the naval services as "daylight torpedo-boats," for their *greatest* value lies in their ability to perform the same task in the "light" as the ordinary surface torpedo-boats and destroyers can do under cover of darkness or fog—that of creeping up close to an enemy, and launching a torpedo unobserved—they have been given, during recent years, so much greater speed, armament, and range of action, that they can no longer be looked upon as small boats just suitable for daylight torpedo attack in favourable circumstances.

Their surface speed has been increased from 10 to 20 knots, making them almost as fast as the surface torpedo-boat. This, combined with manoeuvring powers and general above-water invisibility, has enabled them to take over the duty of the surface torpedo-boat—that of delivering night-attacks on the surface. After nightfall a submarine attack is almost impossible owing to the periscope—the eyes of the submarine—being useless in the dark.

The increase in the armament of the submarine—from the single bow torpedo tube with two torpedoes of short range and weak explosive charge, to the four bow and two stern tubes with eight or ten torpedoes of long range and high explosive charge—has greatly increased their chances of successful attack on surface warships, first, by giving them four or six shots ahead, then the possibility, in the event of all these torpedoes missing, of a dive under the object of attack, and two more shots at close range from the stern tubes (still retaining two torpedoes); and, secondly, by increasing the distance from which the first projectile can be launched, owing to the increased range of the modern torpedo. There are also the advantages derived from the battery of quick-firing guns installed on the decks of modern submarines.

Although at the present time, (1914), these guns are only of small power they nevertheless afford a means of defence—and even of attack under favourable circumstances—against hostile surface torpedo-boats, destroyers, and air-craft. In fact, a flotilla of submarines could undoubtedly now give a very good account of itself if attacked either on the surface or when submerged by one or two prowling destroyers. The increase in the power of the guns carried by submarines, which will certainly come soon, will enable this type of craft to take up the additional duties of the destroyer —that of clearing the seas of hostile torpedo-boats and carrying out advanced scouting—for which work their ability to travel submerged and in a state of invisibility for distances of over 100 miles makes them eminently suitable.

The enormous increase in the size and range of action of submarines, combined with the improvements effected in the surface cruising qualities, have enabled these vessels to be taken from the "nursery" of harbour and coast defence and placed with the sea-going flotillas and battle-fleets. In the short period of ten years the tonnage of submarines has risen from 100 to over 1,000 tons, and the range of action from 400 miles at economical speed to 5,000 miles. Exactly what this means is more easily realized when it is stated that the earlier types of submarines could scarcely cross the English Channel and return without taking in supplies of fuel, and in rough weather were forced to remain in harbour, whereas the modern vessel can go from England to Newfoundland *and back* without assistance, and can remain at sea in almost any weather, as was first demonstrated by the successful voyage of the British submarines A.E.1 and A.E.2 to Australia, and has since been proved by the operations of the British submarine flotilla in the North Sea.

In addition to the cruising range there is, however, the question of habitability. In this respect the progress has been equally as rapid. In the older boats no sleeping accommodation was provided for the crew, and food supplies and fresh water sufficient only for a few days were carried. In the latest British, French and German vessels proper sleeping and messing accommodation is provided, and supplies of all kinds and in sufficient quantity to last a month are carried. Although work on these craft is still very cramping for the crew, the increase in the deck space and in the surface buoyancy has greatly minimised the discomforts of service in the submarine flotilla.

With regard to safety, it has already been shown that a submarine is only held below the surface by the power of her engines. and the action of the water on her diving-rudders. This means that in the event of anything going wrong *inside* the vessel she would automatically rise to the surface; but should the hull be pierced in any way, either by shot or by collision, and an overwhelming inrush of water result—overcoming the buoyancy quickly obtained by blowing out the water-ballast tanks—then the vessel must inevitably sink, and the question of whether or not the crew can save themselves becomes a problem to which no definite answer can be given, although a special means is provided in all modern vessels belonging to the British Navy. Speaking generally, it may, however, be said that if the disaster occurs suddenly, and the vessel sinks into very deep water rapidly, the chances of lifesaving are extremely small; but if the water is comparatively shallow, as along the coast (100 to 150 feet), the likelihood of many of the crew being able to save themselves with the aid of the *special escape helmets and air-locks* is fairly good.

We now come to the most important improvement made in the fighting qualities of these vessels since first they came into being, *viz.* the wonderful increase in the surface and submerged speed. In the older craft the surface speed did not exceed 8 to 10 knots an hour, whereas it now amounts to 16 to 20 knots, and the submerged speed has risen from 5 knots to 10 to 13 knots. It is a little difficult for any but a naval man to realise exactly what this increase in the speed of submarines really means, and it is equally as difficult to adequately describe it here in non-technical language. It is a mere platitude to say that in order to attack a surface warship the submarine must first get within torpedo range of it; and yet it is on this very point that the strategy and tactics of submarine warfare revolve.

A clever naval tactician once described the submarine as a "handicapped torpedo-boat." The two points on which he based this opinion were—the (then) slow speed of these vessels compared with that of the surface warship, and its almost total blindness when submerged. These two defects were for some years the principal drawbacks of all the submarines afloat; but since that naval expert pronounced submarines to be

Right-Angle Attack by Submarines.

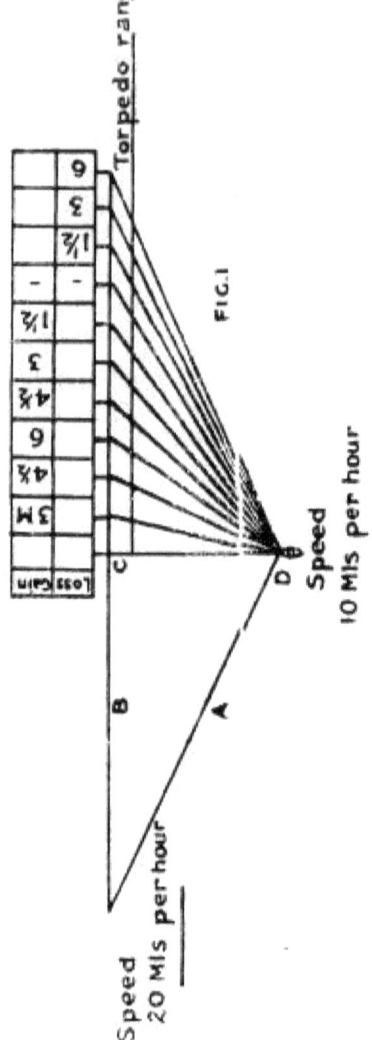

Fig. 1

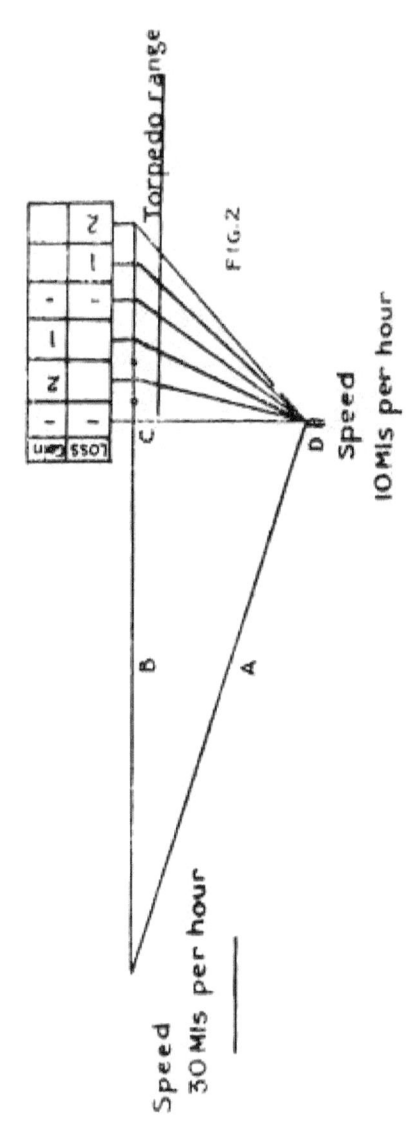

FIG. 2

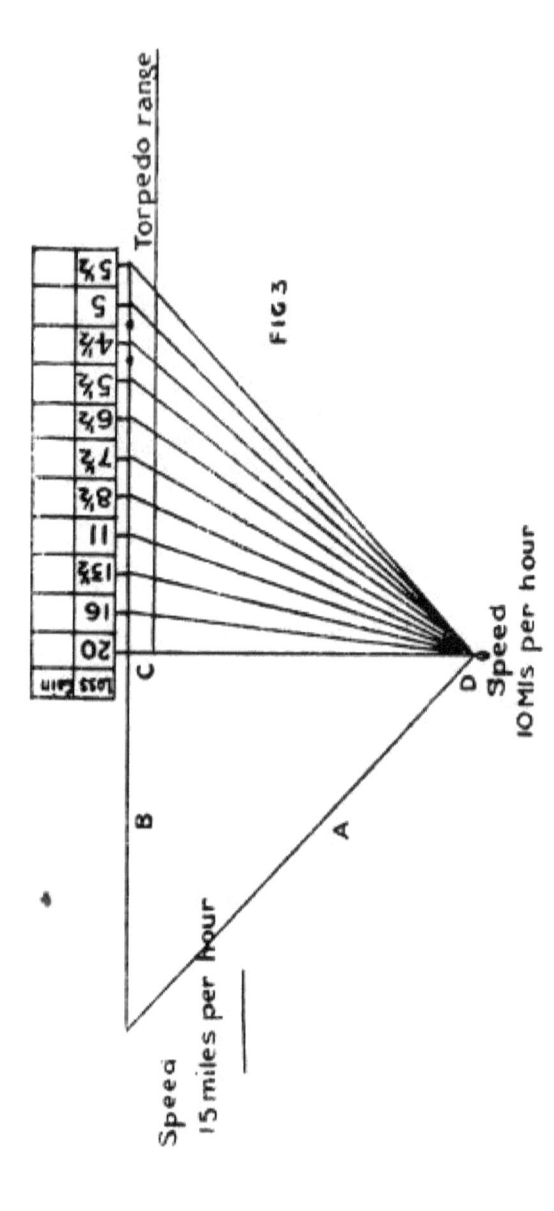

FIG 3

"handicapped torpedo-boats," great changes, great improvements have been made. The speed of the submarine has increased by over 100 *per cent*, and they have been given longer and wider range of vision by the introduction of two and three improved periscopes instead of one elementary instrument. Nevertheless, the speed difficulty is still a very real one, as will readily be seen when it is taken into consideration that the speed of a submarine when attacking submerged is frequently only half, or even a third, of that of her enemy. In order to more clearly illustrate this and lift for a moment the veil of secrecy which enshrouds the methods of attack adopted by this type of craft, it will be necessary to describe what is known as the *right-angle attack*.

Attacking at Right Angles.

The difficulty of attacking a surface warship steaming at right angles to the course of the submarine will be clearly understood by referring to the following diagrams.

The first shows an attack on a warship travelling at 20 miles an hour, such as a big battleship or a cruiser. Any increase in the speed of the surface vessel not only adds to the difficulty of the attacking submarine, but also the direction from which the attack must be made. This feature is shown in the second diagram, which illustrates a submarine attack on a vessel steaming at 30 miles an hour, such as a fast destroyer or fleet scout. On the other hand, a decrease in the speed of the on-coming surface vessel tends to either make easier the task of the attacking submarine, or else to increase the distance from which the attack can be delivered. This is shown in the third diagram, which assumes the speed of the surface vessel to be only 15 miles an hour, such as a merchantman, troopship, food-ship, collier, or old warship.

Fig. 1 represents a submarine attacking a hostile warship (or fleet) steaming at 20 (statute) miles an hour. "A" is the line of vision. The submarine sights the warship at a distance of just over 11 miles on her port bow. "B" shows the hostile vessel's course, which is 10 miles to point marked "C," and each division beyond equals 1 mile.

Directly the submarine, which is assumed to be lying in an *awash condition*, sights the object of attack, she totally submerges and steers forward at a speed of 10 miles an hour. The loss, and gain, of the submarine on the different courses, can be seen in the table above the chart.

★★★★★★

As it is almost impossible for a submarine, when totally submerged, to steer a *perfectly* straight course, the table above each chart shows the approximate average loss and gain on each mile. It must also be remembered that the submarine in actual practice need only reach the torpedo firing line.

★★★★★★

The spaces between the black dots show the most favourable points of attack. It will be noticed in the table that both vessels are equal at point "C," but for many reasons this is not the best point of attack. The gain of about six minutes on the longer course enables the submarine not only to manoeuvre into the best possible position for the attack, but also to discharge more than one torpedo if necessary.

Fig. 2 shows the extreme limit at which a submarine could, with reasonable chances of success, attack a destroyer, or other vessel, steaming at 30 (statute) miles an hour, having sighted her at a distance of 16 miles in the position shown by the line of vision "A."

The distance to "C" is 15 miles for the surface vessel, and 5 miles for the submarine. Here, again, the two vessels would be equal; but the most favourable point of attack is shown by the two black dots—where the submarine has gained two minutes.

Fig. 3.—The submarine sights the object of attack at a distance of 14¼ miles, in the position shown by the line of vision "A." The surface vessel has a speed of only 15 miles an hour (merchantman). In this case the surface vessel accomplishes the 10-mile journey along course "B"—arriving at point "C" 20 minutes in advance of the submarine. The table shows how the submarine, by changing her course and "throwing" the surface vessel on her beam, gradually reduces the loss, until, at the point marked with the two black dots, she is but 4½ minutes behind. At this distance she could fire her torpedoes at long range, with some likelihood of success.

Although these charts show approximately the extreme limits of the right-angle attack, a submarine could, of course, proceed for some distance on the surface at a much faster speed; but considering the rate at which the' two vessels would be approaching each other, the submarine which attempted it would run considerable risk of being detected, and thus destroy her chances of a successful attack. Considering also the time lost in sinking from the "light" to the totally submerged condition, in coming to close quarters, the gain in speed would not amount to as much as may at first seem probable. (*Submarines of the World's Navies*).

These charts are drawn and calculations made assuming the following points:—

(1) The weather—fine and bright
(2) Not taking into consideration strong tides, currents, etc.
(3) The enemy on the alert.
(4) Submarine waits at point "D" in an awash condition.
(5) Owing to 1, 2, and 3 above, the submarine travels from point "D" in all courses in a submerged The most favourable position for a submarine flotilla is to manoeuvre close up to a fleet at anchor, or to get within 1,000 yards of a fleet—steaming across its course; but both of these ideal positions for attack are extremely difficult to obtain, and consequently in all the less favourable positions speed is the deciding factor. Strategems will undoubtedly play an important part in submarine warfare.

An example of this has already been afforded when the German submarines resorted to the dishonest trick of laying in wait behind a trawler engaged in laying mines, over which *the flag of a neutral state* had been hoisted as a blind This resulted in the loss of three British cruisers with over 1,000 lives. It would, however, be quite in accord with the rules of *civilised* warfare for a submarine to shelter behind a "decoy"; to attack simultaneously with a seaplane; or to approach an enemy behind one of its own merchant ships.

The Porpoise Dive.

The manoeuvre known as the "Porpoise Dive" is merely the sudden rising of a submarine in order to enable her commander to get a better view of the surface than it afforded by the periscope. The submarine on approaching the object of attack rises quickly to the surface by the action of her horizontal rudders, then dives again, only remaining above water for a few seconds to enable her commander to get a glimpse of the enemy, and to take bearings. The submarine can then get within torpedo-range, with simply the tiny periscope projecting from the surface. This manoeuvre is now seldom necessary, owing to the long and wide range of vision of the two or three periscopes fitted in modem submarines.

Difficulty of the Fixed Torpedo Tube.

With the exception of one or two vessels, which it would be unwise to specify, all the submarines engaged in the present war have what are called *fixed submerged tubes.* This means that the tubes from which the torpedoes are discharged are fitted *inside* the submarine *on a line with the centre of the boat*, and cannot be moved or aimed in any way apart from the boat itself. It therefore becomes necessary for the submarine to be *aligned* by the leering rudders on the object of attack before the torpedoes can be discharged. In simpler vein, torpedoes can only be fired by a submarine straight ahead or straight astern. Hence a submarine, with a hostile warship coming up on its beam, is compelled to turn and face its opponent (or turn its stern towards her) before delivering an attack.

Submarine Flotilla *v.* Surface Fleet.

It is absolutely necessary for submarines acting in company to have each its allotted task; and for a wide space of water to be left between each boat; as it is impossible, at present, for one; submarine to know the exact position of another when both vessels are submerged. Therefore, if each boat was not previously instructed how to act, there would not only be the likelihood of the greater portion of an attacking flotilla firing their torpedoes at one or two vessels of the hostile fleet and allowing the remainder either to escape or to keep up a heavy and dangerous fire unmolested, but also of collision and of torpedoing each other by accident. There is no means of intercommunication between submarines when submerged, and a battle between submarines is almost impossible.

Surprise Attack.

In this case invisibility is the element of success. Admiral Sir Cyprian Bridge, G.C.B., in a letter to the author once said:

"When submerged the concealment of the submarine is practically perfect. If she has not been sighted up to the moment of diving, she will almost certainly reach, unobserved, the point at which she can make her attack."

And this opinion—shared for many years by all expert—has been amply proved in the present, (1914), war.

A submarine must, however, blend with the surrounding sea in its ever-varying colours, lights and shades, in order that she may be as invisible as possible when cruising on the surface. The French Naval Authorities experimented oft Toulon with a luminous paint of a sea-green colour; but this, although causing the hull to be almost totally invisible in certain weather, was found to be useless, as, on a bright day with a blue sky, the green showed up clear against the bluish tint of the surrounding sea. After many months of experimenting, a pale, sea-green, non-luminous paint was chosen as the best colour for French submarines. The British Admiralty also carried out a few experiments in this direction, and came to the conclusion that a dull grey was the most invisible shade. The German authorities decided in favour of a grey-brown.

When travelling submerged, with only the thin periscopic tube above the surface, it is almost impossible to detect the approach of a submarine *before* she gets within torpedo range; and when cruising on the surface she is equally as invisible at a distance of a few miles. These qualities enable the submarine in nearly all cases where her speed permits, to effect a surprise attack on a hostile battleship or cruiser *when not closely screened by fast destroyers*, whose duty it is to be ever on the watch for submarines.

As to the tactics which would be employed by a submarine (or flotilla) in attacking a hostile warship (or fleet), it is impossible to say, for, like the impromptu attacks of all "mosquito craft," the exact method, or manoeuvre is arranged to suit the circumstances, and it is very seldom that two such attacks are carried out alike. Generally speaking, however, a hostile warship could be easily sighted, on a fairly clear day, from the flying-bridge of a submarine at a distance of 10 miles; but it would be practically impossible to detect the submarine from the deck of a warship at that distance. On sighting her object of attack the submarine would sink to the "awash" condition, and proceed for from 2½ to 5 miles, as might be deemed expedient. She would then submerge and steer by her periscopes, each of which has a field of vision of 60 degrees. He would be a very keen look-out who would be able to detect the few square inches of periscopic tube at a distance of three miles.

As this distance lessened, it might be advisable, if the sea was *very* calm and if the object of attack was stationary, for the submarine to slacken speed, so as to prevent any spray being thrown off by the periscopic tube. Assuming, however, that the optical tube was seen by the enemy, it would be extremely difficult to hit it with gun-fire at a distance of one or two mites, or to damage the boat itself, which would probably be immersed to a depth of 12 or 15 feet. At a distance of about 2,000 yards, or just over one mile, the submarine would discharge her first torpedo, following it up with another at closer range from the second bow tube. A rapid dive would then probably be necessary in order to avoid the hail of shot which would plough up the waters around her. If the first two torpedoes missed their mark the submarine might either dive completely under the object of attack and then fire her stern tubes at close range, or else manoeuvre below the surface for an attack from some other point.

One of the effects produced on fleets or individual warships in war time by the ever present possibility of submarine attack is, however, that they never remain at anchor or even stationary in an exposed position, and seldom—if wise—proceed without destroyers as advance and flank guards. These precautions double the difficulties of a successful submarine attack.

CHAPTER 9

Anti-Submarine Tactics

In all warfare, new weapons of attack are, sooner or later, met by new methods of defence. The submarine and the aeroplane are at present the Only weapons against which there is no true means of defence, and yet one is being used as an antidote for the other without, however, any very striking success so far. The seaplane may be able to distinguish the dark patch in the sea caused by the hull of the submarine *in clear water*, but she cannot destroy it, neither can she signal the *exact* locality to an accompanying destroyer flotilla, owing to the speed with which seaplane and submarine pass over and under each other; furthermore, in rough weather or in shallow muddy water no sign oi the submarine when submerged is visible from above.

The great value of the seaplane as an antidote for submarines lies, however, first in the fact that the water of the open sea is usually clear, and the *submarine shadow* is visible from above, and, secondly, in the great speed of these aircraft which enables them to quickly cover miles of sea in their search for hostile submarines and to report their presence in a given locality by wireless to all ships operating within range.

When the enormous superficial area of a zone of war, such as the North Sea and English Channel, is duly considered, however, the difficulty in quickly and reliably locating from the air the few scattered "submarine shadows" will be easily realised. To make this method of locating submarines even fairly reliable an enormous fleet of seaplanes would be required. Again seaplanes do not, in themselves, constitute a means of defence against submarine attack, they merely increase the likelihood of detection, but, in actual warfare, it has now been proved that for every submarine detected by seaplanes two others pass quite unobserved.

Many means of attack on submarines have been proposed; and no doubt some of these, in certain cases, would prove effective; but none can be relied upon. Therefore, one of the points in favour of the submarine still remains without its antidote. This is the *morale effect*; for if there is no absolutely reliable means of defence, there can be no feeling of security for surface warships or merchant vessels when anywhere within the danger zone of the submarine.

Let us now examine briefly what practical methods of defence a modern warship has against submarine attacks. Great speed is undoubtedly a surface ship's most reliable defence; and when combined with a frequent change of course, would greatly reduce the chances of a successful underwater attack. Should hostile submarines be on the line of advance they would not know whether to wait and chance the enemy approaching within torpedo range or whether to run to starboard or port. This is, if the surface warship was steaming in an erratic course—not a zigzag course, for then it might be possible to estimate, within torpedo range, the position of the ship at a given point if the "tacks" were regular.

Should submarines be seen approaching, a surface vessel would do well to turn her stern to the attacking flotilla, presenting as small a target as possible, and deflecting the torpedoes by her propeller race.

The escape of the Battle Cruiser *Queen Mary* and the Light Cruiser *Lowestoft*, during the action in the Heligoland Bight, as described in the dispatch of Vice-Admiral Sir David Beatty, K.C.B., demonstrates what may be done by the skilful use of the helm on surface warships to frustrate submarine attacks. So interesting, and informative as to the actual fighting between British warships and hostile submarines, in this dispatch that I give it here in full. It should, however, be studied in conjunction with the comprehensive report—the first in the history of Naval warfare detailing submarine attack and reconnaissance—from Commodore Roger J. B. Keyes, C.B., of the British submarines, given in the introduction.

H.M.S. *Lion*,
1st September, 1914.

Sir,—I have the honour to report that on Thursday, 27th August, at 5 a.m., I proceeded with the First Battle Cruiser Squadron and First Light Cruiser Squadron in company, to rendezvous with the Rear-Admiral, *Invincible*.

At 4 a.m., 28th August, the movements of the Flotillas commenced as previously arranged, the Battle Cruiser Squadron and Light Cruiser Squadron supporting. The Rear-Admiral, *Invincible*, with *New Zealand* and four destroyers having joined my flag, the Squadron passed through the pre-arranged rendezvous. At 8.10 a.m. I received a signal from the Commodore (T), informing me that the flotilla was in action with the enemy. This was presumably in the vicinity of their pre-arranged rendezvous. From this time until 11 a.m. I remained about the vicinity ready to support as necessary, intercepting various signals, which contained no information on which I could act.

At 11 a.m. the squadron was attacked by three submarines. The attack was frustrated by rapid manoeuvring and the four destroyers were ordered to attack them. Shortly after 11 a.m., various signals having been received indicating that the Commodore (T) and Commodore (S) were both in need of assistance, I ordered the Light Cruiser Squadron to support the Torpedo Flotillas.

Later I received a signal from the Commodore (T), stating that he was being attacked by a large cruiser, and a further signal informing me that he was being hard pressed and asking for assistance. The Captain (D), First Flotilla, also signalled that he was in need of help.

From the foregoing the situation appeared to me critical. The Flotillas had advanced only ten miles since 8 a.m., and were only about twenty-five miles from two enemy bases on their flank and rear respectively. Commodore Goodenough had detached two of his light cruisers to assist some destroyers earlier in the day, and these had not yet rejoined. (They rejoined at 2.30 p.m.). As the reports indicated the presence of many enemy ships—one a large cruiser—I considered that his force might not be strong enough to deal with the situation sufficiently rapidly, so at 11.30 a.m. the battle cruisers turned to E.S.E., and worked up to full speed. It was evident that to be of any value the support must be overwhelming and carried out at the highest speed possible.

I had not lost sight of the risk of submarines, and possible sortie in force from the enemy's base, especially in view of the mist to the south-east.

Our high speed, however, made submarine attack difficult, and the smoothness of the sea made their detection comparatively easy. I considered that we were powerful enough to deal with any sortie except by a Battle Squadron, which was unlikely to come out in time, provided our stroke was sufficiently rapid.

At 12.15 p.m. *Fearless* and First Flotilla were sighted retiring west. At the same time the Light Cruiser Squadron was observed to be engaging an enemy ship ahead. They appeared to have her beat.

I then steered N.E. to sounds of firing ahead, and at 12.30 p.m. sighted *Arethusa* and Third Flotilla retiring to the westward engaging a cruiser of the *Kolberg* class on our port bow. I steered to cut her off from Heligoland, and at 12.37 p.m. opened fire. At 12.42 the enemy turned to N.E., and we chased at 27 knots. At 12.56 p.m. sighted and engaged a two-funnelled cruiser ahead. *Lion* fired two salvoes at her, which took effect, and she disappeared into the mist, burning furiously and in a sinking condition. In view of the mist and that she was steering at high speed at right angles to *Lion*, who was herself steaming at 28 knots, the *Lion's* firing was very creditable.

Our destroyers had reported the presence of floating mines to the eastward and I considered it inadvisable to pursue her. It was also essential that the squadrons should remain concentrated, and I accordingly ordered a withdrawal. The battle cruisers turned north and circled to port to complete the destruction of the vessel first engaged. She was sighted again at 1.25 p.m. steaming S.E. with colours still flying. *Lion* opened fire with two turrets, and at 1.35 p.m., after receiving two salvoes, she sank.

The four attached destroyers were sent to pick up survivors, but I deeply regret that they subsequently reported that they searched the area but found none.

At 1.40 p.m. the battle cruisers turned to the northward, and *Queen Mary* was again attacked by a submarine. The attack was avoided by the use of the helm. *Lowestoft* was also unsuccessfully attacked. The battle cruisers covered the retirement until nightfall. by 6 p.m., the retirement having been well executed and all destroyers accounted for, I altered course, spread the light cruisers, and swept northwards in accordance with the commander-in-chief's orders. At 7.45 p.m. I detached *Liverpool* to Rosyth with German prisoners, seven officers and 79 men, survivors from *Mainz*. No further incident occurred.—I have

the honour to be, Sir, your obedient servant.
(Signed)   David Beatty,
Vice-Admiral.

The Secretary of the Admiralty.

Quick-firing guns of the 3-inch and 6-inch type are certainly the best weapons for an attack on submarines. In combination with "sharp look-outs," they could be used with effect from the elevated positions on the fore part of warships. The periscopic-tube of the submarine always proves a target for gun-fire; but a grey steel tube, 3 inches in diameter, at a distance of 1,000 yards requires "excellent" marksmanship to hit. That it can be done is proved by the sinking of the German submarine U.I 5 by the British Cruiser *Birmingham* in the North Sea. The effect of a shot carrying away the periscope is to blind the submarine, at least in one eye, she can then be *run-down* by the surface warship or destroyed by rapid gun-fire at close range.

Of course, if submarines were caught napping on the surface the guns of surface warships could quickly sink them; but another incident, similar to that which opened the naval engagements of the Russo-Japanese War, cannot be looked for in the naval engagements to come.

For a fleet engaged in bombarding or blockading, one of the best methods of defence would be to lower the torpedo nets, not close round each vessel, but suspended from "picket-boats" at a distance from the bombarding or blockading fleet. "Picketing" is also considered a good defence during daylight, but neither of these methods are reliable. A submarine might be able to dive unobserved under, or past, the destroyers acting as pickets, and it is this chance which causes these under-water craft to be a source of constant anxiety.

The torpedo-boat destroyer should prove a nasty enemy to the submarine. In warfare it is the duty of these 30-knot vessels to look after their underwater opponents.

It has been suggested that internal armour could be fitted to warships below the water-line, which would render the hulls able to withstand mine or torpedo explosions. At present this is practically impossible, as the great weight of this additional armour, combined with the ever-increasing size of guns and weight of above-water protection, would necessitate a vessel of such enormous displacement as to be quite impossible, if the important factor—high speed—has also to be maintained. , The defence of harbours against submarines is a problem which does not present nearly so many difficulties as the defence of moving ships. Portsmouth, for example, is closed by means of a submarine boom-defence, which is stretched across the mouth of the harbour.

The entrance to the River Elbe (leading to the Kaiser Wilhelm Canal) is effectively closed to British submarines by boom-defences, mines, and submerged wire entanglements. Narrow waterways, such as the Straits of Dover, can be closed by the laying of contact-mines, and even broader seas can be made dangerous to submarines by the same method. An example of this is afforded by the laying of a British mine-field somewhere between the Goodwin Sands and the Dutch Coast, to prevent German submarines from penetrating into the English Channel.

There are so many reliable means of defending harbours and narrow waterways against submarines that it is unnecessary to say anything further here. But to protect moving ships at sea, under all conditions, certainly presents a most profound puzzle.

CHAPTER 10

The Submarine Torpedo

The submarine torpedo has become one of the principal naval arms. Not only does it supply the chief offensive power of the submarine, the torpedo-boat and the destroyer, but it is also carried as a separate arm, with a special highly-trained crew, by almost every warship afloat. At the beginning of hostilities the Naval Powers engaged owned considerably over 80,000 of these weapons, and *one* factory in England alone can make them at the rate of two a day. During the first few weeks of the *Great War* the torpedo was responsible for the sinking of warships to the value of over one million sterling. Had the German Fleet been on the high seas instead of in harbour and protected from torpedo raids by carefully-prepared submarine defences, there is little doubt but what several more of the enemy's ships would have been sunk by this weapon.

The fact that at first the British light cruisers suffered rather heavily—though in total loss of ships and men less than the German Navy—does not point to any advantage derived either from the type of torpedo used or from skill in this mode of warfare possessed by the Germans, but clearly to the timidity of the German main fleet, which was at the very beginning of hostilities withdrawn from the zone of war and placed behind fortifications, where it was safe from torpedo attack. The British Fleet, true to the policy of "attack and not defence," began operations the moment war was declared, with results so brilliantly successful, and of such far-reaching and world-wide importance, that enumeration is well-nigh impossible.

But while all these operations were in progress the British Fleet was more or less exposed to torpedo attack by any hostile submarines or fast surface craft which might succeed in getting past the cordon of protecting destroyers, while the German Fleet was safe, but ignominiously impotent. That the naval losses of Great Britain, with all her fleets at sea, have not been far greater than they have is in itself a victory of the greatest magnitude—a victory due entirely to consummate naval skill.

The modern torpedo varies in length from 14 to 19 feet, and weighs up to half a ton. It has an extreme range of 4,000 yards, or just over 2¼ miles. There are three types of torpedoes in use by the fleets at war. The British use the *Whitehead Torpedo*, the French the Whitehead and the *Schneider*, the Russians and the Japanese use the Whitehead; the Germans have a type of their own, known as the *Schwartzkopf*, and the Austrian arm is principally the Whitehead. All these types are alike in their essential features, and therefore need not be described separately.

The latest pattern 18-inch Whitehead torpedo is propelled by compressed air stored in that section of the weapon known as the *air-chamber* (see diagram). The air on being released is heated and expanded in a tiny three or four-cylinder engine which operates twin screws, moving "clockwise" and "anti-clockwise." The "war-head" contains about 200 pounds of wet gun-cotton which is exploded on the torpedo striking an object. The essential features of the Whitehead torpedo are shown in the diagram. (*Submarines of the World's Navies*).

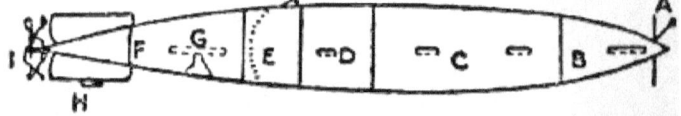

Sketch showing the essential parts of a Whitehead torpedo. *A*. Pistol, detonator, primer, which causes the explosion of " B " when the torpedo strikes an object. *B*. Explosive head, filled with wet gun-cotton. (The " war-head " is substituted by a weighty dummy during practice.) *C*. Air chamber with compressed air, at a pressure of approximately 1350 lbs. per square inch, for action. The chamber is tested to stand a pressure of 1700 lbs. per square inch. *D*. Balance chamber, containing mechanism for regulating the depth of submergence at which the torpedo is adjusted to run. *E*. Engine-room, containing propelling machinery (I.H.P. 60 in latest 18-in. type). *F*. Buoyancy chamber—a practically empty chamber—to give the necessary buoyancy to the torpedo. *G*. Gyroscope. An instrument for correcting any deviation of the torpedo from the line of fire. *H*. Rudders, and mechanism for operating. *I*. Twin-screws, operating "clockwise" and " anti-clockwise.'

This torpedo maintains a speed of 42 knots for 1,000 yards, 38 knots for 2,000 yards, 32 knots for 3,000 yards, and 28 knots for 4,000 yards. Thus, if discharged at a distance of half a mile it reaches its object in about 45 seconds.

Torpedoes are fired—or ejected—into the sea from surface or submerged tubes, and on striking the water are propelled by their own engines in an absolutely straight course towards the target.

The exact mechanism of the submerged tube—which is used in When fired from a surface tube the torpedo sinks immediately to a depth of about 10 to 14 feet, and maintains this depth until it strikes its object. When fired from a submerged tube it rises—if necessary— to the same level. A torpedo always proceeds towards its object of attack at a depth of a few feet below the surface. This, combined with speed, renders it almost impossible to destroy an approaching torpedo by gun-fire. So marvellous is the mechanism of these little weapons that in anything like favourable circumstances they may be *depended upon*, if well aimed, to strike within a yard or two of the spot aimed at. This accuracy is due almost entirely to the gyroscope, which, briefly described, is a rotating wheel automatically controlling the torpedo's course.

Although for many years torpedoes have been carried by nearly all types of service warships, none of them were really ideal for this kind of warfare. A new field for the torpedo was, however, opened out by the introduction of the submarine boat. In order to be effective the torpedo must be discharged from a distance under 4,000 yards—preferably from a point less than half this distance from the object of attack. This means that the vessel carrying the torpedo would have to get within a mile, or at least a mile and a-half, of her object of attack before discharging a torpedo. For a surface vessel to accomplish this in the face of a heavy cannonade from quick-firing guns would be extremely risky.

To make a quick rush to close quarters, if possible, by several vessels from different points, was the only chance of delivering a successful torpedo attack on a hostile warship; unless, of course, she was favoured by fog or darkness *at the right moment*—favourable conditions which would seldom obtain in actual warfare. Again, every increase in the speed of the big surface warship rendered the task of the ordinary torpedo-boat and destroyer more difficult because in the event of a threatened attack the larger vessel would make use of her speed to keep out of torpedo range while her powerful guns were repelling the attacking torpedo-boat.

The *hour* of the torpedo came with it *perfection* of the submarine. All the conditions of an ideal torpedo-boat were fulfilled—*invisibility* rendering daylight attacks possible; *almost perfect immunity from gun-fire* enabling the torpedo to be discharged at closer range; submerged discharge removing the likelihood of the weapon being exploded by accurate gun-fire before being discharged; *speed on the surface* enabling the "carrying" vessel to manoeuvre for position; *moderate speed when submerged* enabling an attack under all reasonably tactical conditions; and *comparatively large displacement* giving good cruising qualities, wide range of action, and enabling a large number of torpedoes and tubes being carried.

Chapter 11

Submarine Mines

If the Russo-Japanese war was the first to fully demonstrate the value of the explosive mine, the Great European Conflict has certainly brought this weapon to the forefront in the rapidly growing science of submarine warfare. During the first few weeks of the naval fighting several warships, beginning with H.M.S. *Amphion*, and many merchant vessels representing millions of pounds sterling, were destroyed by these weapons. Had it not been for the foresight of the British Admiralty in providing a very large fleet of mine-sweepers, aided by seaplanes, there can be no doubt but what the shipping of all countries—neutrals and belligerents alike—would have suffered far greater losses.

The indiscriminate scattering of mines across the trade routes, as carried on by Germany immediately on the outbreak of war, and before hardly any of the ships at sea belonging to neutral countries could be warned to avoid the zone of operations, has never before been so ruthlessly resorted to by a big civilised power.

The system of defence consists of the mooring of these mines in such positions as to make it almost impossible for hostile ships to pass without either striking or coming within the destructive zone of one or more of them. What are known as *floating mines* are those set adrift to be washed about by the tide. They explode immediately on being struck by a passing vessel, and, of course, do not discriminate between friend and foe. The systems of destroying hostile mine-fields consist of *counter-mining*, or placing other mines in the enemy's field and destroying it by their explosion, and by *sweeping*.

The latter method is the one mostly employed in modern warfare. The boats taking part in the *sweep* place themselves one on each side of the mine-field, and between them hangs a long wire rope, weighted

LAUNCHING A GERMAN TROTYL MINE

in the centre to keep it well submerged. They then move forward, sweeping the mines to the surface or exploding them harmlessly. It is, however, very dangerous but highly necessary work.

There are two kinds of submarine mines, one is designed to explode on being struck by a passing vessel, and is called a *contact mine*, and the other is fired from the shore by an electric current, and is known as an *observation mine*. The explosive principally used is wet gun-cotton or Trotyl, owing not only to the safety with which they can be stored and manipulated, but also to the fact that they seldom explode in sympathy with neighbouring mines, requiring to be actually fired. The importance of this will be more fully realised when it is remembered that in warfare it is often necessary to explode certain mines over which hostile ships are endeavouring to pass, while leaving others in fairly close proximity intact, ready to repel a second invasion or to destroy ships nearer to them. The actual explosion is caused by an electric current, either from the shore or from a battery in the mine itself, causing the detonation of fulminate of mercury in conjunction with a small priming charge of dry gun-cotton. Mines are often laid in a series, connected to a battery on the sea-bed in the centre of the line of defence.

The *observation mine* is mostly used for defending the approaches to harbours, as an observer on shore can watch the movements of hostile warships and explode each mine when the vessel passes over it. *Contact mines*, on the other hand, are used wherever an enemy's fleet is likely to pass. They are anchored to the seabed by means of a cable and heavy weight, and are allowed to float a few feet below the surface. They explode immediately on contact At times an unscrupulous or demoralised enemy will simply throw a number of these mines overboard and allow them to float at the mercy of wind and tide. They then become a terrible danger to the shipping of all nations, as once they are left unwatched it is extremely difficult to tell with any degree of certainty where they will eventually proclaim their presence by devastating explosions. Happily for the whole seafaring world, this method is seldom resorted to, as mines set adrift in this way become a danger to both friend and foe. In the Russo-Japanese war several ships were destroyed by their own mines.

There are many different kinds of submarine mines, both of the observation and the contact type. Some are spherical in shape and others cylindrical. Some are moored close down to the sea-bed with a very heavy explosive charge (200-500 lbs. of gun-cotton), and have

A German Submarine Trotyl Mine on the deck of a Mine-layer
These mines contain the famous T.N.T., or trotyl explosive

a small buoyant globe floating above them, which, when struck, fires the mine below. Others, known as secret-mines, are kept continually moored in the waterways leading to important naval harbours, and are only allowed to rise sufficiently high from the sea-bed to be struck by passing vessels in times of emergency. The type most generally used is, however, the ordinary *offensive contact mine*, which contains a powerful explosive charge and is anchored in the path of hostile warships. These mines are usually automatically sown in large numbers over a wide area of sea by the mine-laying fleets.

CHAPTER 12

Mine-Laying Fleets

The *regular* mine-laying fleets of the powers at war are composed of the following vessels, all of which are fitted with special apparatus for the work. Submarine mines can, however, be laid by any vessel, and it is therefore almost impossible to say exactly what ships are engaged in this work. Both Germany and Austria have converted a large number of their merchantmen into minelayers. England, in reply, has converted a large number of small steamers into *mine-sweepers*. Russia is a strong believer in explosive mines, and has strewn the gulfs of Finland and Riga with them. Japan, being on the offensive, is employing more mine sweepers than layers. France has an elaborate system of submarine mine defence for all her important harbours, and maintains a small fleet at each base, known as the "defence mobile," These vessels are all capable of both mine-laying and sweeping.

The submarine mine is primarily the defence of the weaker naval power, and therefore a fleet acting on the defensive, either temporarily or permanently, requires more mine-layers than mine-sweepers, but the reverse is naturally the case with a fleet acting on the offensive. Although this may be taken as a general rule, it does not imply that a strong naval power like Great Britain, whose policy is attack and not defence, needs no mines or mine-layers. On the contrary, the laying of *counter* mines is one of the ways of destroying an enemy's minefield; and even the strongest fleet cannot guard every portion of a long coast line with many harbours exposed to attack. The judicious laying of mine-fields will often prevent raids by hostile submarines and torpedo-boats; and will limit the theatre of operations, as was done by the British Navy in the southern portion of the North Sea in October, 1914. The axiom that a really strong navy needs to be strong in *every* branch, therefore holds good in this, as in all other respects.

The British mine-layer H.M.S. *Iphigenia*
The mine-dropping gear can be seen in the stern

Mine-Laying Fleets.

Great Britain.

Apollo. Thetis. Andromache.
Latona. Naiad. Intrepid. Iphigenia.

These are all second class cruisers of from 3,400 to 3,600 tons, built about 1891-2, which have been converted into mine-layers. They are equipped with a very large number of submarine explosive mines, which can be automatically lowered into the water as the vessels steam along. Their speed is about 15 knots, and their armament consists of four 4.7-inch quick-firing guns. Their complement is about 150 officers and men.

Germany.

Pelikan (1890). *Nautilus* (1906).
Albatross (1907). *Arkona* (1903).

All these vessels, with the exception of the *Arkona*, which was a protected cruiser, have been specially built for mine-laying work. Their displacement is about 2,000 tons. The *Pelikan* has a speed of 15 knots, the *Albatross* and *Nautilus* of 20 knots, and the *Arkona* of 21½ knots. They are all fitted with special gear for dropping the large number of mines Carried, and their armament consists of from four to eight 21-pdr. quick-firing guns. Their complement is about 200 officers and men.

Austria.

The Austro-Hungarian Navy possesses only one regular mine-laying warship—the *Chamaleon*, which was being completed when war was declared. She is a vessel of 1,800 tons displacement, with a speed of 20 knots. Her mine-launching gear is of the most modern and efficient type, and she is armed with several quick-firing guns.

Since the beginning of hostilities Austria has converted several old warships and merchantmen into minelayers.

France and Russia.

Neither of these powers possess proper mine-laying vessels, but on the outbreak of war several old warships and small merchant steamers were used for that purpose.

Chapter 13

Mine-Sweeping Fleets

For clearing away the mines dropped by an enemy special vessels are employed. Each vessel is fitted on both sides with a curious contrivance known as the "picking-up gear." This apparatus is lowered into the water, and "picks up" any mines which may lie in the path of an oncoming fleet. When a mine-field is discovered by either destroyers or seaplanes these vessels are immediately dispatched to destroy it; and they are aided, in the case of the British Navy, by a large flotilla of steam trawlers. Many of these auxiliary vessels are not fitted with the *picking-up gear*, but go to work in pairs.

Two vessels, connected together by a long wire rope weighted in the centre to keep it submerged, range themselves on each side of a mine-field, and by steaming ahead in a parallel line sweep up the mines floating between them. This process can be carried on simultaneously by a large number of trawlers, covering a very wide area of sea. In the meantime the attached destroyers and seaplanes can be searching for new fields. It often happens during sweeping operations that mines are brought into contact with each other and violent explosions occur. Sometimes the vessels engaged in this hazardous work will themselves strike one of the mines, but it is more often the *searching* flotillas which meet with sudden disaster in this way. Fully equipped mine-sweepers usually precede a fleet of battleships and big cruisers through dangerous and narrow seas, within the likely zone of hostile mines.

The British Mine-Sweeping Fleet comprises the following vessels;—

Circe (810 tons), *Jason* (810 tons). *Speedy* (810 tons), *Leda* (810 tons), *Gossamer* (735 tons), *Seagull* (735 tons). *Skipjack* (735 tons), and *Speedwell* (735 tons).

These eight vessels are obsolete torpedo-gunboats which have been specially fitted out for the work of mine-sweeping. There is also a large flotilla of steam fishing trawlers engaged. Some of these vessels were purchased by the Admiralty before the war, and were also equipped for mine-sweeping; but many others were, by special arrangement, handed over to the navy on the outbreak of war. The whole of the mine-sweeping fleet is manned by a special section of the Royal Naval Reserve, known as the "Trawler Section," which consists of about 142 *skippers* and 1,136 men. This is, of course, in addition to the several thousand naval sailors employed on the regular mine-sweepers, named above, and also to those employed on the large number of additional small steamers taken over for this work by the Admiralty at the commencement of hostilities. It is estimated that the task of keeping the North Sea clear of mines during the first four weeks of the Great War required over 100 vessels and 5,000 sailors, in addition to the usual destroyer and submarine patrols with their crews, and also to the seaplanes with their pilots and observers.

Almost any steamship can be quickly converted into an effective mine-sweeper, and for this reason it is impossible to give here more than the very briefest information concerning the vessels employed in these operations by the other Naval Powers at war. Russia had fifteen special mine-sweeping vessels building when war broke out; but, doubtless, many small merchant ships have since been used for this purpose. France employed a number of minesweepers in the Adriatic; and Japan used some in clearing the approaches to Tsing-tau. Germany and Austria, of course, did not need many vessels of this kind, as the Allied Navies laid comparatively few mines and German oversea commerce ceased to exist almost as soon as war was declared. It was in the North Sea, during the first phase of the naval war, that the value of a big British mine-sweeping fleet made itself so wonderfully apparent.

CHAPTER 14

Comparative Fighting Value of the Submarine Fleets at War

Tempered and tried in the forge of war the submarine has at last been lifted from the experimental stage of naval construction to the fore-front of fleets in being. For over twenty years naval experts, marine engineers and scientists have been wrestling with the vast and complex problems of submarine construction, navigation and warfare, and have, at a cost of many lives and many millions sterling, produced submersible warships of steadily increasing size and power, until today, (1914), 264 of these vessels, of over a dozen different and more or less secret designs, with displacements ranging from 100 to 1,000 tons are in the fighting line of the Fleets at war. Thousands of sailors have been trained to fight beneath the seas; torpedoes, guns, engines, and even the air to breath, have been adapted for submarine work. A comparison, therefore, of the strength and fighting power of the submarine fleets engaged for the first time in this great struggle for the mastery of the seas is of more than passing interest.

BRITISH NAVY.

Sea-Going Vessels.

Submarines of 1,000-1,500 tons ("F" class), range 6,000 miles, speed 20/12 knots, armament 6 torpedo tubes and 2 q.-f. guns: (nearly completed)   6

Submarines of 800 tons ("E" class), range 5,000 miles, speed 16/10 knots, armament 4 torpedo tubes and 2 q.-f. guns: (in commission)   19

Submarines of 500-600 tons ("D" class), range 4,000 miles,

speed 16/10 knots, armament 3 torpedo tubes and 1 q.-f. gun: (in commission)   8

Submarines of 300-400 tons ("C" class), range 1,700 miles, speed 14/9 knots, armament 2 torpedo tubes: (in commission)   37

    Total Sea-Going Submarines   70

Coast Defence Vessels.

Submarines of 300 tons ("B" class), range 1,000 miles, speed 12/8 knots, armament 2 torpedo tubes: (in commission)   10

Submarines of 200 tons ("A" class), range 350 miles, speed 11/7 knots, armament 2 torpedo tubes: (in commission)   8

Total Coast Defence Submarines   18

Total number of vessels in British Flotillas   88

It must, however, be pointed out that six vessels of the sea-going "F" class have not yet taken their place in the active flotillas; and that eight vessels of the "E" class were on duty on foreign stations when war commenced.

French Navy.

Sea-Going Vessels.

Submarines of 600-1,000 tons (*Diane* class, *Bellone* class) and *Gustave Zédé* class), range 4,000-5,000 miles, speed 18/10 knots, armament 4 to 6 torpedo tubes and 2 to 4 q.-f, guns: (completing)   7

Submarines of 500-600 tons (*Clorinde* class), range 3,500 miles, speed 15/9½ knots, armament 4 torpedo tubes: (in commission)   10

Submarines of 600-800 tons (vessels: *Mariotte, Archimède, Charles Brun*, and *Admiral Bourgeoise*), range 3,000-3,500 miles, speed 15/10 knots, armament 4 torpedo tubes: (in commission)   4

Submarines of 600 tons (*Fresnel* class), range 2,000 miles, speed 12/9 knots, armament 4 torpedo tubes: (in commission)   22

Submarines of 500-600 tons (*Pluviôse* class), range 2,500 miles, speed 12/9 knots, armament 4 torpedo tubes: (in commission)   11

Total Sea-Going Submarines   54

Coast Defence Vessels.

Submarines of 450 tons (*Circe* class), range 1,000 miles, speed 11/8 knots, armament 2 torpedo tubes and 2 torpedoes in holders: (in commission)   2

Submarines of 400 tons (*Emeraude* class), range 1,000 miles, speed 12/8½ knots, armament 2 tubes and 4 holders: (in commission)   6

Submarines of 300-400 tons (*Argonaute* and *Aigrette* class), range 700 miles, speed 10/9 knots, armament 1 to 4 torpedo tubes: (in commission)   3

Total Coast Defence Submarines   11

Harbour Defence Vessels.

Submarines of 150-200 tons (*Triton* class, *Française* class, and *Lutin* class), range 100-600 miles, speed 11/8 knots, armament 3 to 4 torpedo tubes or holders: (in commission)   9

Submarines of 50-100 tons (*Naiade* class), range 100 miles, speed 8½/5 knots, armament 1 torpedo tube and 2 holders: (in commission)   20

Total Harbour Defence Submarines   29

Total number of vessels in French Flotillas   94

Russian Navy.
Sea-Going Vessels.

Submarines of 800-1,500 tons (*Tigr* class), no particulars: (completing)   12

Submarines of 500-600 tons (*Kaschalot* class), range 3,000 miles, speed 16/10 knots, armament 3 torpedo tubes and 1 q.-f. gun: (in commission)   7

Submarines of 400-500 tons (*Alligator* class), range 3,000 miles, speed 15/10o knots, armament 4 torpedo tubes: (in commission)   4

Submarines of 300-400 tons (*Akula* class), range 2,500 miles, speed 16/10 knots, armament 3 torpedo tubes: (in commission)   1

Submarines of 200-300 tons (*Karp* class), range 1,000 miles, speed 12/8 knots, armament 2 torpedo tubes: (in commission)

	2
Submarines of 200 tons (*Makrel* class), range 800-1,000 miles, speed 10/8 knots, armament 2 torpedo tubes and 2 holders: (in commission)	2
Total Sea-going Submarines	28

COAST AND HARBOUR DEFENCE VESSELS.

Submarines of 150-200 tons (*Minoga* class, *Lossos* class, Sig, *Sterliad* class, *Som* class, *Ostr* class, and *Graf Cheremetieve* class), range 400-600 miles, speed 11-9 knots on surface and 6-7 knots submerged, armament 1-3 torpedo tubes and holders: (in commission)	19
Total Coast Defence Submarines	19
Total number of vessels in Russian Flotillas	47

JAPANESE NAVY.
Sea-Going Vessels.

Submarines of 500 tons (Nos. 16-17), range 3,500 miles, speed 18/9 knots, armament 6 torpedo tubes and holders: (completing)	6
Submarines of 300-400 tons (Nos. 10-15), range 1,700 miles, speed 14/9 knots, armament 2 torpedo tubes: (in commission)	6
Submarines of 300 tons (Nos. 8-9), range 1,500 miles, speed 13/8 knots, armament 2 torpedo tubes: (in commission)	2
Total Sea-going Submarines	14

COAST AND HARBOUR DEFENCE VESSELS.

Submarines of 180-200 tons (Nos. 6-7), range 800 miles, speed 10/8 knots, armament 1 torpedo tube: (in commission)	2
Submarines of 100-150 tons (Nos. 1-5), range 500 miles, speed 9/7 knots, armament 1 torpedo tube: (in commission)	5
Total Coast Defence Submarines	7
Total number of vessels in Japanese Flotillas \	21

GERMAN NAVY.
Sea-going Vessels.

Submarines of 900 tons (U.25—U.30 completed, and U.31—U.37 completing), range 4,000 miles, speed 18/10 knots, armament 4 torpedo tubes and 4 q.-f. guns: (in commission and completing) 13

Submarines of 800 tons (U.21—U.24), range 3,000 miles, speed 14/9 knots, armament 4 torpedo tubes and 3 q.-f. guns: (in commission) 4

Submarines of 400-500 tons (U.19—U.20), range 2,000 miles, speed 13½/8 knots, armament 3 torpedo tubes and 2 q.-f. guns: (in commission) 2

Submarines of 300 tons (U.9—U.18), range 1,500 miles, speed 13/8 knots, armament 3 torpedo tubes and 1 q.-f. gun: (in commission) 10

Submarines of 200-300 tons (U.2.—U.8), range 1,000 miles, speed 12/8 knots, armament 2 torpedo tubes: (in commission) 7

Coast Defence Vessels.

Submarines of 200 tons (U.1), range 700-800 miles, speed 10/7 knots, armament 1 torpedo tube: (in commission) 1

Total number of vessels in German Flotillas 37

Austrian Navy.
Sea-Going Vessels.

Submarines of 800 tons (U,7—U.11), range 3,000 miles, speed 14/9 knots, armament 4 torpedo tubes and 3 q.-f. guns: (completing—delivery doubtful) 5

Submarines of 300-400 tons (U.5—U.6), range 1,500 miles, speed 12/8 knots, armament 2 torpedo tubes: (in commission) 2

Submarines of 300 tons (U.1—U.4), range 1,500 miles, speed 13/8 knots, armament 3 torpedo tubes: (in commission) 2

Submarines of 200-300 tons (U.1—U.2), range 800 miles, speed 12/8 knots, armament 3 torpedo tubes: (in commission) 2

Total number of vessels in Austrian Flotillas 6

When war commenced all the vessels of the German Flotillas (30 to 37) were concentrated in the North Sea and Baltic. The Austrian Flotilla of six vessels was in the Adriatic. Great Britain had in home waters 74 submarines and 14 others on duty in the outer seas. France had several of the 92 vessels composing her powerful flotillas at her oversea colonial naval bases. Russia had 14 submarines in the Baltic, 11 in the Black Sea, and 12 in the Far East. The Japanese Flotilla (17) was concentrated in Japanese waters.

www.ingramcontent.com/pod-product-compliance
Lightning Source LLC
Chambersburg PA
CBHW031600170426
43196CB00031B/261